A New Pension Settlement for the Twenty-First Century
The Second Report of the Pensions Commission
Appendices

Copies of the main report, these appendices and the Executive Summary are available at:
www.pensionscommission.org.uk or from The Stationery Office.

Contents

Contents

Contents

vi

Foreword

The Second Report of the Pensions Commission sets out our conclusions on the likely evolution of the UK pension system if policy is unchanged, and our recommendations for a new policy direction.

This document contains the Appendices to the Second Report. Appendix A provides an update of Appendix A of the First Report and focuses on data developments related to pensions policy. The other Appendices set out in more detail some of the analysis, research and consultation responses that we have considered as we have worked towards our recommendations for a new pensions settlement for the 21st century.

Data adequacy to support evidence-based policy

The Pensions Commission's terms of reference asked us to comment on the adequacy of available data to support evidence-based pension policy: *"To keep under review the regime for UK private pensions and long-term savings... assessing the information needed to monitor progress."*

Our First Report included an appendix looking at this issue. It came to the conclusion that present data sources were significantly deficient as a basis for some aspects of evidence-based policy making. We also noted that some improvements were planned. This review of data adequacy has two main aims:

- to review data improvements and progress made since our First Report, following the areas we considered previously;

- to highlight areas where data would need to be developed to monitor pensions policy in the future if our recommendations, or other reforms, were implemented.

This Appendix focuses on:

1. Data on individual wealth and savings behaviour and on individuals' pension scheme participation

2. Data from employers, schemes and administrative sources on trends in pension provision, membership and contribution rates

3. The Department for Work and Pension's (DWP) modelling capabilities

4. Aggregate national data on total levels of pension contributions and benefits

5. Data on demographics issues and the healthy/unhealthy ageing debate

6. Other areas of analysis

7. Some general principles and developments that would be required to monitor and evaluate pensions policy in the future in light of our recommendations or other reforms

8. Summary of recommendations and conclusion on data improvements

1. Information on wealth, savings and pensions

In our First Report we outlined in detail the ideal dataset for policy development in this area and noted the importance of the following data:

- pensions stocks and flows;

- membership of different types of scheme;

- non-pension financial assets and liabilities; and

- housing net assets and flows.

To be able to analyse this data effectively a range of individual and household characteristics, including employment status, age and income also needs to be available. We also emphasised therefore the importance of:

- longitudinal data;

- identification within couples of individual and shared wealth;

- an ability to link data between different sources; and

- individual measures of assets that produce a good comparison with aggregate data.

Details of the main data sources were outlined in full in our First Report. We now review the developments made and planned since Autumn 2004.

British Household Panel Survey (BHPS): The 2005 wealth module will include additional questions on type of current occupational pension, length of membership and contributions made, expectations of income in retirement from any previous occupational or private pensions and views on the likely sufficiency of retirement income. These questions were last carried in the 2001 survey as part of the ageing and retirement module but have been reintroduced in the wealth module following a request from the DWP.

Family Resources Survey (FRS): A review of the current pension module is underway with the aim of introducing a revised set of questions from April 2006. The research conducted to date has focused the review on improving identification of pension types and scheme membership. Work is continuing to produce a derived measure of net housing wealth. The Pensions Commission hope that the new module will collect good quality pensions data.

As a result of the 2004 FRS Strategic Review, a project has been set up to link records held on the FRS with administrative data held by DWP. This will include both DWP benefit records and HM Revenue and Customs (HMRC) employment records. The employment records include information on employment start and end dates, earnings data and also self-assessed data for the self-employed. A strategy is now in place to take the project forward and this will develop over the next three years. From April 2006 the FRS questionnaire will be developed to include questions to seek informed consent from respondents for DWP to use their personal details to link to administrative data held by the Department. One anticipated benefit from linking the administrative and benefit data is to improve the quality of the survey data by for example confirming benefit receipt. It is expected that some initial linked results will be available in late 2007. These improvements to analytical capability will be beneficial to all areas of policy development and monitoring within the Department, including pensions and we therefore support the project. At the moment DWP envisages that the biggest early gain from this development would be in the measurement of benefit take-up, in particular Pension Credit.

Annual Survey of Hours and Earnings (ASHE): In October 2004 the Annual Survey of Hours and Earnings (ASHE) replaced the New Earnings Survey (NES). It is the best source of information on the distribution of earnings. Coverage of the survey has been improved and survey results are weighted to compensate for differential non-response rates. A new questionnaire was piloted in 2004 and has been introduced for the 2005 survey. For pensions, the new questionnaire has changed the definitions of pension types and has added new questions on pension contributions from the employer and the employee. The results from the new questions on pension contributions will be analysed to assess their quality and fitness for publication as a National Statistic, hopefully in the first half of 2006. In our First Report we welcomed the piloting of the new questions on employer and employee contributions. The Pensions Commission hope that the new questions are successful as collecting good quality information on employer, and indeed employee, contributions is difficult. If this approach is not successful the issue may need to be reconsidered.

General Household Survey (GHS): All members of the European Community are now required to collect some cross-sectional and longitudinal statistical information on income and living conditions (EU-SILC). From April 2005 these requirements are being met using the GHS. The GHS was identified as the best vehicle for this work because there are many overlaps in the topics covered. One of the main features of the EU-SILC requirement for the GHS is the provision of both cross-sectional and longitudinal data to investigate major issues of social concern. This requirement has resulted in a change to the GHS sample design to a four yearly rotation, an increase in the sample size, and additional core questions. To reflect its longitudinal element, the GHS is now known as GHS(L). The change of design may limit analysis of pensions issues for certain groups, for example ethnic minorities and divorced women, in the future from this data source. This suggests that other sources such as the FRS will increase in importance.

English Longitudinal Study of Ageing (ELSA): This survey is continuing with wave 2 data expected to be available from the UK Data Archive in January 2006. Fieldwork for waves 3, 4 and 5 should follow as planned in 2006, 2008 and 2010, therefore building a good longitudinal dataset for analysis.

Pension wealth calculations (accrued state and private pension wealth for each individual, and predictions of wealth accrued by the time they reach State Pension Age) for the wave 1 sample have been carried out and analysed, and a description of the methodology has been published as a working paper by the Institute for Fiscal Studies. Pension wealth calculations have been calculated based on imputed earnings histories since the access to the linked National Insurance (NI) records is not yet operational. Pension wealth data is now available as a supplementary public release data file from the UK Data Archive. The Commission believe that the ELSA project is vital in collecting data to monitor trends in pension accumulation and retirement trends as recent analysis using it has shown, and so adequate funding for the survey in the future should be ensured.

Expenditure and Food Survey (EFS): For the first time the Office for National Statistics (ONS) has published results on an equivalised income basis for a number of types of retired households. Tables of household expenditure by different household types by equivalised gross income decile groups are published in *Family Spending 2004*. We noted these plans in our First Report. We believe that this development should help improve analysis of consumption patterns of the retired in the future.

Household Assets Survey (HAS): ONS continues the development phase of a household wealth and assets survey. A feasibility study was undertaken in June 2005. Results from this study suggest respondents generally accept the content of the survey. A pilot study will be conducted in early 2006 on a larger sample, and will provide a test of the revised content of the survey, and a dress rehearsal for all survey procedures. It is anticipated that the survey will go into the field in July 2006, with first results being available later in 2007.

Other ongoing work includes investigating methods to supplement the survey sample to adequately capture those at the higher end of the wealth spectrum. Potential linkages to administrative data are being explored. Administrative data provides a rich source of information on an individual's pension wealth, income, taxation and benefits. It is hoped technical and legal issues can be resolved to further enhance the value of the survey. In our First Report we noted that this survey should be a major priority, and we continue to believe this. The Pensions Commission welcome the progress that has been made, and fully support these developments. This is a very important project, and if the survey could be developed with a longitudinal element this would enhance the usefulness of the data.

2. Other sources on pension provision, membership and contribution rates

In our First Report we outlined in detail the ideal dataset for policy development in this area. In short we noted the importance of the following data:

- membership of each type of scheme, together with details of those schemes; and

- data from employers on the pension schemes they provide, participation rates and contribution rates.

The Government Actuary's Department (GAD) Occupational Pension Schemes Survey (OPSS): Since the First Report of the Pensions Commission, GAD has published a new survey of occupational pension schemes (OPSS 2004). The results of the survey, which relate to April 2004, were published in June 2005, and are available from the GAD website. GAD is currently working towards a further survey (OPSS 2005), for which results will relate to April 2005. It is anticipated that this will be published in May or June 2006.

In the longer term, the Morris Review of the Actuarial Profession, which also included a review of GAD, recommended that responsibility for the survey be moved to either the Pensions Regulator or to the ONS. The Government accepted the latter recommendation, and from 2006 onwards these surveys will be conducted by the ONS.

However, the survey will become less effective over time as more pensions are provided in a Group Personal Pension (GPP) form, rather than under the trustee-based occupational form, on which the GAD survey exclusively focuses. We noted in our First Report that GAD and the new Pensions Regulator should give consideration as to how such data can be gathered and to the co-ordination of their data gathering. Those with responsibility for the survey in future therefore need to consider if there is a practicable way to collect useful information on membership and contribution rates in GPPs in a manner consistent with how the survey collects this information for occupational schemes. The Commission hope this useful survey will continue in the future. The ONS will want to see how this survey fits in with their current data collection plans and liaise with the Pensions Regulator.

Employers' Pension Provision survey (EPP): DWP aims to conduct further surveys in 2007 and 2009. As noted in our First Report the Commission hope that this survey will continue to be undertaken every two years in the future.

HM Revenue and Customs (HMRC) statistics: Following the recommendation in our First Report, HMRC published a consistent series of contributions to all non-occupational pension schemes derived from various administrative sources from 1990/91 to 2003/04. This includes contributions to personal and Stakeholder Pensions, retirement annuity and free-standing additional voluntary contracts. The series forms part of its suite of National Statistics on pensions and savings and will be updated annually. In addition, at the end of May 2005 HMRC also published for the first time a full set of distributional tables of funds held in personal and Stakeholder pensions for 2002/03. These break down fund size by earnings, age, gender and region of residence. These will also be updated annually. The Commission welcome these developments.

Lifetime Labour Market Database (LLMDB2): Providing all of the legal obligations are met, the LLMDB2 will be linked, by National Insurance number, to a 1% extract of the Work and Pensions Longitudinal Study (WPLS). The WPLS is DWP's linked database, incorporating information on individuals' benefit receipt and New Deal activity over time as well as employment information from HMRC about work activity, earnings and savings. This will allow a combined analysis of interactions with both the National Insurance Recording System (NIRS2) and the benefit system, offering the chance to explore, in more detail, benefit claimants' behaviour. The Commission support the use of linked administrative data where the quality justifies this.

In our First Report we welcomed the better information that was likely to emerge from data sharing between DWP and HMRC made possible by the Pensions Bill at that time. Following the introduction of new data-sharing provisions in the Employment Act 2002 and the Pensions Act 2004 the DWP is able to receive more data on employment from HMRC.

As well as supporting the working age agenda, the database will significantly improve the analytical evidence base for pensioners. It will inform both private and state pension policy, and will provide an important source for monitoring pensions' developments in the future both for existing and prospective pensioners. It will also improve capability surrounding Pension Credit take-up campaigns.

Market data from the pensions industry: The Association of British Insurers (ABI) collects a variety of data from insurance companies about premiums flowing into long-term savings including pensions. It collects data on "new business" for policies sold during the year, and also for "business in force" (including premiums for policies put in place in previous years). The new business figures are under constant review, and in 2005 the distribution channels have been amended to take into account the changes in distribution following depolarisation in late 2004. Additionally, new product lines have been included to allow collection of data on the new Stakeholder suite of products from April 2005.

The annual returns that enable the ABI to report on business in force are undergoing a major review at the end of 2005. The main reason for such a review is the introduction of International Accounting Standards in 2005 that are initially being adopted by some, although not all, of its members. The new standards will have a significant impact on the way income and benefits paid figures are collected and reported. The data requirements of insurers, the ABI and other organisations will be considered during this review.

The Commission hope that the review provides an opportunity to review consistency of treatment of different parts of pension business to maximise the accuracy and usefulness of the survey.

ABI statistics need to be interpreted carefully in order to develop a true picture of trends in pension saving since:

(i) The "business in force" figures are broken down into "regular premiums" and "single premiums". While the latter include some genuine flows of new money from personal sector savers, they also include a large element of money transferred from existing pension policies with other providers. Adjustments to exclude these transfers can be made using other data available to the ABI.

(ii) The "new business" figures may also include money being transferred from existing policies (although this is identified separately). Even if this is not the case "new business" premiums may be matched by the cessation of payments to an existing policy.

There are no plans to enhance the reporting of transfers further within the new business forms at present.

The Pensions Regulator: The Pensions Regulator is the new regulator of work-based pension schemes in the UK. Created under the Pensions Act 2004, the Regulator has wider powers and a new proactive and risk-focused approach to regulation. As part of the new organisation's approach to regulation, a scheme return form has been created that all work-based pension schemes with two or more members will be required to complete. By July 2005, 8,000 scheme returns had been mailed out to all Defined Benefit (DB) schemes with five or more members. A further 4,000 revised scheme return forms will be mailed to all DB schemes with between two and four members in January 2006. The mailing of returns to Defined Contribution schemes is scheduled for 2006, as work needs to be carried out to tailor the form appropriately. The Pensions Regulator intends to publish statistical information from the scheme returns during the second year of its operation, providing an overview of the membership, status and finances of pension schemes in the UK.

In addition to this, the Pensions Regulator plans to collect other data to assist in the development of the Regulator's approach to scheme risk mitigation. One such project that is currently underway focuses on scheme governance. An external working party has been established to assist in the set up of this work. Findings from this work will be published in Spring 2006.

The Pension Protection Fund (PPF) will be using the pension scheme data collected by the Pensions Regulator to build up a database in order to conduct modelling work for calculating the levy. The aim is to see how the levy may be calculated for relevant schemes from 2006/07. This work will inform its thinking and help with further calculations of the Risk Based Levy.

In our First Report we welcomed the plans that the Pensions Regulator had outlined for its scheme return. However, we were concerned that this was developed with little if any input or consultation with other relevant analysts, for example from DWP. We were also concerned that the content of the detailed return was necessarily limited to the regulatory information required. This seems to be an opportunity lost to collect additional, useful analytical information on work-based pension schemes through this administrative process, or to looking at reducing the burdens on survey respondents by bringing together the return information with other surveys such as the GAD and EPP surveys. The Commission believe there is a lesson to learn here for the future if new administrative systems are developed.

Annual Business Inquiry – Financial Questionnaire (ABI2): During our work over the past year we became aware of another official survey that included questions on employer pension contributions. The Annual Business Inquiry is carried out by the ONS. UK businesses are sampled according to their employment size and industry sector. The sample is drawn from the Inter-Departmental Business Register (IDBR). The sample design is a stratified random sample, and almost 80,000 businesses are contacted in total. Response rates for the survey are good. The Annual Business Inquiry is conducted in two parts: one dealing with employment (ABI1), the other with financial information (ABI2). The main reason for splitting the form into two parts is that the employment data are available much earlier than the accounting data. The financial inquiry covers about two-thirds of the UK economy. Currently this situation is under review and work is continuing to see if data quality from the financial sector can be improved so that the data can be used, and if the Annual Business Inquiry can be expanded to include the agriculture sector. The coverage of the employment inquiry is wider. Financial data collected include information on company turnover, capital expenditure, employment costs, including employer pension contributions, value of purchases and employment information.

Companies are sent a paper questionnaire. The majority of respondents receive a standard form type but derivations of this standard form are used for certain industries. For most of these full form types there is a corresponding short form type, which does not contain the detailed breakdowns requested on the full forms. This short form is sent to a proportion of respondents in each size band in order to minimise the burden on businesses. The proportion varies by size so that most small businesses receive the short form while all large businesses receive the full form.

In particular interest to the Pensions Commission, and other pension analysts, the short form only asks for total employment costs whereas on the full form costs are divided into four categories: gross wages and salaries, employers' NI contributions, employer contributions to pension funds, and redundancy and severance payments.

The financial questionnaire was reviewed in May 2004, with recommendations including investigation of possibilities to expand ABI2 coverage, review the use of long forms and whether it was feasible to increase the number of variables included on the inquiry form. Work is planned in the near future to review the sample, both in terms of sample size, distribution and long/short form types. The form content itself is reviewed annually.

The Pensions Commission believe that this could be a useful source to investigate the level of employer pension contributions at an aggregate, and sectoral level, if employer pension contributions were separately identified on the short form. Indeed, having the more detailed information on the components of employment costs available would help to monitor the effect of the introduction of the National Pension Savings Scheme (NPSS) we propose on wages and employer pension contributions.

3. DWP modelling capabilities: Pensim2

We noted last year that the Pensions Commission would need access to the DWP's 'dynamic microsimulation' model, Pensim2, to estimate the likely impact of different policy regimes on the long-run level and pattern of pensioners' incomes. We have indeed made extensive use of the Pensim2 model in developing our recommendations, and more detailed information on the model itself, and the use we have made of it, is described in Appendix F. We recommend that DWP publish a paper describing the model and what it does, including a range of analysis to illustrate its capabilities and limitations.

In the debate over options for pension reform that we hope will follow our report, Pensim2 will be an important tool for government and we would regard maintaining DWP's capacity to use and develop the model as of very high importance. Ideally it would be very helpful if a version of the model were available to specialist external analysts. Clearly this facility would need to balance providing access and limiting the resource costs of supporting users. We recommend that the DWP investigates the best way to provide such access.

4. Aggregate national data on pension contributions and benefits

ONS published an article in July 2005, and subsequently in the September edition of *Economic Trends*, describing the progress that has been made in the surveys of pension funds and insurance companies; updating estimates of pension contributions; and explaining how the new estimates and methodological improvements have been incorporated in the National

Accounts dataset released on 30 June 2005. We noted its previous article in August 2004 describing how the surveys to pension funds and insurance companies had been modified in Appendix A in our First Report.

In summary, changes to pensions measures have now been incorporated into the latest view of the economy published in the National Accounts. The impact of the changes on national accounts aggregates was broadly in line with the provisional estimate published in the August 2004 *Economic Trends* article.

In our First Report we welcomed the work of the Pension Statistics Task Force (PSTF) in improving the aggregate data. We hope that this work will continue.

In our First Report we proposed that HM Treasury, DWP, ONS and HMRC should consider whether there were wider lessons to be learnt from the severe problems that had occurred in aggregate pension statistics looking in particular at (i) cross-departmental co-ordination, (ii) high-level credibility checks and (iii) resource adequacy within ONS.

The PSTF was wound up in October 2005 and was replaced by a new Pensions Analysis Unit in ONS. This new unit will build on the work of the PSTF, developing a work programme designed to deliver better use and analysis of existing pensions data and to improve the quality, range and accessibility of these data.

The new unit will continue to produce analysis and publications on pension statistics, including updating *Pension Trends* (see below), to support the pensions debate and enable greater understanding of issues, and to work to achieve improvements in relevant data sources. These cover a wide range of ONS sources including financial surveys, ASHE, the planned Household Assets Survey and estimates used in compilation of national accounts. The Pensions Analysis Unit will continue to develop relations with customers and stakeholders, consulting on potential developments and issues as well as keeping up-to-date on developments within the pensions sector.

The Commission hope that the new unit will become a centre of expertise in pension statistics and will encourage developments in a range of relevant data sources in the coming years, working together with interested analysts and policymakers. It is vital that the Pensions Analysis Unit maintains good links with data providers and policymakers so it is aware of key policy issues and developments. The PSTF Advisory Group has met regularly during the past year and we recommend that a similar group consisting of representatives of the main data providers, and other experts, should continue as one way for analysts to keep in touch with developments and plans across departments.

5. Demographics, health and longevity issues

As we have noted in terms of pensions reform good quality data on demographics issues, including healthy ageing, are vital. Some developments are already planned in this area, but more needs to be done.

Demographics situation following Morris Review: The Morris Review of the Actuarial Profession published its final report on 16 March 2005, including a review of the future role of the GAD. This included a recommendation that the responsibility for the national population projections and associated demographic work be transferred to the ONS. The Government has in principle accepted this recommendation. A recent announcement confirmed that the transfer will take place on 31 January 2006 when the National Statistics Centre for Demography is created within ONS. The Commission hopes that a centre of expertise in demographics can be developed which will work with policymakers to continue progress in this important area. In addition it is vital that communication of the trends in life expectancy, and in particular what they mean for individuals are made clear so that they can make the choices they need to about the savings/retirement trade-off.

International migration: As individuals become more mobile during their working lives, and there are indications that more people are planning to retire abroad, but would still be eligible for pension provision from the UK, we believe that this is an area that requires further investigation. If significant numbers of people living overseas, who do not appear in the national population projections, are eligible for UK pensions this could have an effect on forecast pension expenditure and measures of adequacy. And if patterns of migration are changing this increases the uncertainty in the projections. We recommend that the National Statistics Centre for Demography, in conjunction with relevant policymakers and analysts throughout government, should undertake a feasibility study into this area to see if any existing data sources could be developed to monitor these issues more effectively in relation to future pension reforms.

The ONS Longitudinal Study: The ONS Longitudinal Study (LS) is a dataset containing linked census and vital event records for 1% of the population of England and Wales. The LS started in 1974 with a sample drawn from the 1971 Census, based on those born on one of four birth dates. The same dates were used to identify and link LS members' records from the 1981, 1991 and 2001 censuses. Approximately 500,000 LS members are found at each census. New LS members enter the study through birth or immigration and leave through death or emigration from England and Wales.

The LS was first established to inform a range of research and policy topics. Its primary objective was to permit more accurate prospective analyses of mortality. Linkage of census and death records has allowed the LS to produce more reliable statistics on socio-demographic differences in mortality. At death registration, the socio-demographic information collected is limited and information from an informant is likely to differ from that obtained when the person was still alive. The LS is continually updated with information on life events, including births to sample mothers, cancers, widow(er)hoods and deaths. The latest data released in September 2005 included births and deaths occurring up to 2003, immigration and emigration up to 2004 and cancer registrations up to 2001.

ONS is currently reviewing life expectancy methodology and the attribution of social class over time. Preliminary findings from this work will be available in Spring 2006. We welcome this development.

The ONS Longitudinal Study is a key source of information. When it was established in the 1970s the Census was the best available source of information to investigate these issues. However, the meaning of social class has changed over time, and this is an issue in interpreting the results. New administrative sources may have opened up opportunities to look at mortality issues by a variety of other factors or characteristics, in addition to social class, for example earnings levels, which are not available from the Census. Therefore as a supplementary approach to the ONS LS we recommend that a feasibility study be undertaken by DWP and the National Statistics Centre for Demography to investigate whether alternative administrative sources could be used to look at past life expectancy trends, identify key factors influencing longevity, and investigate whether future projections can be made on this basis. We believe this is an area where data holders such as DWP would need to work carefully with demographic experts, and the results of such a feasibility study should be made publicly available.

We have noted previously the importance of the ELSA data in collecting information on pension wealth, but another important element will be the information it collects on both physical and mental health issues. It will therefore be possible to investigate issues around health inequalities in more detail in the future. And the longitudinal element of the survey will enable the process of ageing to be examined too. With its multi-disciplinary focus incorporating high-quality measurement of health and a longitudinal design, ELSA provides a unique opportunity to understand these relationships. As noted above we believe that the ELSA project is vital in collecting data to monitor trends in health issues, and so adequate funding for the survey in the future should be ensured.

In our First Report we proposed that DWP and the Department of Health (DH) should consider how best to share insights and co-ordinate research into the healthy/unhealthy ageing debate, and that the relevant research councils (Medical Research Council (MRC) and Economic and Social Research Council (ESRC)) should also note the issue as a key one for society.

Since then government departments have collaborated on a number of activities related to healthy ageing. These include:

■ Publication of *Opportunity Age*, the first government strategy on ageing, which highlights the importance of healthy ageing and sets out a series of specific proposals to help deliver policies across a wide range of areas.

- DWP and DH jointly developing outcome indicators, related to Opportunity Age initiatives, which include healthy ageing.

- Publication of the DWP *Five Year Strategy*, which outlines the ageing society as the main future challenge for the Government, and the need to respond to this challenge across the lifecycle. Healthy ageing is a key part of this, and cross-cutting work is starting in DWP in order to prioritise how evidence and analysis can build the foundation for an even longer term strategy aimed at tackling the multi-faceted issue of population ageing.

- The establishment of a cross government research and analysis group where the ageing society, including healthy ageing, has been identified as one of the major challenges facing government.

The ESRC, Engineering and Physical Sciences Research Council (EPSRC), Biotechnology and Biological Sciences Research Council (BBSRC) and MRC, with input from DWP and DH, have developed a major new interdisciplinary research programme on ageing – The New Dynamics of Ageing. One element of this programme focuses on the issue of active ageing, to try and understand how factors occurring earlier in the lifecourse affect well-being in later life. But there are many other strands to this programme, which should shed light on issues relating to ageing. This is a welcome initiative: research and investigation into issues around healthy ageing, and their communication to the public, are important for policy development in many areas, not just pension reform.

6. Other areas of analysis

During the past year plans have also been developed in other areas that may prove useful to the pensions debate.

Public attitudes to pensions and saving for retirement survey: We used the National Statistics Omnibus Survey to collect data on attitudes and expectations of individuals to retirement and pension planning to inform our recommendations (more details of this research are described in Appendix D). We also drew on a number of other surveys and research reports produced by a number of public and private sector organisations. And surveys such as the British Social Attitudes Survey are useful in monitoring trends in attitudes over time. A DWP survey is currently under development to examine public attitudes to pensions and financial planning for retirement. It is anticipated that the survey will be repeated every two years. It aims to provide a picture of the level of knowledge and public attitudes to and confidence in pensions and how these change over time and to examine how attitudes translate into intended or actual saving behaviour. We support this development.

Continuous Population Survey (CPS): ONS plans to integrate the major government household surveys on which it leads into one survey. The five surveys to be integrated are the Labour Force Survey (LFS) and associated boosts, the General Household Survey, the Expenditure and Food Survey, and the

National Statistics Omnibus Survey. The CPS sample will be composed of the cumulative total sample size of the component surveys, making it the largest ever, continuous survey to be conducted in this country. While continuing to meet the information needs currently met by the five separate surveys, the CPS is designed to deliver improvements in the quality, precision, range and coherence of outputs. A central aim of the project is to deliver these quality improvements while maintaining the integrity of key time series. A comprehensive development programme to meet these aims is ongoing, with the survey due to go live in January 2008. The Commission believe it is important that this new development is considered as one strand of the evaluation strategy for the National Pension Savings Scheme (NPSS) that we propose.

Labour market projections: ONS is working on producing labour force, or activity rate, projections updating work that was last published in June 1998. Essentially, the work involves modelling forward trends in activity rates, and then applying these modelled activity rates to population projections from GAD. In modelling the activity rates, ONS looks at a number of groups disaggregating by age, sex, and, for the younger age groups, student status. The aim is to project activity rates out to 2020, and as part of this ONS is trying to make some allowance for the change in the State Pension Age for women between 2010 and 2020. Publication of the results of this work is planned for 2006. The Commission believe this work may be helpful in making future assessments of the dependency ratio and therefore informing pensions policy.

LFS Retirement module: In April-June 2006 an ad hoc module will be included in the LFS considering issues around the transition from work into retirement. This is a special module agreed in consultation with the EU's Member States. The EU sees the promotion of active ageing and prolongation of working life as priorities for action. Therefore the module will attempt to identify how people make or expect to make the transition towards full retirement. There is an interest in knowing more about plans for transitions towards full retirement and plans for exit from work. The module also aims to discover which factors are at play in determining the exit from work, and which factors could make someone postpone the exit from work. The questions are to be asked of LFS sample members aged between 50 and 69 who are either in work or who had been after the age of 49. The Commission hope that this module is useful to analysts and policymakers and, if it is successful, that a repeat module may be considered in the future to identify any change in retirement behaviour over time.

Index of Labour Costs per Hour: The ONS has published experimental data for an index of labour costs per hour and work is continuing with the aim that the series becomes a National Statistic. The new index goes beyond existing earnings indicators to include non-wage costs such as pension contributions. The index will help in monitoring inflationary pressures emanating from the labour market. This index, once fully developed, may be able to help monitor changes in wage growth occurring around the time that reforms, such as our proposed NPSS, were introduced.

Pension Trends: ONS recently published the first edition of *Pension Trends*, which brings together key findings from a wide range of data sources. The main focus is the individual and the demographic, economic and social context for current and future pensioners. Specific topics include: incomes received in retirement, expectations of retirement, state provision and private provision, contributions, pension wealth and other sources of household wealth. The publication also considers pensions from the national accounts perspective and the perspective of the providers: covering businesses, pension schemes and the financial sector, and the investment behaviour of pension funds. We welcome this publication as it brings together existing statistics from a range of sources to illustrate the economic and social issues that shape trends in pension provision, and presents the data in a straightforward way that is accessible to a wide range of users. We hope it will prove a useful publication in the future.

7. Future data requirements to monitor pension reform

This section considers three important areas for future development:

(i)   Monitoring of the four options.

(ii)   General principles to improve data adequacy in the future.

(iii)   Analysis that would be required to monitor and evaluate the introduction of the proposed National Pension Savings Scheme (NPSS).

(i) Monitoring of the four options

In our First Report we stated that faced with the increasing proportion of the population aged over 65, society and individuals must make choices between four options:

■ pensioners will become poorer relative to the rest of society; or

■ taxes/NI contributions devoted to pensions must rise; or

■ savings must rise; or

■ average retirement ages must rise.

We reported what the present situation was for each of these four indicators. It is important therefore that these four indicators continue to be monitored in the future so that people can see what choices both individuals, and society as a whole, are making. The government and others can then try to evaluate the impact of future pension reform in terms of the balance of action between these choices.

A range of data on pensioners' incomes and pensioners' position in the income distribution are already published by the DWP. This should continue in the future. Indeed, DWP has commissioned research into pensioners' experiences of poverty that should help policymakers to understand these issues better. The government should also continue to publish data indicating both current and planned expenditure on pensions and pensioners, and highlighting the range of uncertainty in the figures depending on the demographic scenario used. And a number of the surveys highlighted above will provide information on the value of savings in the future, either at an individual or aggregate level, and the Household Assets Survey could play an important role in this.

Monitoring changes in average retirement ages for various groups will be important in the future, especially to evaluate the impact of the change in women's State Pension Age. We suggest that DWP and ONS analysts work together to agree the best approach to monitor this. And alongside this headline measure attitudinal information and qualitative research will be required on people's expectations of longevity and the length of time they will spend in retirement, and whether people are working longer or changing their retirement plans.

Although a number of indicators relating to the four options are published at the moment, it is important that their publication and consideration is undertaken in the round, with the implications for society and pensions policy drawn out. We recommend that a publication of this sort is developed. Who takes responsibility for this is a matter for the government and will depend on any future institutional reforms. However, this could fall under the remit of our proposed Pensions Advisory Commission (as described in Chapter 11).

(ii) General principles to improve data adequacy in the future

Although the Commission have not been able to consider all of the data implications of our recommendations, and indeed these will become clearer as the fine detail of the proposals are considered, there are some general principles that can be outlined, and should be taken into account, in an effort to ensure that good quality data will be developed and be available in the future. When the implementation of any reform following our recommendations is reviewed in the future the necessary data should be readily available.

Good quality and timely survey and administrative data will be required to monitor future pension reform – both have an important role to play. Current, and planned, surveys will need to review their contents to see if they need to be adapted to take into account any pension reforms. And as administrative data are developed consideration should be given to linking the data to other relevant datasets such as the LLMDB2, so that a more complete picture of what is happening can be developed. The linking to other datasets would also facilitate the provision of Combined Pension Forecasts to individuals.

Relevant provision will need to be made in future legislation to enable sharing of data from administrative and regulatory sources. In particular, to allow data linking of information across key departments so that analysts can use data effectively, while also ensuring that data confidentiality safeguards are maintained. Such changes could reduce the need for specialist surveys in some areas.

We have noted that data developments will take time. Therefore we believe that investigation of the options in more detail and planning for changes need to start to take place now so that baseline data can be collected before the introduction of any new scheme. This should be the responsibility of a single, accountable body, possibly DWP or our proposed Pensions Advisory Commission, and we recommend that this body should develop a fuller evaluation strategy and report publicly on a regular basis on progress being made. We also recognise that in order for good quality data to be available these developments will require sufficient funding and resources being made available in a number of different departments such as DWP, ONS, DH and HMRC.

We also recognise that collecting data from people, and businesses, does impose a burden. We hope that as the statistical approach for monitoring our reforms is developed that all relevant agencies within government, and the relevant regulatory authorities will work together to try and minimise duplication in order to try and reduce burdens. For this to be possible data sharing will be required for both survey and administrative data.

And it is important that in this key policy area that affects everyone, public confidence in the data and analysis published is developed.

(iii) Analysis which would be required to monitor and evaluate the introduction of a National Pension Savings Scheme (NPSS)

In monitoring the introduction of a NPSS there are two broad issues to consider:

■ the development of administrative data to be able to provide business management information; and

■ wider data developments to capture more fully the impact of the scheme on a variety of issues.

The different elements of the system should provide administrative data based on individuals, employers, investment funds and decumulation choices. Therefore, as the detailed design of a new scheme is developed (whichever approach is taken to organising and running the scheme) analysts, policymakers and regulatory authorities should work together to make sure that adequate data collection systems are in place at the time when the new system is implemented. Only by doing this will administrative data be available to monitor the impact of the new system from day one. It will be important that headline figures relating to participation and contributions to the scheme, from both individuals and employers, are available in a timely fashion from the administrative systems that are developed. Regular information on investment choices, returns and pensions payable will also be required. It is important that the scope of information collected is not narrowly defined or geared too much to the early stages of any new pension scheme. Instead a broad range of useful and accurate analytical information for both short and long-term analysis should be collected, while avoiding adding significantly to the administrative requirement on businesses.

In a broader context, the introduction of a new pensions system of the type we recommend would require monitoring and evaluation of its effectiveness on a range of indicators and areas of policy, as well as monitoring the impact on current pension provision. In addition good quality data would be required to inform any future modelling, such as the development of Pensim2, so that forecasts under the new system can be developed. Data would be required to consider the impact on a number of different elements including: people, employers, schemes, and funds. Therefore there will be a need for comprehensive and robust data to both complement, and be compatible with, existing data sources and developed administrative systems. This would require the establishment of new data collection mechanisms and the development of current data sources to take account of the new pension system, and also the regular undertaking of qualitative research to consider aspects of the new system, and attitudes to it, in more depth.

People

Policymakers would want to know what difference the new system makes to individuals and households. A number of questions would need to be considered, both in relation to the new scheme itself, and to the impact on pensions overall:

■ Who is eligible to join or participate?

■ What is the level of participation?

■ Why are people not participating? Are they in their employer's scheme instead? Do people join the scheme at a later date after having opted-out?

■ Are unemployed, economically inactive and self-employed people joining the scheme?

■ What contributions are being made? Are people contributing above the minimum level? If so, who are they?

■ What choices are people making in terms of investment funds, and why?

■ What is the effect on the accumulation/decumulation of other assets people hold?

■ What do people do with their pension pots at retirement, what choices do they make?

All of these questions would need to be considered at both a personal and household level, together with a range of characteristics including age, income, ethnicity, employment status and so on, as well as aggregate numbers. In particular policymakers will want to be able to see if there are vulnerable groups that continue to under save following the introduction of the new scheme, and understand the reasons for this.

And as we noted previously both cross-sectional and especially longitudinal data will be needed to monitor the impact of the new scheme effectively. This suggests that the Household Assets Survey, in particular, could have an important role to play, especially if it is developed with a longitudinal element, along with a number of the other data sources mentioned earlier in this chapter, such as ELSA.

And of course in all these developments safeguards need to be in place consistent with the Data Protection Act and other good practice so that people can be reassured that any information relating to them is being used in accordance with the law.

Qualitative research would have an important role to play by helping to put some of the numerical data into context by exploring people's attitudes, understanding and expectations for retirement and retirement planning. Issues to be explored could include seeing if people have a better understanding of the key issues and choices, what are their views of the reforms and do they have confidence in them. And qualitative research would be required to understand people's views of the new scheme and the decisions they are making.

Employers

Policymakers would need to see what the impact of the new system has on employers and their current pension provision. For example:

■ What schemes will employers continue to provide?

■ What contributions levels are made to existing schemes and the new scheme?

■ Are employers paying above the minimum level of contributions? If so, what are their characteristics, and why are they contributing more?

■ Is there an impact on wages, employment levels?

■ Is there a change in recruitment practices?

■ Is there any effect on overall remuneration and benefit packages?

Again data will be required so that any differential effects by size of firm, and industry sector can be considered. This suggests that the Employers' Pension Provision Survey would continue to be a key data source, as would the Annual Survey of Hours and Earnings, especially its longitudinal element, but additional employer-based data sources may also need to be considered.

Pension schemes

In addition to specific information on the new scheme, information would also be required on the impact of its introduction on existing schemes.

■ Is there an increase in schemes closures?

■ Is there an impact on scheme membership levels?

■ Is there a change in contribution levels?

■ Is there any change to scheme rules for example in terms of accrual rates, access and eligibility, and the benefits available?

Again, differences between the different types of scheme and between the public and private sector schemes will be important. This suggests that the Occupational Pension Schemes Survey could have a role to play, but additional data in this area could be required. And of course, as well as the impact on occupational schemes, the impact on personal pensions would also be important considering issues such as participation levels, contributions, investment decisions and persistency.

Pension funds

The first indicators required to monitor pension funds are measures of contributions, both in terms of stock and flow. And this would include both regular contributions, and lump sum transfers into the accounts. In terms of assessing pension adequacy it is important to know what investment choices are being made as this will have a direct impact on what pension level is achieved. Therefore information would be required on the asset allocation of funds and individuals and the level of assets in funds. In particular policymakers would need to know who is using the default fund for their investments, and whether they actively chose this fund or not. Of special interest would be the performance of individuals' accounts – what are the investment returns, and the distribution of those returns, at an individual and aggregate level? The level of administration costs would also need to be monitored.

Decumulation phase

Again, in terms of adequacy of income in retirement, the choices that people make when it comes to the decumulation phase and the age at which they make this choice are important issues to monitor. For example, policymakers would want to see what types of annuities are bought: joint or single life, index-linked or level, or other types of annuity or income withdrawal products.

Macroeconomic impact

The previous paragraphs have highlighted analysis required to monitor the introduction of the NPSS at a microeconomic level by focusing on the actions of individuals and firms. However, it will also be important to consider the effects to the UK economy as a whole, for example in terms of employment trends, aggregate savings, inflation, wage levels, GDP and so on.

Conclusion

Both survey and administrative data covering a variety of issues, and at both a microeconomic and macroeconomic level, would be required to evaluate the impact of pension reform in the future. And we recommend that a single, accountable body, possibly DWP or our proposed Pensions Advisory Commission should develop an evaluation strategy and review data requirements and developments to contribute to this analysis.

The development of the administrative data available from the new scheme is of vital importance. Analysts need to be involved in the development of the relevant forms and systems so that useful data can be collected in a timely, consistent and comprehensive manner. The ability to use the administrative data for longitudinal analysis is also important in order to get a lifelong picture of pension right accumulation and decumulation.

As New Zealand proceeds with its planned "Kiwisaver" scheme then there should be lessons to be learnt from its introduction and evaluation that can be taken on board by the UK. The situation here should be kept under review.

8. Summary of recommendations and conclusion on data improvements

This section summarises both likely developments already in hand which the Pensions Commission welcomes, and recommendations on further improvements which should be considered.

We welcome in particular:

■ The FRS data-linking project.

■ The anticipated pension contributions data from the ASHE survey.

■ The continuing development of the ELSA project, both in terms of pension wealth, and health analysis.

■ Progress that has been made in the development of the Household Assets Survey, which we continue to regard as a major priority.

■ Developments that have occurred so far in the GAD Occupational Pension Schemes Survey, and we hope this continues to develop when the ONS takes responsibility for the survey in the future.

■ The creation of the Pensions Analysis Unit in the ONS to build on the work of the PSTF, and continue the publication of Pension Trends.

■ The creation of the National Statistics Centre for Demography in the ONS and hope it will become a centre of expertise, working closely with policymakers.

■ The planned research and collaboration in the area of healthy ageing.

■ The planned DWP survey on public attitudes to pension issues.

We make the following recommendations on priorities:

■ We recommend that DWP publish a paper describing Pensim2 and what it does, including a range of analysis to illustrate its capabilities and limitations.

■ We recommend that DWP investigates the best way to provide access to Pensim2 for specialist external analysts.

■ We recommend that the PSTF Advisory Group, or a similar group, should continue as one way to facilitate cross-departmental co-ordination in pension data issues.

■ We recommend that the new National Statistics Centre for Demography in ONS, in conjunction with relevant policy makers and analysts throughout government, should undertake a feasibility study to investigate issues of migration in relation to pension reform.

■ We recommend that DWP and ONS undertake a feasibility study to investigate whether administrative data sources could provide supplementary measures of longevity to complement the ONS Longitudinal Study.

■ We recommend continued monitoring, and publication, of measures of the four options, so that the impact of pension reform in relation to these choices can be measured.

■ We recommend a single, accountable body, possibly DWP or our proposed Pensions Advisory Commission should develop an evaluation strategy as pension reforms develop, and report publicly on a regular basis on progress being made.

We make the following proposals for government consideration:

■ Thought still needs to be given as to whether it is possible to collect information from GPPs.

■ The Annual Business Inquiry should consider if employer pension contributions can be separately identified on the short form.

■ DWP and ONS analysts should work together to agree the best approach to monitor the impact of the change in women's SPA.

■ Analysts, policymakers, and regulators need to work together on the development of administrative systems for the proposed NPSS.

■ Existing surveys are changed to take account of the proposed NPSS.

■ Lessons need to be learnt from the development of "Kiwisaver" in New Zealand as it proceeds.

We welcome the developments made during the past two years, and those planned for the future, which should considerably help future policymakers and organisations considering the area in the future. These are areas affecting very large proportions of national income and assets. We hope that progress will continue to be made in the areas we have identified.

Report on the Pensions Commission consultation

In Chapter 9 of the Pension Commission's First Report, *Pensions: Challenges and Choices,* we asked interested and informed parties to submit their views on a range of issues. During our official consultation period, from 12 October 2004 to 31 January 2005, the Commission received almost 250 written submissions from a range of organisations and individuals including government bodies, businesses, the financial services and pensions industries, experts, academics and members of the public. The Commissioners also met with key representative and interested bodies: the Trades Union Congress (TUC), the Confederation of British Industry (CBI), the Association of British Insurers (ABI), the National Association of Pension Funds (NAPF), the Pensions Policy Institute (PPI), the Equal Opportunities Commission (EOC), Help the Aged, Age Concern, the Pensions Reform Group and the Institute of Actuaries. We also held a series of consultation meetings in Belfast, Edinburgh and Cardiff. Since our official consultation period ended, we have continued to receive numerous letters from interested parties and we held a further consultative event on 21 June 2005.

This Appendix reviews the breadth of comments which have been made to the Pensions Commission since the publication of the First Report. In writing this Appendix, we have tried to summarise the views of people who have contacted us in as accurate a manner as possible but inevitably there is not space to do justice to all the details and nuances of everyone's views. The submissions of many of the organisations that gave evidence are available on their websites and we plan to deposit copies of all the submissions with the House of Commons library. The views expressed therefore should not be taken as the views of the Pensions Commission. And as comments have been received from a self-selecting group of interested parties they should not be read as necessarily representative of the views of the wider public.

Key conclusions

To deliver an effective lasting solution to the problem of pension provision we need to seek a consensus on pension reform. Responses to our consultation clearly demonstrated that although there was considerable consensus on the need for radical changes in pension policy, the consensus on the best way forward was far less clear. On some issues there was a general sense of a single direction for change, but on others opinion was divided.

- **Compulsion or voluntarism:** The Pensions Commission believes that the current state system combined with the current voluntary private savings system are not fit for purpose. It is time for either changes to the state system, significant revitalisation of the voluntary system or an increase in the level of compulsion in the system. Opinion on compulsion, however, is divided. A considerable number of submissions, including those from the ABI, the CBI and the NAPF, are in favour of maintaining the voluntary principle in private pension provision. Whilst they are united, however, around a relatively small number of reasons why compulsion is not the answer, there is far less agreement on the best way to revitalise voluntary savings and the ABI and NAPF, for example, both proposed different reforms to create what they consider to be the best state foundation for private saving.

Many respondents state that they are against compulsion but still argue for more rather than less state intervention in the pension system. Those who are explicitly in favour of compulsion propose a wide range of options for compulsion: from compulsory employer and employee contributions to compulsion on employers to provide advice on savings. Indeed, what became increasingly clear to the Pensions Commission as we digested responses is that the debate around compulsion is not one which has a yes or no answer. Rather there is a scale of compulsion ranging from a completely free market approach to pension saving to a fixed compulsory savings requirement for the working population. Opinion is spread out along this scale.

■ **Changes to the state system:** The majority of respondents are in favour of some sort of increase to the level of the Basic State Pension (BSP) through earnings-indexation and/or a step increase to the level of payout. Several individuals and groups suggest that the state should only provide a simple, flat-rate benefit to all and not involve itself with earnings-related provision. Others, however, are in favour of some sort of role for the state in earnings-related provision. Views on continuing to allow people to contract-out of the state earnings-related system are completely divided.

The large majority of respondents say that they would prefer to see a system which had significantly less or no means-testing. Indeed the clearest consensus was around the need to prevent the further spread of means-testing in the pensions system.

However many of those who favour a significantly increased BSP, reduced means-testing and/or a state organised earnings-related system are not clear about the measures they would put in place to pay for the increase in state expenditure on pensions which would be required to pay for these policies.

A fair but not overwhelming number of submissions argue that the UK should move to a universal rather than a contributory state pensions system and an almost equal number suggest that improvements to the current contributory system would be fairer and more practical than the switch to a universal system.

Several submissions also call for changes to the current system of tax relief and suggest various changes including a flat-rate system of tax relief and the abolition of tax relief in the system. We have returned to several respondents to discuss whether there is a way to successfully reform tax relief in a way that deals with the practical difficulties of implementing changes to the system of tax relief within Defined Benefit and hybrid schemes. We discuss our own conclusions on tax relief in Chapter 7 of the main report.

- **State Pension Age and retirement age:** The issue of the State Pension Age (SPA) is very contentious. Many respondents say it should not rise beyond the planned equalisation of male and female SPA but others say that it should rise, for example, to 70 by 2030. There is, however, almost complete consensus around raising the retirement age, the age at which people choose to leave the workforce, and around facilitating longer working lives for those who choose to work longer. Most respondents say that people do not want to be forced to work longer, but would like to be supported to work longer if they so choose.

This Appendix considers the following issues in more detail:

1. What mix of the Pensions Commission's four options should be the response to the demographic challenge?

2. The appropriate role of the state in pension provision

3. The adequacy and equity of pension provision

4. The complexities of the UK pension system: contracting-out, funding and means-testing

5. Opinions on compulsion

6. Barriers to voluntary saving

7. Revitalising the voluntary system

8. Risk sharing within the pensions system

9. Non-pensions savings and housing wealth

1. The Pensions Commission's four options

In our First Report, the Pensions Commission concluded that faced with the increase in the proportion of the population in retirement, society and individuals had to choose some mix of four options. Either:

1. Pensioners become poorer relative to the rest of society; or

2. Taxes or National Insurance (NI) contributions devoted to pensions must rise; or

3. Savings must rise; or

4. Average retirement ages must rise.

We also concluded that Option 1, poorer pensioners, was undesirable.

The vast majority of responses clearly state that a decline in pensioner incomes should not be part of the solution and that the planned response should be made up of the other three options.

■ The largest group of responses say that the solution may have to involve a mix of higher taxes/NI contributions devoted to pensions, higher savings and higher average retirement ages. The Small Business Council would prefer a mix of about 20% from tax increase, 40% from savings, 40% from later retirement.

■ Several responses rule out one of the three options. An increase in taxation proved the least popular option and the group proposing a solution of higher savings and higher retirement ages includes the ABI, Standard Life and the Association of Consulting Actuaries (ACA). One commentator, however, notes that higher taxes/NI contributions are preferable to increased savings as government provision is likely to be stable in comparison to private provision.

■ We also heard several warnings:

   – The CBI notes that solving the problem just through increased taxation or forced savings could have damaging macroeconomic effects.

   – One respondent expresses concern that all of the options would be a concern for ethnic minorities and it has also been noted that we need to recognise that neither higher savings nor later retirement will help many of the disabled.

2. The role of the State

In the First Report we posed the philosophical question of what role the state should take in pension provision. In their responses, we asked commentators to indicate what they thought the role of the government should be. Should the government limit its involvement to poverty prevention and to making well-informed choice possible? Or should government seek to ensure that people up to some level of income have made provision which they will consider adequate: and if so what should that level be?

Opinions on the appropriate level of state intervention in the pensions system vary widely [Figure B.1]. Professor Tim Congdon writes that above providing the basic minimum, the Government should leave choice to individuals who will look after themselves. Others believe that the state should enable everyone to build up a decent retirement income. Amicus says that the state should intervene to minimise the need for means-testing and limit inequalities in the system. In the private sector, the NAPF says that above an adequate state pension, the state has a clear role as an enabler of private pension provision providing the right regulatory and fiscal regimes. We also heard that the state should provide a framework and mitigate some of the risk, or ensure access to transparent, simple effective pension schemes. It was

Figure B.1 Respondents' views on the level of state intervention in the pensions system

Flat-rate state system	Earnings-related pensions
■ Those in favour of a flat-rate state pension think that the state should provide an equal minimum benefit to all.	■ Those in favour of state intervention in earnings-related pensions propose a range of measures.
■ The NAPF propose a single universal state pension paid at the current Guarantee Credit level, linked to earnings with eligibility based on citizenship, not the contributory principle: on a Citizen's Pension. This should be paid for through the abolition of the State Second Pensions (S2P) and the abolition of the contracting-out rebate.	■ Most of those who support the S2P call for it to be revitalised and made more inclusive. The CBI want the S2P to retain an element of earnings-relation rather than move to a flat-rate system as currently planned.
■ Others say that the S2P should be abolished after transition to higher BSP.	■ The EOC believes that state involvement in second tier pensions should be preserved and revitalised with more comprehensive credits to ensure actual adequacy for low earners, carers and the disabled.
■ Help the Aged believes that further reform of the S2P may simply increase its complexity but provide no immediate gain.	■ The Women's Budget Group also thinks that the S2P should be strengthened and extended to provide a good second pension for women, the low paid and carers.
■ The ABI would like to see a state system of two elements, the BSP and a flat-rate S2P benefit which would include the self-employed based on £15,000 annual earnings but with earnings-related contacting-out that would clearly indicate that those earning over £15,000 year should contract-out of the state system into the private sector.	■ Others argue that the S2P is necessary in order to support those individuals who do not have access to good employer provision. And others would like to see the self-employed included in the S2P.
	■ The CBI suggests that the government should consider an individual approach for S2P with the possibility of partial funding.
	■ There are some respondents who say that the state should provide a cost-efficient earnings-related system in addition to an earnings-linked BSP at the Guarantee Credit level, although how the costs of this would be met are not clear.
	■ Most of those in favour of compulsion advocate a compulsory, straight-forward earning-related pension financed by employer/employee contributions.
	■ The TUC supports a compulsory earning-related system to provide 50% of earnings above £6,000. This would be on top of a BSP of 25% of average earnings which would provide a 100% replacement for low earners and fall to 55% for those earning over £50,000.

suggested that the state underwrite occupational pension schemes. Yet there are also those in favour of compulsion into either a state-run system or into savings vehicles provided by employers and the private pensions industry.

In this Section we summarise responses relating to:

(i)   The level and appropriate indexation regimes for the BSP (or replacements there of)
(ii)   How improvements in the state pension provision should be paid for
(iii)   Raising the State Pension Age and/or average retirement ages
(iv)   Equity between different groups of people
(v)   The accrual regime: a universal or contributory approach
(vi)   Governance of the state system

3. The adequacy and equity of pension provision

(i)   The level and appropriate indexation regimes for the BSP (or replacements there of)

In their submissions, we asked respondents to indicate whether they thought that changes to the state system were necessary in order to make voluntarism work. Regardless of whether organisations or individuals came down in favour of state intervention in earnings-related pensions or not, we received many proposals for changes to the state pension. Several responses clearly say that pension reform needs to start with reform of the state pension system to provide a solid basis for voluntary system. Dr Ros Altmann and HSBC Actuaries and Consultants Limited are two of those proposing urgent radical reform of state pensions. This has also been a common theme in the media commentary. A large group say that simplification of the state system is key to making the whole system work. Norwich Union write that the current complexity in the system undermines saving and support radical simplification of pensions including an end to future accruals to S2P and abolition of contracting-out rebates.

The PPI response to our consultation[1] says that there is a strong consensus that the state pensions system should be modernised to prevent future generation's retiring with lower retirement income than is seen today. They suggest that consensus for reform is that the foundation state pension should be above the means-tested level and there are two ways of achieving this: increase the BSP or move to a Citizen's Pension. They suggest that the latter would be more effective at reducing poverty, inequality and complexity but both are possible, affordable and sustainable, provided transition is managed in certain ways.

---

[1] The PPI's response is based on a body of PPI work analysing different state pension reform options and a stocktake review of pension policy proposals made by organisations with an interest in pensions.

Many respondents say that the State should ensure poverty prevention. Many more, including the NAPF, the TUC and the CBI, say that the government should provide a (guaranteed) adequate basic minimum pension and some of this group said that adequacy should be the aim of the state at whatever cost. Dr Ros Altmann says that the state pensions should provide a social welfare underpin and private pensions should provide the savings aspect of pensions. The British Bankers Association (BBA) states that there should be an adequate basic level of state support prescribed by government while making clear that those who want to save beyond this level should make provision for themselves.

Age Concern believes that pensions should be based on principles of adequacy, fairness, security, clarity and flexibility. Yet the level of an adequate pension can be debated. Age Concern tells us that an adequate income should cover essentials (food, warmth, housing) and allow full social and economic participation in society and give individuals the ability to exercise choice. They believe that raising the BSP to the current level of the Guarantee Credit (£109 per week) would be an improvement but on its own would not provide an adequate pension. An adequate income should be met through a combination of state and private income.

Amicus tells us that the system should provide a replacement rate of two-thirds at average earnings. Other individuals note that desired replacement rates are highly subjective and could not be prescribed. One person writes that pensioners want enough money to allow independence and choice. Another says that the Pensions Commission's analysis of desired replacement rates should take account of the evidence that expenditure decreases during retirement, implying that desired replacement rates are higher at the point of retirement than later in retirement.

In our First Report we said that we thought above a certain level, say the 90th percentile of income, a purely individualist approach to pension provision was appropriate. Help the Aged responded to say that the top 25% of the income distribution should look after themselves and the BBA says that the State does not need to ensure adequacy even up to the 75th percentile.

The Pensions Commission did not specifically ask respondents what they thought the level of the BSP should be. Much of the public debate, however, has been around this. [Figure B.2 summarises opinions.]

Figure B.2 Level of Basic State Pension and indexation: preference stated in submissions

Level	Indexation regime		
	Price Linked	**Earnings linked**	**Not specified**
Current BSP	1 response	1 response	3 responses
Higher than BSP		Popular	Popular
		Lloyds TSB favour an earnings-linked BSP at higher levels than today.	The BBA and Watson Wyatt, amongst others, fall into this group.
		The EOC call for a BSP at the same or higher level.	
		The ACA call for a higher BSP to cover basic living costs financed by a higher BSP.	
		One respondent suggested restoring the BSP to the level it would have been at now if the earnings link had not been broken.	
Guarantee Credit		Popular	Fairly popular
		Generally suggested alongside the abolition of another part of the state pension and a call for a universal pension, paid on grounds of residence rather than contribution record.	
		Advocated by the NAPF, Norwich Union, the Women's Budget Group and Help the Aged amongst others.	
		Age Concern says the BSP should be increased to the level of the Guarantee Credit immediately and then assessed at regular intervals.	

Figure B.2 Level of Basic State Pension and indexation: preference stated in submissions (continued)

Level	Price Linked	Indexation regime	
	Price Linked	Earnings linked	Not specified
Minimum wage (40hr/wk)			A few supporters
25% average earnings		The TUC argues for an immediate rise to the Guarantee Credit level with a further increase to 25% average earnings.	1 response The Prudential are in favour of a higher state pension of up to 25% of national average earnings.
At poverty line			A few supporters

ii) How improvements in state pensions provision should be paid for

We asked respondents who are in favour of increases in the value of the state pensions to indicate how they intend to pay for the increase in state expenditure. We gave respondents 3 choices: higher Tax/NI; higher SPA; or a mix of the two. Figure B.3 show this response.

Several alternative funding strategies have also been proposed including the abolition of the S2P and tax relief. Help the Aged, for example, are in favour of funding an increase in the BSP through a combination of increased taxation, reform of the tax relief system or scrapping S2P. One person suggests increasing compulsory saving to fund a higher state pension and another increasing government borrowing. The TUC is in favour of funding an increase to the BSP through the rebalancing of public expenditure and improving the dependency ratio by achieving an 80% employment rate. The TUC also says that there should be an increase in the overall share of GDP being spent on the state pension funded by savings on other benefits and the CBI also says that government should fund increases in the BSP through reallocated spending and efficiencies in other areas as well as through a higher SPA.

[2] Lawrence Churchill made his response to our First Report in a personal capacity. Mr Churchill is Chair of the Pension Protection Fund.

Figure B.3 Views on how costs of impr ovements in pension provision should be met

	Higher Tax/ NI	Higher SPA	Higher tax/NI & SPA
For	The BBA, Amicus, Age Concern, Help the Aged plus others are in favour funding an increase in the BSP through higher taxes devoted to pensions. A couple of responses suggest introducing an explicit pensions tax. Another suggests that we should tax the baby boom generation. The TUC argues that an increase in the tax bill is acceptable as the Government's share of GDP is currently lower than the EU average.	This option is supported by Lawrence Churchill,[2] Norwich Union, Watson Wyatt and the Institute of Actuaries amongst others. The ACA suggests increasing the SPA in steps to 70 and permit further increases as recommended by a permanent Pensions Commission. The CBI would like to see the SPA increased to 70 between 2020-2030 to reflect increases in life expectancy. Any further change should reflect further changes to life expectancy. The Institute for Public Policy Research suggests increasing the SPA to 67. Another response suggests that we consider allowing employers to link private scheme retirement ages to SPA.	Several respondents are in favour of both higher taxes/ NI contributions and a higher SPA. The NAPF says that the costs of their Citizen's Pension proposal in the longer term would need to be met by either increasing NI costs or increasing SPA. They suggest that the SPA would need to increase to 67 by 2030 and 70 by 2045. Lloyds TSB favour a tax payer funded state pension and a raised SPA to reflect increase life expectancy.
Against	Several respondents are against an increase in taxation including the submissions from Lawrence Churchill and Professor Tim Congdon.	Quite a large group of responses are in this group including the TUC, the ABI, Amicus, Age Concern and Help the Aged. The Prudential are against any increases in the short-term.	

iii) Raising the State Pension Age and/or average retirement ages

We have heard a range of arguments for and against increasing the SPA and many more arguments in favour of higher retirement ages [Figures B.4 and B.5.] The TUC for example are explicitly against raising SPA but in favour of a rise in average retirement ages.

Figure B.4 Respondents' views on higher SPA

For	Against
■ The CBI say that the government needs to increase the SPA to 70 between 2020 and 2030 in order to pay for a higher flat-rate BSP. The CBI notes that government will also need to introduce a series of active labour market policies to increase retirement age especially amongst those aged between 50 and 65. Help is needed to increase older workers skills and help those on Incapacity Benefit back to work.	■ The TUC, amongst others, thinks that a higher SPA will have a distributional effect and the greatest impact will be felt by the low paid.
■ The NAPF suggests that the SPA would need to increase to 67 by 2030 and 70 by 2045 to meet the longer term costs of their Citizen's Pension.	■ It is also thought that a higher SPA will have a disproportionate affect on manual workers.
■ Several respondents including the CBI think that increasing the SPA should give the right signal to people about working longer and reflects longer and healthier lives. The PPI also suggests that increasing the SPA would be of immense significance as an indicator that the government expects people to work longer.	■ Age Concern opposes increases to the SPA on the grounds that reform should not be at the expense of the most disadvantaged.
■ It was also noted the government needs to allow greater flexibility about when to draw state pension.	■ Help the Aged fears that a higher SPA will have an adverse affect on the most disadvantaged whose life expectancies have not increased at the rate of the general population and who may be employed in manual jobs which they cannot physically continue past 65.
■ One submission notes that you could adjust the SPA with life expectancy by pursuing a "cash balance" approach to the state pension promise, allowing people to annuitise the implicit value of their accumulated state pension rights. This approach is also known as Notional Defined Contribution.	

Figure B.5 Respondents' views on raising retirement ages

For	Against
A significant number of respondents are in favour of raising the retirement age voluntarily and making it easier for those who want to, to continue to work late in life.	Comparatively few arguments were made against increasing retirement ages.

For

A significant number of respondents are in favour of raising the retirement age voluntarily and making it easier for those who want to, to continue to work late in life.

■ One person tells us that later retirement is a reasonable if the trade-off is earning a decent pension.

■ Professor Nicholas Barr writes that higher and more flexible retirement ages should be a core part of the solution, both to stabilise the long-run fiscal costs of pensions and to increase security by giving people the opportunity to work longer.

■ Some think that average retirement ages will rise naturally as longevity increases. One view is that the first aim of government should be to keep people in work in their 50s. Another that a flexible approach to working during your 60s and 70s should be pursued and government should encourage and enable part-time work for older workers. The concept of a flexible decade of retirement features in some discussion.

■ The BBA says that those who want to work beyond retirement ages should be able to do so.

■ Help the Aged says that the government should abolish mandatory retirement ages so that people have the choice to work longer if they wish to and take a more vigorous approach to training and employing older workers.

■ The TUC and others agree that government should seek to remove barriers to working after 65 and default retirement ages. The TUC also advocate incentivising flexible retirement by allowing people to work and draw part of their state pension.

Against

Comparatively few arguments were made against increasing retirement ages.

■ A couple of respondents believe that aging is not healthy enough to allow for increased retirement ages and one person notes that working late in manufacturing could be dangerous.

■ Some are concerned about where the jobs will come from to enable people to work longer and we were told that we need to consider the effect of raising retirement ages on economy/ employment levels.

■ One submission notes that later retirement should not be the solution as life expectancy differs according to career and it could increase age discrimination.

Figure B.5 Respondents' views on raising retirement ages (continued)

For	Against
■ The Third Age Employment Network recommended a series of measures by employers, government and employees to achieve a longer working life which will be rewarding for all parties, rather than just a forced response to declining pensions. They believe that as well as abolishing default retirement ages, the government should have ambitious targets for the employment rate for people aged 50-SPA and/or for the contribution to the workforce made by those above SPA. They also observe that issues of occupational health, flexibility and choice and work conditions need to be addressed so that longer working life generates better health. ■ One person writes that government should compel employers to employ older workers. ■ Dr Ros Altmann says that we should rethink the concept of retirement so that it becomes a process of gradually reducing working hours later in life rather than an "event."	

iv)   Equity between different groups of people

Respondents clearly think that ensuring equity is important. There is fairly significant support for a universal BSP, paid on grounds of residency rather than contribution record, to ensure that all pensioners receive at least an element of the state pension. Age Concern proposes that the government should use indexation to ensure that all pensioners benefit from the increasing prosperity of the nation. They also say that pensions should meet the needs of all, including women, carers and low income earners and that everyone should be able to build up a second pension.

There is particular concern about protecting and supporting those who have been traditionally disadvantaged by the pensions system although some responses also note that gender inequalities in pension provision are linked to labour market inequalities and the state should also aim to reduce gender inequalities in income. We were told that, to a certain extent, the problems faced by women are generational and will work out of the system.

We were reminded, however, of the need to consider the position of women carefully with any proposed changes to state or private provision. The EOC says that the pensions system must ensure parents, carers, the low paid and those in part time employment have the opportunity to build up additional pension rights. The Parents and Carers Coalition calls for better recognition of carers at all ages and a new Carers Allowance for carers aged over the SPA.

It is argued by some that the system should fully include the self-employed and those outside the labour market. Standard Life suggests that the government could cover payments into private pensions whilst carers are outside the labour market to compensate those with caring responsibilities. We were also asked to look at the uprating policies for pensions in payment to UK nationals residing abroad.

v)   Accrual: independent or couple based: universal or contributory

How people accrue pension rights is a significant concern. There is strong consensus on the need for individuals to accrue a pension in their own right, which is supported by the TUC, the ABI, the ACA, Aegon and Lloyds TSB amongst many others. Aegon also says that S2P should be extended to the self-employed. There is less agreement about what should happen to spouse benefits. Age Concern says that survivor's benefits should be protected throughout any transition to a new individualised system. Legal & General is in favour of continuing to allow spousal rights and one submission argued that private pensions should be restructured so that each spouse benefits from all contributions made during a marriage. Others note however that households would benefit more than single pensioners from a push for a greater level of individual rights. It was noted that taxation could be used to redress this effect. The Women's Budget Group says that when we have reached a position that all women and carer have accrued their own substantive pension rights then spousal and survivor benefits should be phased out.

There is a fairly strong, but by no means dominant, group in favour of a move to a universal pension which includes the ABI, who would like to see improved eligibility for the BSP by either basing it on residency or a shorter working life and/ or rewarding periods of caring as if they were paid employment, Help the Aged, the NAPF and Norwich Union who would all like to see a universal state pension at the level of the Guarantee Credit, the Citizen's Pension model. Age Concern would like to see a system where both men and women are entitled to a full basic pension in their own right at the level of the Guarantee Credit through either major reform to the contributory system or the introduction of a residence based pension. There are various arguments, however, both for and against a universal, residency based pension [Figure B.6].

Figure B.6 Respondents' views on universal state pensions

For	Against
■ The major argument in favour of universality is that it will benefit those disadvantaged groups who are unable to build up a full work record, in particular women.	■ Although they saw the merits of the Universal system, several respondents think that a Citizen's Pension is too expensive.
■ A move to universality could also pave the way for the abolition of the NI system.	■ It was also argued that universality should not be introduced at the cost of supplementary state provision which is designed to benefit the at risk groups.
■ It was also noted that high income pensioners would not benefit overly from a higher, universal BSP as they will return 40% to HM Treasury in tax.	■ Another view is that moving to a universal pension will change the incentives to work and could increase the tax burden on those in work as others exit the labour force.
	■ One response also notes that a universal BSP will give as much money to those who have **not** contributed to the system as to those who have and questions whether this is fair.
	■ The ACA note that it could be difficult to identify a "fair" residency requirement for the state pension within the European Union.

Most of those who are in favour of the contributory system, however, suggest changes to enhance the current contributory system. Several specific changes to the current contributory system to benefit women, carers and part-time workers have been suggested, including:

■ Revitalising the credit system and recognising caring more thoroughly;

■ Moving to weekly rather than annual credits;

■ Simplifying Home Responsibilities Protection (HRP) or converting HRP to a credit system;

■ Abolishing the 25% rule on entitlement to the BSP so that the system provides some benefit for just 1 year of contributions;

■ Reducing the number of hours of employment required to contribute to the NI system; and

■ Allowing people with several part time jobs to combine their earnings for NI purposes.

We also received numerous letters commentating on the increasing inequalities in the pension system between private sector pensions and the scheme provisions for public sector employees, MPs and Senior Executive schemes and a large number of these called for reform of these "top-hat" schemes.

vi)   Governance of the state system

Several responses comment on the governance of the state system and those that do mostly call for a depoliticised state system. Proposals range from a new non-political organisation to implement pension policy, to a new governance body modelled on the Monetary Policy Committee to a more permanent Pensions Commission which could monitor the long-term trends, assess progress to reduce under-saving or even be required to set the level of the state pension and the SPA.

4. The complexities of the UK state system: contracting-out, funding and means-testing

The debate over contracting-out of the S2P is probably one of the most contentious with a set of strong arguments on either side [Figure B.7].

Figure B.7 Respondents' views on contracting-out

For	Against
The TUC, the ABI, the Prudential, Legal & General, Aegon, Standard Life, HSBC Actuaries and Consultants Limited and the CBI amongst others are in favour of the continuation of the contracting-out option. Many, however, would like to see reform of the system to simplify the system and increase the incentive to contract-out.	Those who would like to see contracting-out abolished include the NAPF, the Women's Budget Group, Watson Wyatt and the ACA.
■ The ABI is strongly in favour of contracting-out. They argue that abolishing contracting-out will reduce the level of pre-funding in the system which will make it more difficult to meet future needs more difficult. They also believe that reforming contracting-out with clear incentives to contract out will kick start private pension saving and make small pension pots more attractive to pension providers. They argue that abolishing contracting-out is likely to cause more occupational schemes, particularly Defined Benefit (DB) schemes, to close.	■ The NAPF argues that the complexity which contracting-out creates is a barrier to voluntarism as it adds costs and complexity to workplace pension provision: it is little understood by scheme members and advisors will not provide financial advice to consumers on contracting-out. They argue that DB schemes would actually welcome the abolition of contracting-out as the loss of the rebate would allow them to re-evaluate their DB promise.
■ The CBI want to retain contracting-out to maintain incentives for employers to retain DB provision and the contributory principle.	■ Dr Ros Altmann argues that phasing-out contracting-out is essential to unwind the confusion between state and private pensions and the money spent on contracting-out could pay for a universal residency based pension.
■ Standard Life argues that abolishing contracting-out to increase expenditure in the short-term would simply imply further increase of the burden on later generations.	■ The ACA thinks that the level of the rebate currently provides no incentive to opt-out.
■ The Prudential advocate higher contracting-out rebates.	■ Watson Wyatt says that contracting-out is now so complex that if it were abolished pension provision in the state and private would not suffer.
■ A couple of organisations argue for abolishing the S2P but maintaining a contracting-out system to allow people to opt out of the top slice of BSP.	■ Others argues that contracting-out should be restricted and should only be allowed into DB schemes.
	■ The Women's Budget group thinks that contracting-out should be abolished. The S2P, however, should be strengthened and extended to provide a good second pension for women, the low paid and carers.

There is also some debate over whether the pensions system should be funded or unfunded/ Pay As You Go. The largest body of opinions argue for a mixed funding/ PAYG strategy [Figure B.8].

Figure B.9 Respondents' views on whether the pension system should be PAYG or funded

PAYG	Mixed	Funded
■ Watson Wyatt calls for the abolition of the NI system, saying that pensions should be paid for out of basic taxation	■ Age Concern says that we should preserve the current balance of funding and PAYG systems so that no one scheme takes on all of the risk. ■ The Pension Reform Group advocates a Universal Protected Pension which would combine the BSP and a new funded element to reduce the demands on future tax payers and create property rights. Additional contributions could be made to the existing NI system but then would flow into funded savings. This funded part should have its own independent governance structure administered by trustees who would select private sector professional fund managers to manage the fund. ■ Another submission argues that saving to pre-fund the system will only contribute to solving the problem if the savings promote future economic growth.	■ Some argue that the NI system should become a real funded system. ■ Some respondents propose the introduction of a Government-run pension fund to provide "private" savings. ■ The London Stock Exchange writes that investment in equities has given the best return over time.

One area where there is significant consensus is around means-testing with the large majority calling for at least a halt to the spread of means-testing in the system [Figure B.9].

Figure B.9 Respondents' views on means-testing

For	Against
■ Legal & General, despite being against means-testing in general, note that means-testing is inevitable and that the current tapered withdrawal of benefits is better than previous Minimum Income Guarantee system. ■ We were also reminded of the need to strike balance between cost of abolishing means-testing and the disincentive effect which it creates. ■ The ABI believe that means-testing acts as a disincentive to save, but acknowledge that it is not possible to remove it all together.	■ Around 50 submissions to us say that the government should either reduce the spread of means-testing in the system or remove it all together. This groups included Professor Nicholas Barr, Lawrence Churchill, Standard Life, the NAPF, Legal & General, the CBI, the ABI, Dr Ros Altmann, the Pensions Reform Group, the ACA, Aegon, Lloyds TSB, Age Concern, Norwich Union, Watson Wyatt, HSBC Actuaries and Consultants Limited, the Institute of Actuaries, the Prudential, and Help the Aged. ■ The NAPF believe that the current high level of means-testing is a disincentive to save and is unsustainable in the longer term. ■ Age Concern says the need for means-testing should be reduced through improvements to the pension system. **Disincentive effects:** ■ The main argument against means-testing is that it disincentvises saving and increases the complexity of the pensions system. ■ We are told that means-testing puts those who save a modest amount at a disadvantage compared to those who do not and so means-testing incentivises individuals to spend now. One more specific view was that means-testing disincentivises saving for people over 50 who have not saved before. ■ Help the Aged say that means-testing confuses those of working age as to whether it is worth their while to save or not.

Figure B.9 Respondents' views on means-testing (continued)

For	Against
	Complexity:

Complexity:

- Financial services companies and actuaries told us that means-testing makes giving financial advice difficult and expensive and creates a fear of mis-selling. The NAPF believes that there is a fear of mis-selling for those earning below £15,000 as it is unclear (until the point of retirement) that it was worth savings in a private pension. The BBA believes that advisors are particularly at risk of mis-selling to those on incomes below £28,000 owing to the current complexity of the system.

- Aegon says that the FSA needs to provide clear advice on when personal pensions should be sold to low earners. They also said that people need clear information on the impact of not saving and the complexity which means-testing introduces to the system makes this difficult to provide.

- It has also been noted that individuals need clear advice about the level at which savings will compromise entitlement to benefits.

- We have been told that means-testing is inappropriate as a long-term solution, its cost will be unsustainable over the long term and it should only be a safety net for a few people.

- The Prudential state that the government should set out a planned reduction in means-testing consistent with providing a higher BSP worth 25% of average earnings.

- The Pensions Reform Group argues that their reform proposal (the Universal Protected Pension) will allow the government to place a time limit on means-testing in the pension system and eventually remove it altogether.

- The BBA call for further evaluation of the economic costs of means-testing as the population ages.

5. Opinions on compulsion

The Pensions Commission was set up to recommend to government whether there was the need to move beyond the current voluntary approach to private pension saving towards a more compulsory system. In our First Report we noted that the state pension system did in fact contain an element of earnings-related compulsion in the S2P. The key question which we posed, therefore, at the end of our First Report was whether respondents believed it appropriate to introduce further compulsion above that which already exists in the system. In response we heard numerous arguments both before and against varying degrees of compulsion as well as comments on auto-enrolment as a viable alternative to a fully compulsory system [Figure B.10].

Figure B.10 Respondents' views on compulsion

For	Against
■ We are told that compulsion is inevitable if there is no clear case for voluntarism.	Many respondents and organisations are wary of compulsion, including Lawrence Churchill, Standard Life, the NAPF, the CBI, the ABI, the BBA, the ACA, Aegon, Lloyds, HSBC Actuaries and Consultants Limited, the Prudential, Help the Aged and the Institute of Actuaries. The NAPF, the CBI and the Institute of Actuaries and Watson Wyatt specifically say that there should be no further compulsion above the level which already exists in the system. Age Concern and the Prudential are wary of compulsion into private pensions.
■ Compulsion has also been described to us as the only option which addresses the issue of moral hazard with advice.	
■ The EOC is in favour of compulsion if necessary to achieve adequacy for all.	
■ The Prudential thinks compulsory matching up to a given level could be a viable option.	We were warned that compulsion is unpopular, inequitable and unfair on low earners. The PPI doubts that a practical system of compulsion into private pension saving can be designed that will achieve the objectives of good pensions for all.
■ The Small Business Council is in favour of some element of compulsion or inducement so people can be encouraged not to chose to rely on the state safety net as long as it does not take the freedom of individual choice away. They suggest that one approach might be increasing NI contributions and paying these into personal accounts and warn of the burden on SMEs of compulsion on employers.	And there are numerous, more specific arguments against compulsion:
The various proposals included:	■ Age Concern says that lifecycle issues mean that saving is not always the best option and their submission is one of several which note that compulsion limits choice and could lead to an increase in the level of debt.
■ Compulsory minimum pension contributions.	■ The ABI argues that rather than introduce a further compulsory system we should make the S2P more generous (which will in turn reduce means-testing and remove a disincentive to save). They add that it would be better to reduce the level of borrowing than introduce compulsion.
■ Increased compulsion through the state collection of NI and tax to improve the BSP and the S2P.	
■ Compulsion with age-related contributions.	

Figure B.10 Respondents' views on compulsion (continued)

For	Against
■ One individual proposes that we should move to a system of compulsory wealth accumulation when individuals have an income above a set minimum and decumulation when they do not, with no distinction between asset class.	■ The NAPF, the CBI, the ABI, the ACA, amongst several others, are concerned that compulsion could level provision down to a minimum. The CBI says that compulsion may not lead to an overall rise in the savings rate.
We were also given various provisos for compulsion [See below].	■ Others are concerned with the potential to mis-sell with compulsion.
Opinions on compulsion also depend on who compulsion should apply to.	■ We are told that low income earners should not be compelled to save in risky products and that investment risk should not be transferred to individuals.
On employers:	■ The CBI thinks that compulsion is not in the interests of the very low paid who will find themselves no better off.
■ Standard Life and HSBC Actuaries and Consultants Limited say we could allow companies to make scheme membership a condition of employment.	■ The ABI notes that there is a political risk for government in setting the level of compulsion and Standard Life say that there is a political risk if compulsion does not deliver adequacy.
■ Norwich Union suggests compelling employers to auto-enrol people into pension schemes which meet minimum requirements.	■ Some respondents think that compulsion could be seen as a payroll tax and could reduce employment.
■ Help the Aged says employers should be obliged to provide schemes or contribute to second tier pensions.	■ The Prudential thinks that it could destroy employer-based schemes.
■ Legal & General tells us to compel employers to provide pensions or match employees contributions into a scheme of their choice.	■ The ABI, the CBI and the NAPF are also concerned that tax incentives for saving could be removed if savings were made compulsory.
■ One individual suggests that rather than introduce a compulsory system we should penalise employers who do not provide a good scheme.	■ There is a strong belief that compulsion will place a burden on small and medium sized employers which is supported by the CBI and the SBC. The CBI says that compulsion will place an unacceptable burden on SMEs who are ill-equipped to help employees make key decisions. The BBA say that wholesale employer compulsion will have a negative impact on small and medium sized employers. The SBC emphasise that any solution should avoid placing extra burden on small and micro-sized businesses.

Figure B.10 Respondents' views on compulsion (continued)

For	Against
For employees/individuals: **For both:** ■ The TUC advocates compulsion on 15% of earnings above £6,000. They want to split contributions on a ratio of 2:1 employer: employee and pay these into a 2nd tier scheme of the individual's choice: either a private scheme or a revitalised S2P. ■ The EEF proposes that a compulsory national scheme funded initially by 2% employer: 2% employee contributions, rising to 4% each over 10 years with an exemption for those already paying into good quality provision.[3] ■ One individual proposes compelling employers to contribute to pensions for all their employees and compelling employees to contribute when they are over 35. Individual contribution levels should be phased in so they pay full rate by age 40. The Government should credit the low paid and limit investment choice to reduce risk.	■ The CBI believes that compulsion could distort economic activity and make firms reluctant to grow. ■ The ABI believe that any increase in savings achieved via compulsion will come primarily from low earners and those not contributing to a pension or contributing very little. They say that the later have higher debt to income ratios so need to be able to opt out of saving if it is not appropriate for them.

---

[3] The EEF proposes that this compulsory system be introduced on top of an enhanced basic state pension paying 21% of average earnings at 65 and 25% of average earnings at 75.

Provisos for compulsion

We were also able to use responses to compile a list of proposed conditions for compulsion if it were to be introduced: many of which were proposed by organisations and individuals who were against compulsory private savings in principle.

■ The ABI says that if the government introduces compulsion then the level should be adequate, the system must be transparent and durable, the administration must be secure and efficient, individuals should be able to chose the level of risk for their investment and the decumulation phase should balance flexibility with security and retain choice via the open market option. The risk of levelling down should be mitigated with additional incentives.

■ Help the Aged warns that compulsion should not be introduced only on employees.

■ Lawrence Churchill says that if necessary we should compel individuals to save a certain amount but not prescribe the method of saving. If we do chose to recommend compulsion we should also consider assisting individuals through compulsion on employers.

■ There was the view that compulsion would be welcomed by many as long as it would benefit savers rather than financial institutions.

Other provisos include:

■ Any compulsion should be spread across individuals, employers (who should be compelled to make a certain level of contributions), the state (who should be compelled to stand by the promises made), and the financial services industry (who should be compelled to be prudent with funds).

■ People should only be compelled to save into very safe products. One individual also says that compulsion would be fair only if the government underwrites the risk.

■ Even in a compulsory scheme where government collects contributions to pass on to providers, consumers should be allowed to choose between regulated products.

■ People with access to a decent DB scheme should be exempt from any national compulsion.

■ If government compels individuals to save then it needs to subsidise those at low incomes.

■ Any compulsory system also needs to limit investment choice to reduce risk.

■ A compulsory system would need large collective investment vehicles as default in order to keep costs down.

■ A compulsory system needs to protect SMEs and the self-employed.

Auto-enrolment:

Several respondents to the Report also commented on the policy of auto-enrolment: automatically enrolling individuals into pension schemes but allowing them to opt-out if they so choose. The CBI and Norwich Union say that they are in favour of applying the principle of auto-enrolment to pension schemes. Auto-enrolment has also featured heavily in much of the public media debate and has many supporters. The ABI are also in favour of encouraging auto-enrolment. The Prudential is in favour of auto-enrolment where employers make contributions.

6. Barriers to voluntary saving

Our First Report highlighted several barriers to saving: savings behaviour; the costs of saving and the complexity of the system. Responses to our consultation indicate that many employers do not want the responsibility of a company pension scheme and that the lack of security puts respondents off saving in a pension. And several submissions describe the removal of tax credits on pensions as a raid on pension fund dividend income by the government and now, as a reason not to save. One submission notes that in order to solve the pensions problem, government has to overcome the unrealistic expectations and widespread scepticism of the public.

The fact that people have seen their pensions decrease in value is described as a reason not to save. Standard Life believes that the costs of saving in the UK are very competitive given the distribution model and advice rules that apply. However cost savings could be made by adopting a new distributions model and the lighter touch sales regime. Others think that financial services professionals charge too much for the return they achieve and one individual suggests that performance related management charges should be introduced for schemes. The TUC thinks that establishing multi-employer/industry wide schemes will reduce costs.

Trust is a significant problem, with organisations and individuals noting a lack of trust in the government, the financial services industry and employers [Figure B.11].

Figure B.11 Lack of trust in various bodies

Government	Financial Services	Employers
■ We heard that the government does not address risks or stand by its promises.	■ We have been told that the financial services do not provide a good return and are not prudent with funds.	■ We have been warned that individuals do not trust employer schemes and this lack of trust is in part due to employers changing the level of contributions.
■ One individual writes that people will not save until the government helps those who have previously lost out in pension scheme collapses.	■ Another says that we need to encourage the industry to communicate clearly to overcome issues with trust.	
■ Another says that the problem is partly caused by the government giving out mixed messages.		
■ We also heard that the government needs to guarantee that it will not change its plans again.		
■ One individual thinks that restoring the tax credits on pension fund dividend income will restore trust.		

7. Revitalising the voluntary system

A large number of submissions state that they are in favour of revitalising the voluntary system including those from the NAPF, Legal & General, the ABI, the CBI, the BBA, Aegon, Lloyds TSB, Norwich Union, Age Concern, HSBC Actuaries and Consultants Limited and the Prudential. Their ideas about how to revitalise the system, however, vary widely and some respondents propose ways forward which involve more compulsory measures than others.

We asked respondents specifically to indicate whether they thought the voluntary system could work for low income earners and here there was considerable disagreement [Figure B.12].

Figure B.12 Respondents' views on whether voluntarism can work for low income earners

Yes	No
■ Aegon believes that it is viable for the industry to serve low income groups through the employer.	■ The CBI believes that some low income people will be better off relying on state provision. The CBI would like to see a voluntary "pension partnership" for low earners where employees and employers each make a minimum of 3% contributions which is matched at 3% by government for first 5 years.
■ HSBC Actuaries and Consultants Limited thinks that it will become possible to serve low income earners as the lighter touch sales process and higher charge cap take effect.	
■ Lloyds TSB thinks that Reduction in Yields could fall if contributions (voluntary and NI rebates) were collected and handled at a national level.	■ We heard that it was not possible to serve low income earners in employer-sponsored pensions in small and medium firms. One submission argued that low persistency and low premiums mean that it is not possible to serve low income earners and that this will always be the case. We were also told that charges are too high for low income earners and the market ignores the lowest income earners.
■ Another submission suggests that if employers set up multi-employer schemes it would be possible to serve low income earners.	
■ Watson Wyatt says that the workplace can be an efficient route to facilitate pension saving by people on low incomes.	■ Lloyds TSB says that low income earners are focussed on subsistence and have nothing spare to save.
	■ The BBA says that individuals earning less than £20-25,000 do not want to take risks with their saving.
■ We have also been told that it would only be possible if the government met the cost of advice or if pay levels increase at the bottom of the income distribution.	■ The Prudential says that stakeholder pensions are not economically viable for some market segments.
■ Legal & General believe that it is commercially viable to market to low income groups through the workplace.	

Making voluntarism work

Although many organisations come out in favour of voluntarism, they suggest a broad range of ways to revitalise the voluntary system. Legal & General says that we need to stimulate the demand for saving. Another respondent suggests that we use insights into behavioural economics to encourage more people to save in pensions. Most organisations suggest a package of measures which would be necessary. Watson Wyatt, for example, says that the system needs better, more rational incentives for saving, less regulation, and better financial education.

In this Section, however, we have split the suggestions by the following themes:

i)   Advice, information, education;

ii) Incentives;

iii) Employers and the labour market;

iv) Regulation; and

v)   Products and scheme design.

i)   Making voluntarism work: Through advice and information

A large group of respondents argues for better advice and information on pensions and a drive to improve financial capability. Several responses suggest that improving information and advice on saving will kick start voluntary saving. Others argue for improved information and advice even though they do not believe that this would have a significant impact on the level of saving. We have been told to increase levels of information and communicate the need to save to create a new savings culture.

Norwich Union says that the government need to make it easier to give financial advice. Several respondents think that there should be generic advice separate from the sales process, particularly for low earners. One person suggests that the government should fund, but not operate, independent, face to face advice. Others think that information and advice should come through the work-place, by, for example, improving information to help employees understand the value of employer contributions. A few respondents, including Legal & General, think that providing comprehensive pension statements could help.

The CBI, the ABI, the ACA and Age Concern and several others all think better education would go at least some way to improving the level of voluntary saving. Aegon suggests that the industry, with government encouragement, needs to run a campaign of education and information to change consumer attitudes on the importance of saving. The Institute of Actuaries also believes that financial literacy is important and that we need a simple information campaign to communicate the need for individuals to provide for their own retirement. Several submissions suggest that better financial education will improve the situation but not solve the problem and most people will still need professional advice. It was suggested that better education should be a long term goal but it will not be the short-term answer.

ii)   Making voluntarism work: Through incentives

Several respondents note that there should be good rational incentives for people to save and the government should increase these. We have been reminded that incentives need to be simple and stable. It is suggested by some that incentives should be focused on those with low incomes or on individuals approaching retirement. Dr Ros Altmann says that both individuals and employers need better, fairer incentives, targeted at those who need them most. The London Stock Exchange notes that removing stamp duty on equities will increase pension values and incentivise saving.

Tax relief is the most contentious form of incentivising saving, Figure B.13 studies respondents' views on tax relief.

Figure B.13 Respondents' views on tax relief

For	Against
■ A few respondents suggest that we should leave the current system as it is but the majority of those in favour of tax relief thought that the current system needs revising or remarketing. ■ Several respondents think tax relief should be simplified and/or used to incentivise long-term saving. Lawrence Churchill suggests that tax could be used to enhance rates of return. ■ The CBI says the government should increase awareness of tax relief. ■ The ABI says tax relief should be rebranded with a clear message. ■ Age Concern and Help the Aged, amongst others, think that tax relief should favour low to middle income earners. ■ Several responses argue for a reduction in higher rate tax relief or a single rate of tax relief. ■ The Small Business Council suggests using tax relief to support employers who contribute to employee pensions. ■ The CBI, and others, suggest using tax relief or credits to help businesses contributing to pensions.	Several responses criticise the current system of tax relief and cite the following reasons: ■ Tax relief favours the rich; ■ Tax incentives are not generally understood; and ■ The annual payment of tax allowance is inefficient and unfair. Several other responses argue for the abolition of tax relief: ■ One individual suggests that the government should abolish tax relief and put money saved towards benefits. ■ Another thinks that no tax relief is necessary above £30,000 annual earnings. ■ The Women's Budget Group proposes limiting tax relief to 22% and then phasing it out. ■ One respondent suggests that it would be better to not give tax relief during the accumulation phase and to not tax pensions in payment.

iii)   Making voluntarism work: Through employers/ labour market

Legal & General, Aegon and the Prudential amongst several others think that work place/employer provision is key to revitalising the voluntary sector. Several organisations, including Age Concern, think that employer contributions are key and that government should encourage and incentivise higher contribution levels:

■ The CBI and the Norwich Union, amongst others, would like the government to incentivise employers to contribute to schemes. HSBC Actuaries and Consultants Limited would also like to reward employers for sharing risk with employees. The ACA thinks that there should be incentives for those employers whose schemes meet certain requirements. The Prudential would like the government to incentivise smaller employers to contribute to schemes.

■ The CBI believes that a tight labour market will make employers provide better benefits and that employers should match employees contributions where they can afford to. They call for the introduction of a Pensions Contribution Tax Credit and they are particularly in favour of incentivisation for SMEs and suggest a range of methods: seed-corn funding, industry wide schemes, subsidised IFA advice and incentives for contributions for low earners.

■ The ABI also calls for a Pension Contribution Tax Credit which could be targeted at SMEs to encourage employer contributions to pensions. They also suggest incentivised financial advice in the workplace.

■ There was also a call for the government to introduce lower taxes on employers and employees to encourage private provision and increase incentives for pension funds.

■ Other suggestions include making one to one advice at work mandatory, incentivising employer provision through the NI system and encouraging salary sacrifice and taxing those companies who do not provide DB schemes and using this money to fund protection for those who do. The TUC think that we should look at creating multi-employer schemes and the NAPF argue that there is a clear role for multi-employer schemes in which economies of scale could be generated to the benefit of sponsoring employers and scheme members.

iv)   Making voluntarism work: Changes to regulation

Some respondents, including the ACA, suggest that radical simplification and reduction of regulation or making regulation more proportionate could help revitalise the voluntary system. The NAPF says that the volume, cost and prescriptiveness of the regulatory system are a major cause of the decline of occupational pensions and the government should simplify regulation to allow the private sector to flourish. More specifically, one submission says that the government need to rewrite FRS17 to make it more realistic for DB schemes. HSBC Consultants and Actuaries Limited call for genuine simplification of the pensions regulatory regime.

v)   Making voluntarism work: with products and scheme design

Several respondents have written to us with proposals about scheme design in the private saving sector. The greatest call was for increased flexibility and portability of products. The ABI argues that pot proliferation and lack of persistency in saving are significant problems and we should look at ways to enable employers to pay contributions into an individual's pension pot and make transferring funds easier. The CBI, amongst others, would support a system of pension pots owned by individuals into which employers could pay pensions contributions. The BBA believe that the introduction of individualised long-term savings pots into which specific retirement contributions could be made would reinvigorate saving and provide more flexible ways of doing so. Standard Life suggests establishing a means through which employer contributions could be collected and channelled into an individual's pot to encourage persistency. Aegon is sceptical as to the overall benefits of establishing a central clearing house by which to do this. HSBC Actuaries and Consultants Limited say there should be flexibility in relation to retirement patterns, for example, final salary schemes should be able to convert pensions into a pot of money so as to facilitate staggered vesting. The ACA says employers should be able to change scheme rules retrospectively to reduce unexpected costs due to longer life expectancy including raising the normal retirement age. They would also like to see the promotion of lower cost DB schemes offering "foundation level" benefits.

The second most frequent set of demands is for simpler, more transparent products. Professor Nicholas Barr writes that we need simple reliable savings products to facilitate voluntary pension saving. One submission told us specifically that people want a no-risk, modest-return, tax-free product with a guarantee that it will pay out. Another suggests launching simple ISA like products for pension saving which will not require a sales process. And yet another says that we should introduce a Personal Savings account for all based on a compulsory 10% contribution which could be collected through the NI system.

Other proposals include introducing schemes where the value of the pension is affected by the average life expectancy at time of retirement or schemes that operate like bank accounts and allow people to access assets. We have been warned that pension fund design must lock a certain amount of the fund into bonds. Help the Aged also says that pensions should be designed to be split on divorce.

Life-cycle issues are also important to some respondents. One individual proposes investing at birth for a pension pot. More respondents say that people should be able to bequeath pensions wealth or bequeath their estates into pension-type savings for the recipient.

8. Risk

Achieving the appropriate risk-sharing balance between the state, employers, the financial services industry and individuals will be a key in any pension reform. In our First Report, the Pensions Commission highlighted the shift in pension provision from DB to DC and asked whether the large shift of risk to individuals which is currently occurring is acceptable and/or avoidable. No respondent said that this shift in risk is acceptable. Many, however, including the ABI, think that it is unavoidable. Watson Wyatt notes that high levels of regulation, required benefits and recent changes to pension legislation such as the set up of the PPF have encouraged the shift to DC pension provision and the consequent shift in risk holding. Legal & General, however, thinks that risk has shifted to individuals because they do not appreciate others taking it on their behalf or understand the consequences of risk.

Looking ahead, there was a range of opinion about who should bear risk [Figure B.14].

Figure B.14 Who should bear risk in pension provision?

State	Employer	Individual
■ We were told that the government should guarantee risk in any compulsory system up to a stated level of income.	■ The ACA notes that employers are unwilling to take on mortality risk.	■ One individual warned that we need to reassure individuals that the factors on which they calculate risk will not be changed by government.
■ Standard Life thinks that the state should take on more of the risk for low earners.	■ Amicus says that we need to look at ways to encourage employers to provide DB schemes. Another respondent said that we need to protect DB schemes from employer raids, and should consider a move to career average schemes.	■ The Prudential and the London Stock Exchange say that we need to improve consumer understanding of risk and reward.
■ One submission argues that the state should take on longevity and inflation risk and another says that risk should be borne by society through the state.		
■ The ACA and the Prudential, amongst others, say that the Government should issue ultra long-dated or longevity bonds.		
■ The NAPF also says that the government should consider the merits of issuing long-dated or longevity bonds to help schemes manage longevity risk.		
■ The Institute of Actuaries, however, would welcome ultra-long gilts but is not convinced that government should issue longevity bonds.		

Figure B.14 Who should bear risk in pension provision? (continued)

Most respondents argue for some sort of risk sharing arrangement:

- Age Concern thinks that we should seek to preserve the current balance of risk sharing, and the CBI, the ABI and Help the Aged all believe that we need a clear, comprehensible division of risk between individuals, employers, financial institutions and state.

- HSBC Actuaries and Consultants Limited argue that employers should take investment risk and individuals should take on mortality risk and that employers should be rewarded for sharing risk.

- The TUC suggests introducing industry wide schemes to pool risk between small and medium employers.

- The NAPF, the TUC, the CBI and Age Concern, amongst others, say we should encourage risk-sharing pensions and hybrid schemes such as cash balance or career average schemes. The CBI and the NAPF note that in order to do this, the government should not apply the regulations for DB schemes to hybrid schemes. The NAPF also say that government should give encouragement to pension arrangements where risks are shared between employers and members such as cash balance or career average schemes and the regulation of such schemes needs careful consideration.

- One submission argues that government should spread risk in DB by allowing companies to change employee contribution levels and allow pensions to be partially funded on a PAYG basis where companies have large deficits. Government should also underwrite DB schemes and meet the cost of this through a charge on those employers not providing DB pensions.

- The EOC feels that individuals should not have to take on investment risk for their subsistence income.

Investment risk is also a significant issue in funded pension saving. We have been told that there should be no investment risk in basic pension provision and that above this asset allocation should be as diverse as possible. We were warned that a policy based mainly on private saving could result in cohorts of poor and rich pensioners because of the volatility of the stock market.

Annuities

The Pensions Commission has noted that the public debate has a tendency to focus on the accumulation phase of pension saving and the issues surrounding the decumulation phase are less well discussed. Yet any policy designed to increase savings in DC schemes will place increased demand on the annuities market which the insurance industry will have to absorb. The ABI tells us that there is some concern about the capacity of market which would be eased by a wider base of supporting investments including new and innovative instruments. It is also noted that consumers want a guaranteed income in retirement but also want return of unused capital when they die. It is this desire for a pot to bequeath which seems to turn the issue of annuities, and particularly compulsory annuitisation at age 75, into a contentious one. We have heard various arguments both for and against annuities [Figure B.15].

Figure B.15 Respondents' views on annuities

For	Against
■ Legal & General tells us that the annuities market is robust but the government should back it with long-dated or longevity bonds.	■ The ACA says we should consider alternatives to annuities.
■ The Prudential says that annuities are the most financially efficient way of converting retirement funds into an income for life..	■ Standard Life warns that the annuity rate risk is significant for people with DC pension arrangements.
■ One submission proposes a government backed standard retirement annuity. Another calls for the introduction of a flexible, deferred annuity which is underwritten by the State.	■ Watson Wyatt writes that there is a risk associated with individuals preferences for single life flat annuities given the growth in DC schemes. **Change:**
■ Aegon says it should be possible to pool pension pots at retirement to enable couples to purchase a joint life annuity	■ Six responses call on us to abolish the requirement to purchase an annuity at 75. ■ Age Concern argues that it should be compulsory to disclose the purchase of a single life annuity.

9. Non-pensions savings and housing wealth

In our First Report we concluded that non-pensions assets and housing assets in particular, are significant and could play a significant role in pension provision on average but that they do not provide a sufficient solution to the pension problem because of the uneven distribution of assets. We asked respondents whether they agreed with our assessment and received a range of responses [Figure B.16].

Figure B.17 Respondents views on non-pension savings and housing wealth

More significant than the Commission thinks...	Not the whole solution...
■ Professor Tim Congdon writes that all saving within the UK should be considered relevant. Overall national savings are about at the level to produce 60% of earnings in retirement. The problem to tackle is unequal distribution of assets.	■ The NAPF and the CBI both agree with our conclusion that non-pension assets and housing will not provide a total solution.
■ The ABI, the ACA and the Prudential think that non-pension assets and housing are more important than the Commission states. The ACA thinks that the market for equity release is likely to grow. The BBA also say that housing assets are increasingly a key consideration when providing for retirement.	■ One individual notes that some people are in theory keen to use some assets for retirement but also that the Commission is right to be cautious about the extent to which people on low incomes will be able to liquidate assets. Inheritance is least likely to go to those who need it.
■ Lawrence Churchill writes that housing wealth could be more important if asset prices rise faster either because of a shortage of supply or driven by fiscal incentives.	■ Age Concern think that inheritance will increase the unequal distribution of wealth.
■ One submission notes that non-pensions assets are important for the self-employed.	
■ Another individual writes that the housing market is easier to understand and value of asset easier to determine.	

Sectoral and national savings

This Appendix presents an analysis, conducted by the Pensions Commission, of trends in sectoral and national savings. It responds to several comments made in response to the First Report, which suggested that different conclusions might be reached if the Commission focused on total household or total national savings rather than pension savings alone. [See Figure C.1 for a summary of some of these comments.] In fact Chapter 5 of the First Report did look at the **stock** of household sector wealth held in non-pension financial assets and houses. But it did not present an integrated analysis of all categories of saving **flow** including those by non-household sectors.

This Appendix therefore now presents an integrated analysis of all categories of national saving. It is intended as a stimulus to discussion, and as an exploration of some difficult issues of interpretation. The tentative conclusions, proposed for debate, are set out in Figure C.2.

The Appendix is structured in six sections:

1. The relationship between sectoral and national savings: theory and the overall present position

2. Aggregate national savings and pension adequacy

3. Apparent long-term trends in sectoral and national savings

4. The economic meaning of equity value increases in excess of aggregate net savings

5. Household financial savings, pension and non-pension: some key trends

6. Household saving in houses: capital investment and price appreciation effects

Three annexes covering technical issues are available on the Pensions Commission's website (www.pensonscommission.gov.uk: Sectoral and National Savings Discussion Paper). They cover:

■ Annex A: Understanding the external position

■ Annex B: Complexities in the measurement of the corporate savings rate

■ Annex C: Response to specific points made by Tim Congdon

1. Sectoral and national savings: theory and present position

The UK's gross national saving represents the extent to which, in any given year, the UK does not consume that year's GNP, but saves it, either via investment in the UK or via the acquisition of a claim on the rest of the world. National savings mathematically equals household saving plus corporate saving plus general government saving [Figure C.3].

Figure C.4 sets out the figures for gross savings for the three sectors and at the national aggregate level in 2002, with a gross national saving of £156 billion in 2002. Figure C.5 shows the derivation of net saving (gross savings minus capital consumption) and of "net lending", the financial balance of each sector given by gross saving minus investment. The minus £17 billion for the national net lending figure in 2002 represents the fact that in 2002 the rest of the world sector net acquired £17 billion of claims on the UK.

Figure C.1 Comments received on the savings analysis in the First Report

- Analysis of aggregate national savings would reveal long-term adequacy and therefore prove individual rationality in savings decisions.

- Analysis of aggregate national savings would reveal that the problem of inadequate savings is worse than first appears because of government dis-saving.

- Personal sector total wealth is now higher than ever: therefore any inadequacy of pension saving must be being offset by non-pension saving.

- Saving via the accumulation of housing assets could create adequate consumption in retirement resources for many people.

- Measured national savings underestimate real economic savings since an increasing proportion of economic investment (e.g. in R&D and know-how) is not captured in accounting measures.

Figure C.2 Some possible conclusions

- It is not possible to draw strong inferences about the adequacy of savings for retirement from the level of the aggregate national savings rate...

- ... but trends in the rate are likely to carry implications for trends in savings for retirement adequacy [See Section 2].

- The UK **gross** national rate may be on a slight downward trend but the **net** savings rate appears trendless with capital consumption trending down [See Section 3].

- Over the last 25 years UK households have enjoyed significant "wealth accumulation without saving" as a result of equity price appreciation unexplained by capital investment: but this effect is unlikely to repeat in the future [See Section 4].

- If there is a deficiency of household pension saving, it is not being offset by household direct accumulation of claims on corporate capital [See Section 5].

- But what has occurred in the last 25 years is a steady increase both in household debt liabilities and in household cash (and equivalent) assets with, effectively, increased financial flows from one part of the household sector to another (via banks and building societies) [See Section 5].

- This increase in household to household lending has arisen from and is dependent on the increased value of housing assets relative to GDP, which in turn has implications for the design of optimal pension policy, even though it derives (primarily) from price appreciation effects which (rightly) do not appear in national accounts measures of household sector or national saving [See Section 6].

Figure C.3 National saving and sectional saving

- Household sector saving (pension and non-pension)

      +

- Corporate sector saving (non-financial corporate and financial corporate)

      +

- General government saving

      =

- National saving

Figures C.4 and C.5 show significant gross saving by the household sector but also significant investment; this is primarily in residential housing. They also show that the biggest gross saving figure is in the non-financial corporate sector, matched by investment in productive business capital. And they show that in 2002 government was a significant dissaver at the net savings level. But it is important to understand that **all** wealth is ultimately owned by the household sector, and that all saving/dissaving is ultimately on behalf of the household sector. Government dissaving creates a liability which the household sector will eventually have to pay for through taxes; and corporate saving accrues to the benefit of the household sector, since it increases the value of corporate capital held by households even when households make no new acquisitions of corporate capital [Figure C.6]. Provided a number of equilibrium conditions apply [Figure C.7] and in a closed economy, any change in household wealth held in corporate capital which is not explained by household net acquisition/sale of corporate capital must be exactly explained by corporate sector net saving done on the household sector's behalf.

It would thus be possible in a closed economy in equilibrium to think about the UK's wealth holding and savings patterns as taking the form shown in Figure C.8.

■ The household sector owning, directly or indirectly, two ultimate forms of wealth: the housing stock and the capital resources of companies (represented in real terms by buildings, machines, brands, patents etc. and in financial terms by equities and bonds).

■ The household sector saving/investing via net investment in housing or via net investment in corporate capital.

■ And different groups within the household sector lending and borrowing to one another (via financial institutions), with the value of housing used as security.

This model captures the essence of the savings process, and is a useful one to keep in mind in trying to make sense of the multitude of different figures available. But it is complicated in the real world of open economies and disequilibrium conditions by three factors:

■ First, that for the last 25 years the claim on the value of the corporate sector has increased far faster than can be explained by the combination of household net acquisition of corporate capital plus corporate net saving on the household's behalf [see Section 4 below]. The household sector has as a result got richer much faster than can be explained by measured savings captured anywhere in national accounts.

■ Second, a similar effect has been seen in housing, with the market value of residential housing rising far faster than can be explained by net new capital investment in housing [see Section 6]. Again households have got richer faster than can be explained by measured saving.

Figure C.4 Sectoral and national saving: 2002 £ billion

	Households	Non-financial corporations	Financial corporations	General government	National
Gross operating surplus and property income		261			
- Distributed income		-135			
- Taxes		-25			
Gross disposable income/ total resources*	735	101	21	210	1057
Final consumption	-692		-11	-209	-901
Gross saving	43	101	10	2	156

Source: Blue Book

Note: *Figure shown is after the reallocation of pension fund saving to household sector i.e. total resources.

Figure C.5 Gross saving, net saving and capital investment: 2002 £ billion

	Households	Non-financial corporations	Financial corporations	General government	National
Gross savings	43	101	10	2	156
- Capital consumption	-36	-65	-4	-10	-115
= Net saving	7	37	6	-9	41
Gross saving	43	101	10	2	156
+/- Other	3	3	0	-5	1
- Capital investment	-50	-103	-7	-15	-174
= Net lending +/-	-4	0	3	-17	-17

Source: Blue Book

Figure C.6 Understanding corporate saving and household wealth

■ All wealth ultimately belongs to people: government wealth in a collective sense, but corporate wealth in an individual property claim sense.

■ Saving by the corporate sector must therefore increase household wealth in some way.

■ The route is that:
  – Net saving by corporations increases the retained wealth of companies, and thus the market value of companies.
  – It does not show up in the income, gross saving, or capital investment of households.
  – But it delivers to households unrealised capital appreciation, so that on average the value of equities held (in pension funds or outside) rises by more than the next acquisition of equities.

Figure C.7 Corporate sector net saving and equity price appreciation: equilibrium conditions

■ If all "investment" which increases the value of a company is covered by the accounting definitions of "capital investment"...

  ... and if "capital consumption" correctly captures the investment needed to keep the value unchanged...

  ... and if all net saving exactly earns the rate of return which shareholders expect/require...

■ ... then the market value of equities equals the book value (Tobin's Q=1).

■ And the change in market value each year equals the change in book value which is the net savings.

■ So that corporate sector net savings equals unrealised capital gain by the household sector.

Figure C.8 Wealth holdings in a closed economy in equilibrium

The household sector
(directly or indirectly) owns

The household sector
(directly and indirectly)
saves/invests

↓

↓

■ The housing stock

■ Via net investment
  in housing

the household sector lends
and borrows within itself,
via banks and building
societies with house value
as the main security

+

+

+

■ Corporate capital
  (bonds + equities)

■ Via net investment in
  corporate capital

■ Thirdly, in an open economy there are a complicated set of claims by the various UK sectors on the rest of the world, and by the rest of the world on the UK sectors.

Sections 4 and 6 explore the complexities created by share price and house price appreciation; Annex A (available on the Pensions Commission's website) explains some key trends in the external accounts which need to be understood if misinterpretations are to be avoided. But before turning to these complexities, Section 2 considers what inferences for pension adequacy can and (crucially) **cannot** be drawn from aggregate national savings analysis. Section 3 then considers the apparent long-term trends in sectoral and national savings.

2. Pension adequacy and aggregate national savings

This section considers what implications for pension system adequacy can and cannot be inferred from analysis of the national aggregate savings rate. It makes the following points:

(i) All forms of saving need to be considered in assessing the adequacy of resources for retirement.

(ii) Whether saving for retirement is "adequate" cannot be inferred directly from analysis of the **level** of the aggregate national savings rate. Analysis of the "adequacy" of a pension system can only proceed via bottom-up analysis of the savings stocks and flows of specific groups of people.

(iii) An argument can however be made that a low savings rate may make political conflicts over future income distribution, and in particular over the taxation/generosity balance with the state PAYG system, more severe. How far this is true depends on how pensioners define income "adequacy" in retirement.

(iv) But trends in the national savings rate are likely to carry some implications for trends in pension adequacy.

(v) And analysis of the implications for the national savings rate is a useful discipline in assessing proposals for pension policy changes.

(i) Pension and non-pension savings equally relevant

"Pension" saving is simply that element of total saving which happens to occur within the legal form of pension funds or pension policies (and which because taking that legal form benefits from pensions-specific tax rules). But accumulated "pension" saving is no more valuable as a potential source of "consumption in retirement" resources than any other form of savings accumulated by the time of retirement. It is therefore clear that we should analyse all forms of savings (direct and indirect) through which households can accumulate assets: pension savings, non-pension financial savings, and real assets (in particular houses).

In the rest of this section we will therefore refer to "savings for retirement" to cover all forms of savings which individuals accumulate and which they could draw upon during retirement.

(ii) The level of national savings and the adequacy of savings for retirement

There is no way to infer the adequacy of savings for retirement directly from the level of national savings. To understand this we start with definitions:

■ National savings represents the aggregate national excess of current income (GNP) over current consumption. Positive net national savings (after capital consumption) increase the capital stock and, in combination with technological progress, deliver increased GDP. The national savings level captures the combined effect of savings by or on behalf of some households and dissavings by or on behalf of other households.

■ "Savings in retirement" represents the accumulation of assets by people of working age. These savings are then to a degree decumulated during retirement providing consumption in retirement resources.[1] For the individual who leaves no bequeathal indeed, dissavings in retirement exactly equal savings during working life. Such a person has no net savings across the whole lifecycle, but may still have a perfectly adequate pension.

Given these definitions, there are three reasons why the **level** of national savings has no necessary implications for the adequacy of pension savings.

■ First, it is at least theoretically possible for an economy to have a nil net savings rate but to have a quite adequate system of funded savings for retirement (and thus no requirement for a PAYG system). Such an economy would typically be a zero growth economy (since the capital stock would not increase). But workers could be significant net savers, accumulating savings for retirement throughout working life, and then selling off these accumulated assets to the next generation of workers

---

[1] More precisely pensions actually derive from the combination of asset decumulation plus investment income earned on the remaining asset balance.

during retirement. The zero adequate savings rate could be the sum of perfectly "adequate" net savings by workers matched exactly by the dissavings of retirees.

If we introduce growth in GDP and in incomes the model gets more complex. Accumulation by workers now exceeds decumulation by retirees thus producing the positive national savings required to deliver a growing capital stock. But it remains the case that the total scale of savings for retirement (the accumulation by workers) will greatly exceed aggregate national savings. And the potential adequacy of "savings for retirement" depends more on the size of the capital stock which can be bought by workers and sold by retirees, than by the flow of net savings in any particular period.

■ Second, it is **possible** that the capital stock which is bought by workers and sold by retirees can increase relative to national income even if there is no net national saving. This can for instance occur via the route discussed in Section 6, an increase in the price of houses unexplained by net investment in housing. This increase does not represent national savings in either accounting or real economic terms[2], but it may well mean that workers devote increased resources to the purchase of houses while retirees can achieve higher retirement incomes through the sale of houses (either those that they themselves purchased or those that they inherit). Gross workers' saving devoted to the purchase of housing assets can thus rise, but with no increase in the national savings rate, because there is matching decumulation by retirees.

■ Third, conversely, it is clearly possible for a high national savings rate to co-exist with inadequate savings for retirement for many people, since some people may save more than adequately for retirement while others save inadequately.

For all these reasons it is impossible to infer from the level of national savings whether a system of savings for retirement is "adequate". A low savings rate country could, at least theoretically, have a workable and stable system of inter-generational resource transfer based on the accumulation and decumulation of either corporate capital or houses; and a country with a high savings rate could have a high proportion of the population making inadequate funded provision for their retirement, with savings very unevenly distributed.

---

[2] See Gale and Sabelhaus, "Perspectives on the Household Saving Rate", Brookings Papers on Economic Activity 1: 1999, for a discussion on this and other complexities in the measurement of saving.

The only way to measure the "adequacy" of "savings for retirement" by the current generation of workers is therefore on a bottom-up basis, analysing for different groups of people the stocks of assets (of all types) already accumulated, the flows of savings (of all types) occurring, and likely accumulated funds available at point of retirement.[3]

(iii) A low savings rate may increase future political tensions

An important counter-argument can however be made that the level of the savings rate matters because of its effect on the growth rate, and because a higher growth rate ameliorates political conflicts over the distribution of income. An increased national savings rate, by increasing the capital stock, can increase future productivity and thus GDP. Not all the benefit of this future GDP growth will flow to providers of capital: some will flow to future workers, who will enjoy higher wages, and to future government tax revenues. The total economic cake out of which retirees can receive state PAYG pension is therefore increased: any given real pensioner income can be afforded at a lower tax rate on workers: or for any given tax rate on workers a better real value PAYG pension can be afforded. Conversely a low savings rate means less future resources and therefore greater conflict.

An article in the National Institute Economic Review 2005 ("Are we saving enough?") illustrated this argument. It argued that a net national savings rate of 5.0%, combined with a capital stock of 4.28 times Net Domestic Product, implied that in the long-term the UK economy could only grow at 1.2% real per year. Therefore (even absent any demographic effects on dependency ratios) unless pensioners are willing to accept only 1.2% per year real growth in pensioner incomes between this generation and the next, there are political problems ahead: either unhappy pensioners, or unhappy workers on whom pensioners (via their voting power) will impose increased taxes.

---

[3] Note however that any such analysis is crucially dependent on the assumptions made as to (i) the level of income replacement that people will consider adequate (ii) the age at which they retire (iii) the rate of return on investment.

The validity of this argument, and thus of the assertion that an increased national savings rate is required to ameliorate future pension problems depends on whether assessments of pension income adequacy are determined by reference to real income during life (plus some desired absolute level of growth) or to the average level of income in society when people reach retirement [Figure C.9].

■ If the former then a more rapid rate of growth clearly eases pension adequacy problems: retirees can feel adequately provided even if the percentage of GDP flowing to retirees falls since the denominator (GDP) rises.

■ If the latter case (adequacy defined relative to average incomes) more rapid GDP growth does not ease any perceptions that provision is inadequate.

The issue of the definition of adequacy was discussed in Chapter 4 of the First Report: it is relevant to the debate on whether state pensions should be earnings indexed during retirement or price indexed. A reasonable judgement is that perceptions of adequacy probably lie between these two extremes: if they do then a higher rate of growth does to a degree mitigate pension inadequacy problems. It is noticeable for instance that countries which have achieved very high rates of GDP growth (e.g. Ireland in the last few decades) seem able to deliver pensions which many individuals consider "adequate" even while keeping pension expenditure as a percentage of GDP very low: pensioners have high real incomes relative to expectations determined by their own lifetime earnings, even though low relative to the general level of prosperity now achieved. But while this suggests that in general a higher rate of national savings and thus of GDP growth must help avoid tensions in the state pension system, it still leaves us with no straightforward way to infer overall pension system adequacy (covering both the PAYG and funded elements of the system) from the level of the national savings rate.

(iv) Trends in national savings rates relevant to pension adequacy debates

While however there is no straightforward way of inferring savings for retirement adequacy from the **level** of national savings, it is **likely** that **trends** in the national savings rate do carry some implications for trends in the adequacy of savings for retirement. An increase in the national savings rate is one possible element in the response to the demographic challenge. It can however produce disadvantages if pursued too far.

In our First Report we talked of four possible responses to rising life expectancy and a rising dependency ratio: a fall in relative pensioner incomes, a rise in taxes, a rise in the retirement age or a rise in savings. If the fourth option is taken, the current generation of workers will sacrifice current consumption in working life to deliver a higher level of total consumption in retirement than enjoyed by previous generations (i.e. where total real consumption in retirement is the annual rate of real consumption multiplied

Figure C.9 Definition of pension adequacy: implications for the importance of the aggregate savings rate

A. Pension adequacy defined relative to average earnings. 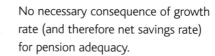 No necessary consequence of growth rate (and therefore net savings rate) for pension adequacy.

B. Pension adequacy defined relative to growth target (eg. 60% of current average earnings + 1.2% real growth per year). 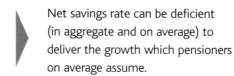 Net savings rate can be deficient (in aggregate and on average) to deliver the growth which pensioners on average assume.

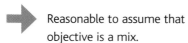 Reasonable to assume that objective is a mix. 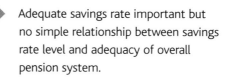 Adequate savings rate important but no simple relationship between savings rate level and adequacy of overall pension system.

by more years). This increase in accumulation by workers will clearly deliver an increase in total national savings in the short-term, and may, under certain conditions, increase it in the long-term.

- In the short-term the total national savings rate will rise because worker accumulation has already risen, while increased retiree decumulation lies in the future.

- In the long-term, the total national savings rate **may** stay higher because each subsequent generation of workers may also have a higher accumulation savings rate, and while the total retiree decumulation rate will also increase, in a growing economy the former effect outweighs the latter. (The total capital stock/GDP ratio will also increase to a new level and the aggregate net savings rate required to maintain this higher equilibrium level will increase.)

- The caveat "may" is included however because the long-term effect is dependent on the preferences of the future workers i.e. on how the next generation of workers choose to make the trade-off between savings levels, retirement age and income in retirement. And it is possible that one generation which seeks to save its way to adequate income over a longer retirement, is followed by another which prefers to work later rather than save more. If this occurs the attempt of the current generation to save its way to prosperous and longer retirement may be frustrated by the next generation's low demand for assets. The lower relative income option will then come about by default.[4]

This caveat does not however change the conclusion that a rise in the national savings rate will (in a growing economy) be the inevitable consequence of any solution to a problem of inadequate pension provision which avoids higher retirement ages or higher taxes.

Conversely if the aggregate national savings rate is falling, it is **likely** that problems of inadequate savings for retirement are increasing. A falling aggregate national savings rate could arise **either** (i) because accumulations by current working-age people were falling: this would tend (subject to its precise distribution) to increase any problems of inadequate pension provision; or (ii) because net decumulations by existing retirees were increasing. This would however reduce inheritance receipts by the current working generation, again therefore reducing aggregate resources potentially available for consumption in retirement.

It is therefore valuable to analyse (as we do in Section 3 of this Appendix) the trend in the national savings rate, and to draw possible references of that trend for the number of people with inadequate savings for retirement, even if the level of the aggregate national savings rate can tell us little about the

---

4 See Adair Turner "The Macroeconomics of Pensions" lecture to the Actuarial Profession September 2003 for a more detailed analysis of this possible effect.

absolute scale of the problem. And it is the case that an increased national savings rate is one possible response to the demographic challenge of increased life expectancy.

One potentially negative effect of too large or rapid an increase in the national savings rate should however be noted. An increased rate of aggregate national savings **may** have negative consequences for the rate of return achieved. This would be the case in a closed economy since, everything else equal, an increase in capital/labour ratio will tend to decrease the return to capital and increase the return to labour. Such an effect could however be significantly mitigated in an open global economy, in which the additional savings could be invested outside the country. But if other countries are also simultaneously attempting to save their way to prosperous longer retirements, the falling rate of return effect could apply at the global level. Appendix B of the First Report described published analyses of these issues and estimates of the possible scale of any return reduction effects. It concluded that it was extremely difficult to produce precise convincing estimates, but that directionally there must be some tendency for higher savings to be associated with lower returns. This argues for caution against relying entirely on an increase in savings as the only response to the demographic challenge.

(v) Analysis of national savings rate effects: a useful discipline

As discussed above, analysis of trends in the national savings rate can provide useful though imperfect indications as to whether savings for retirement by the current working generation are rising in response to the demographic challenge: they provide a double-check against the bottom-up analysis (also imperfect because of data problems) which must be the key route to assessing the "adequacy" of saving for retirement.

But analysis of aggregate national savings, and in particular of the combined effects of changes in the household and government savings rates is also useful to guard against "free lunch" fallacies, i.e. policies which might appear to provide responses to the demographic challenge but which on closer inspection do not. Thus, for instance, the economic impact of any proposal to switch from an unfunded PAYG scheme to a funded scheme needs to allow for the impact on public finances. If the switch involves the government foregoing tax/NI revenue but maintaining state pension payments to the existing generation of pensioners, there will be no increase in national savings, since increased public debt will offset the additional funded savings. Only if the switch involves someone sacrificing current expenditure (e.g. by having to pay both PAYG contributions and new contributions to a funded scheme) will additional future resources to support consumption in retirement have been created.

3. Sectoral and national savings: apparent long-term trends

Over the last 25 years, household sector gross and net saving (combining pensions and non-pensions, financial assets and housing assets) have oscillated significantly, but some commentators would argue that the underlying trend is down, with very low rates sustained over the period since 1999 [Figure C.10].

Corporate net saving, conversely, has if anything been on a slight upward trend, with corporate gross saving apparently trendless, but with the accounting measure of "capital consumption" on a steady downward path as a percentage of GDP [Figure C.11].

General government saving meanwhile has been highly cyclical, and at least in the late 1980s and early 1990s inversely related to household savings [Figure C.12].

Figure C.10 Household gross and net saving as a percentage of gross national disposable income: 1980-2004

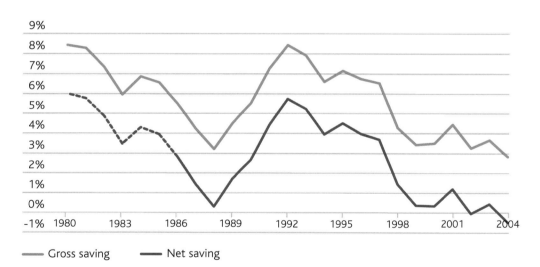

Gross saving   Net saving

Source: Blue Book

Note: Net saving figures prior to 1987 have been estimated using other household data.

Figure C.11 Non-financial corporations gross saving, capital consumption and net saving as a percentage of gross national disposable income: 1980-2004

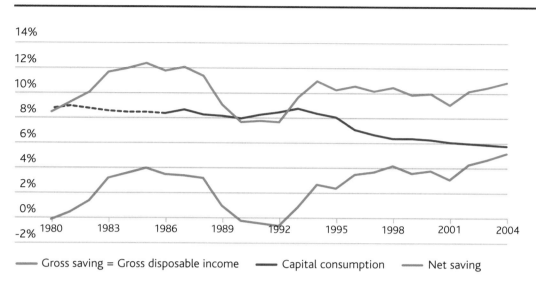

— Gross saving = Gross disposable income   — Capital consumption   — Net saving

Source: Blue Book

Note: Capital consumption figures prior to 1987 have been estimated using other non-financial data.

Figure C.12 General government gross and net savings as a percentage of gross national disposable income: 1980-2004

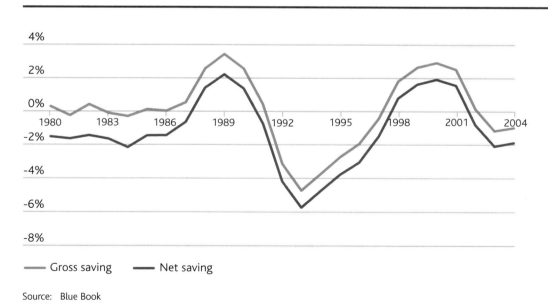

— Gross saving   — Net saving

Source: Blue Book

Putting the three sectors together to produce aggregate national savings, shows an oscillating gross savings line, with, if anything, a slight downward trend over the last 25 years [Figure C.13]. Over the still longer term this downward trend appears more clearly with national gross savings appearing to grow between the late 1940s and the late 1960s, but on a long downward trend thereafter [Figure C.14].

At least over the last 25 years, however, this downward trend is not apparent at the **net** national savings level, with the fall in gross savings offset by the fall in measured "capital consumption" [Figure C.15].

The interpretation of these trends, and their relevance if any for public pension policy is uncertain. As Section 2 argued it is not possible to draw any significant inferences about the adequacy of a pension system from the **level** of aggregate national savings. But it also suggested that trends in the national savings rate **probably** imply trends in adequacy.

Figure C.13 Gross saving by sector as a percentage of gross national disposable income: 1980-2004

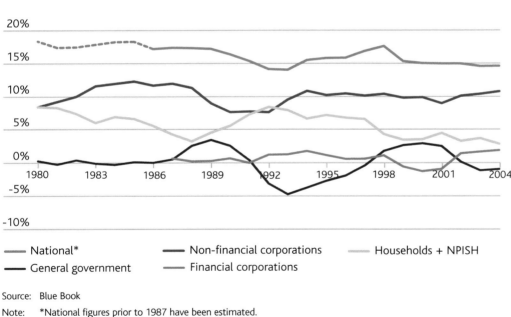

Source: Blue Book

Note: *National figures prior to 1987 have been estimated.
NPISH = Non-profit institutions serving households.

Figure C.14 National savings ratio, 1948-2003: gross capital formation plus the current account surplus as a percentage of GDP

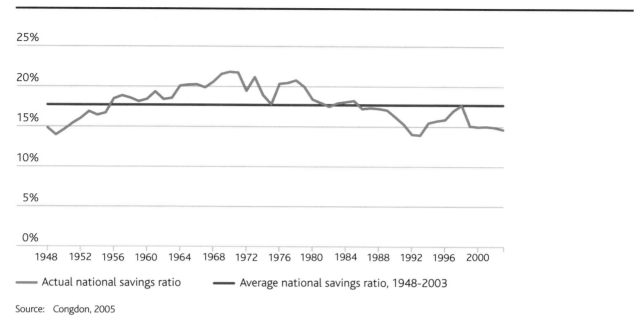

—— Actual national savings ratio   —— Average national savings ratio, 1948-2003

Source: Congdon, 2005

Figure C.15 National gross saving, capital consumption and net saving as a percentage of gross national disposable income: 1980-2004

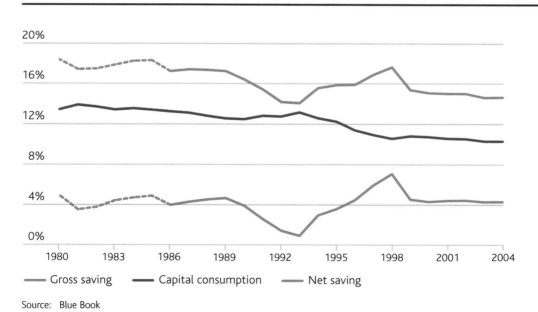

—— Gross saving   —— Capital consumption   —— Net saving

Source: Blue Book

Note: National figures prior to 1987 have been estimated using other national data.

The tentative conclusions we draw from these figures are therefore:

■ While there may have been some underlying decline in the UK's national gross savings rate over recent decades, it is not so dramatic as to make the national savings rate a central issue in pension policy.

■ Conversely however, there is no sign that the national savings rate is rising, and therefore no prima facie evidence to support assertions that the flat level of pension savings (described in the First Report) is masking more dynamic savings trends elsewhere in the household sector or in other sectors.

■ Net national saving is probably best described as trendless over the last few decades, but only because "capital consumption" as a percentage of national income is declining. The real economic meaning of this accounting measure is however unclear. It is explored in Annex B (available on the Pensions Commission's website).

4. Increases in value of corporate capital in excess of net savings

In a closed economy operating under the equilibrium conditions described in Figure C.7, the total value of corporate capital (equity and bond/debt combined) would rise each year by an amount equal to Net Household Acquisition of Corporate Sector Securities PLUS Net Saving at Corporate Level. All of the annual increase in the **stock** of corporate capital which the household sector ultimately owns would therefore be explained by an annual **flow** of savings, saved either by households themselves or by corporates on their behalf. The increase in the stock of wealth would be explained by savings flows measured somewhere in national accounts.

A striking feature of the last three decades however is that the total value of the corporate capital stock has increased far faster than can be explained by any measured savings flow occurring either at the household or at the corporate level [Figure C.16]. Households have therefore enjoyed a wealth gain without having to save (either directly or via corporates retaining earnings on their behalf).

Figure C.16 Capital investment and asset price appreciation: UK non-financial corporations: 1987-2003 £ billion

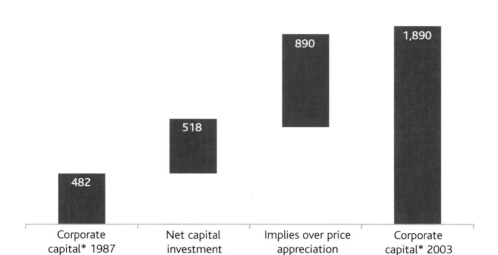

Source: Blue Book
Note: *Value of equity liabilities plus net cash, debt and bond liability.

This is one reason why UK households have been able to reduce their aggregate capital claims on corporate capital relative to the total value of UK corporate capital, while increasing the value of these claims relative to UK GDP (and thus to their average earnings)[5].   Thus, for instance:

■ Over the period 1987-2003, UK household claims on corporate equity (UK or overseas) whether held directly or via pension funds and insurance companies have fallen in value from 88% to 75% of the value of UK corporate equity [Figure C.17][6].

■ But the value of these claims as a percentage of UK GDP has increased from 98% to 120% [Figure C.18].

■ This is in part because the value of all UK company equity relative to GDP has increased from 105% to 155% [Figure C.19]. Over the longer-period since 1975 (and looking solely at quoted equity) this ratio has increased from 25% to 125%, and remains, despite the equity price falls of 2000-2002, well above the levels seen at any time since 1963 [Figure C.20].

---

[5] The other reason is the factor explained in Annex A – the fact that UK corporates increasingly hold claims on non-UK GDP, matched by increasing overseas claims on UK corporate capital.

[6] Ideally the analysis should focus on the total level of claims on corporate capital, whether in debt or equity form. Data availability makes that analysis extremely difficult. But it is clear that the trends in ownership of equity have not been offset by counteracting effects in the ownership of debt/bond claims.

Figure C.17 UK household sector claims on UK corporate equity

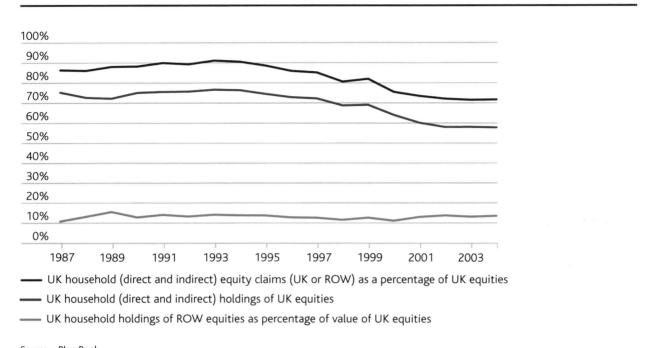

— UK household (direct and indirect) equity claims (UK or ROW) as a percentage of UK equities
— UK household (direct and indirect) holdings of UK equities
— UK household holdings of ROW equities as percentage of value of UK equities

Source: Blue Book
Note: "Indirect" claims mean claims held via pension funds and insurance companies.

Figure C.18 Household (direct and indirect) holdings of equities (quoted and unquoted) as a percentage of GDP

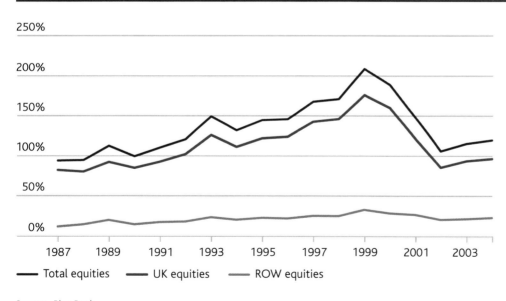

— Total equities — UK equities — ROW equities

Source: Blue Book

Figure C.19 Consolidated equity liabilities (quoted and unquoted) of UK corporations as a percentage of UK GDP

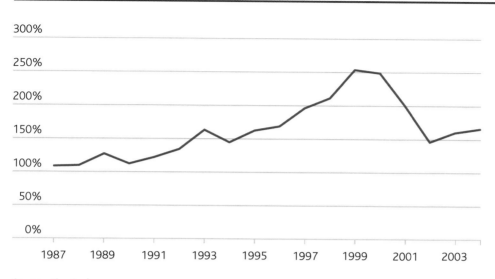

Source: Blue Book

Figure C.20 Equity and bond liabilities of UK corporates as a percentage of GDP: 1963-2003

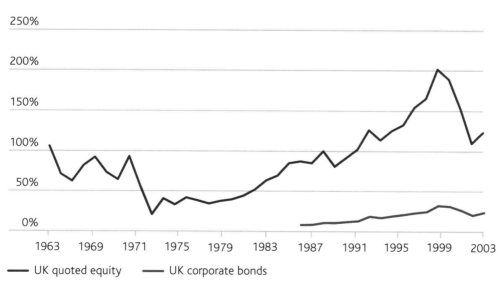

—— UK quoted equity   —— UK corporate bonds

Source: Blue Book

Key questions are therefore:

(i) What is the explanation and the economic meaning of these increases in wealth unexplained by savings flows: do they mean that concerns about inadequate savings flows are overstated, either at the aggregate national level, or at the level of individual savers?

(ii) Can such wealth increases without savings be expected to be enjoyed in future?

(i) The economic meaning of increases in equity wealth increases unexplained by savings

There are at least four possible reasons why the value of UK corporate capital could have increased relative to GDP. Three of these could deliver wealth increases to households not captured by national savings measures.

■ First, UK corporates could have accrued larger claims on GDP produced by the rest of the world, as a result of increasing UK corporate investment overseas. As Annex A describes, (available on the Pensions Commission website) this has been a major phenomenon of the last 10 years. But this would **not** in itself deliver increased wealth to UK households since it would tend to be matched by UK households owning a decreasing percentage of UK corporate capital (e.g. when BP purchased AMOCO with shares the percentage of BP owned by non-UK households automatically increased).

■ Second, the profit share of national income could have increased, so that capital owners own a claim on an increased share of GDP. In fact gross operating surplus as a percentage of GDP has been remarkably constant over the very long-term. But it did fall during the 1960s and reached levels well below trend in the mid-1970s [Figure C.21]. A significant element of the equity market rise of the mid-1970s to 1980s, may therefore be explained by the recovery of the profit share of national income to its long-term average.

■ Third, expectations of future growth rates in profit could have risen, either because of a **further** anticipated rise in the profit share of national income or because of expectations of higher GDP growth. These changed expectations could be either rational or irrational.

■ Fourth, the real discount rate which shareholders apply when calculating their required return from investments in corporate capital could have declined because of either:

  – A fall in the required risk-free discount rate. This has clearly occurred in the 1990s, with real returns on risk-free government bonds now below 2% versus 3% to 4% in the mid-1980s.

Figure C.21 Gross operating surplus of UK corporations as a percentage of GDP: 1948-2004

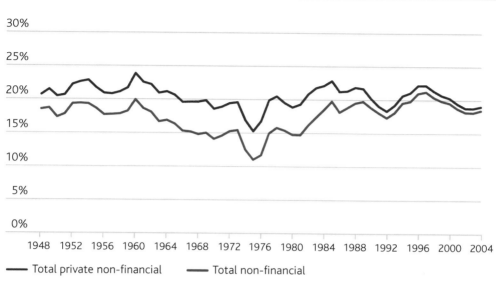

Source: Blue Book

— Or a fall in the perceived riskiness of corporate capital investments and thus of the risk premium applied to equity. This changed perception could also be either rational or irrational. But it could be argued that there were at least some rational reasons for a reduction in perceived risk between the mid-1970s and today, with the emergence of greater political consensus on the merits of a capitalist system, and with the achievement of far greater macroeconomic stability.[78]

The relative role of these explanations, and in particular the balance of rational and irrational effects, is a large and hotly-contested issue. But over the last 30 years rational explanations could explain at least some of the rising value of equity relative to GDP (via the increase in the profit share of GDP, the fall in real risk-free discount rates, and the reduction in domestic political risk.)

---

[7] The very low levels of equity market valuation relative to GDP seen in 1975 may for instance have reflected the interaction of high inflation with taxation systems insufficiently adjusted to exclude inflation effects.

[8] Note that it is also at least theoretically possible that the perceived riskiness of corporate capital investment has stayed stable but that the extra return which individuals need to compensate for risk has reduced (i.e. that there has been for some reason a change in the psychological cost of risk).

(ii) The key question therefore is: can corporate capital wealth increases without savings be expected in future? The most reasonable expectation would seem to be no. There do not appear to be good reasons to expect that the rational drivers of past increases in the corporate capital to GDP ratio will be repeated in future. There is no obvious basis for anticipating that the profit share of GDP will now move sustainably above its 50 year trend level: there is no reason to believe that real risk-free yields will fall even further from present low levels (even if they stay at those levels): and there is no reason, if the rational equity risk premium has fallen, to anticipate its further decline.

Any forecast of equity values and returns entails significant uncertainty, but the mean expectation must be that the value of corporate capital relative to GDP will be steady, which in turn implies two results:

- First that from now the best assumption must be that increases in the stock of household claims on corporate capital will be equal to savings flows occurring either within the household sector or within the corporate sector on the household sector's behalf.

- Second that the prospective return on equity is best estimated by looking at the returns achieved over the very long-term e.g. over the whole of the 20th century, rather than over the last 30 years. This (as Appendix B in the First Report argued) suggests equity returns of more like 6% real per year rather than the 10% to 12% real enjoyed in the 1980s and 1990s. [9, 10]

5. Household pension and non-pension saving

The UK household gross savings rate fell from 8% in 1992 to 4% in 2002, while the net savings rate fell from about 6% to 1% [see Figure C.10]. This was predominantly a cyclical effect, with [as Figure C.11 showed] corporate savings rising in the inverse direction, and the gross national savings rate unchanged between 1992 and 2002. The idea that there is a problem of aggregate under savings at national level is not therefore suggested by these figures.

Within household sector savings however two elements dominate - pension savings and savings for house purchase. There is therefore no evidence to support the assertion that deficient pension savings by some individuals are being compensated for by non-pension **financial** saving. The important role which house price appreciation plays in enabling increased cash borrowing and lending **between** different groups **within** the household sector is however clearly illustrated by the figures.

---

[9] **Any** attempt to infer future equity return from past performance rests however on a large number of debatable assumptions.

[10] Note that provided our estimates of return on equity investment include the capital gain element, projections of accumulated future stocks of wealth held by individuals can be based on their own savings (i.e. accounted for in the household sector) as increased by this total rate of return. We do not need separately to allow for the saving on their behalf occurring within the corporate sector since this saving is captured via the capital gain element of total return on equity.

These points are expanded below.

The structure of household savings is illustrated by the 2002 figures set out in Figure C.22. In that year the household sector had gross savings of £42.9 billion. But capital investment by the household sector was higher at £50 billion, and the sector was therefore a net acquirer of financial liabilities i.e. a net disposer of financial assets. The net figure of -£3.9 billion however arose from an £10.9 billion net acquisition of occupational pension fund assets, offset by a £14.8 billion net disposal of all assets held outside occupational pension funds. Since this net disposal includes a positive figure for personal pensions (but one which it is impossible to precisely determine) the imbalance between **all** pensions and non-pensions will be even more striking.[11]

Gross savings into occupational pensions funds fell gradually between 1980 and 2002, as a result both of falling contributions flowing in (i.e. accumulation) and rising pensions flowing out (i.e. decumulation). But these occupational pension savings have dominated the household sector's net acquisition of financial assets throughout the period, with the net acquisition of financial assets outside occupational pension schemes negative in most years (and the net acquisition of non-pension financial assets i.e. excluding also personal pensions, almost certainly significantly negative in every year) [Figure C.23].

It is important to understand however that these national figures fail to capture the full reality of savings behaviour since they net out accumulations by some people and decumulation by others (see Section 2 above for a general discussion of the difference between savings at the individual level and savings at the national level). In particular they fail to reveal the dominant feature of household sector non-pension financial behaviour over the last 20 years, which is the accumulation of large cash liabilities by some households, significantly offset at the aggregate level by the accumulation of cash balances by other households [Figures C.24]. In terms of the framework set out in Figure C.8 the household sector has been steadily liquidating claims against corporate capital held outside pension funds, but some parts of the household sector have increasingly lent cash (via the banks and building societies) to other parts of the household sector.

In stock of wealth terms the liquidation of corporate capital claims was offset until 2000 by the equity price effects described in Section 4. But following the equity price falls 2000-2002, and looking over the whole of the period 1980-2002, the increasing dominance of the "cash recycling" effect **within** the household sector, relative to its claim against corporate capital, becomes clear [Figure C.25].

---

[11] Within National Income and Accounts gross savings can be divided between Occupational Pensions Saving and All Other Savings (which includes Personal Pensions). The net acquisition of financial assets can be divided between "Pension Funds, Personal Pensions and Life Policies" and "All Other Savings" (excluding both Personal Pensions and Non-pension life policies). It is not possible to derive precise figures for all non-pensions savings (i.e. **excluding** personal pensions but **including** non-pension life policies).

Figure C.22 Household saving and investment figures: 2002 £ billion

Gross saving		42.9
	+ capital transfers	3.1
	- capital investment	-50.0
Net acquisition of financial assets		-3.9
Of which **Net acquisition of non-occupational pension financial assets**		-14.8 ⟵ Net disposal of financial assets outside occupational pension funds
Assets acquired in occupational pension funds		10.9

Source: Blue Book

Note: Effects of errors in the household sector gross savings, arising from Blue Book errors in estimates of total pension savings, are yet to be determined.

Figure C.23 Gross household sector savings: occupational pensions and other as a percentage of gross national disposable income: 1980-2004

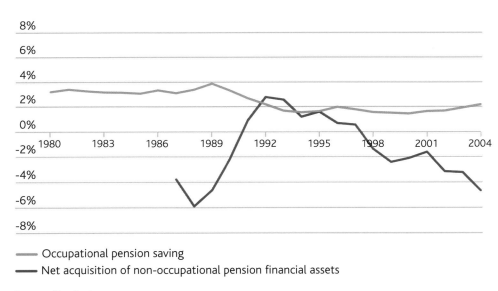

—— Occupational pension saving

—— Net acquisition of non-occupational pension financial assets

Source: Blue Book

Figure C.24 Household non-pension, non-life NAFA/NAFL as a percentage of gross national disposable income: 1987-2004

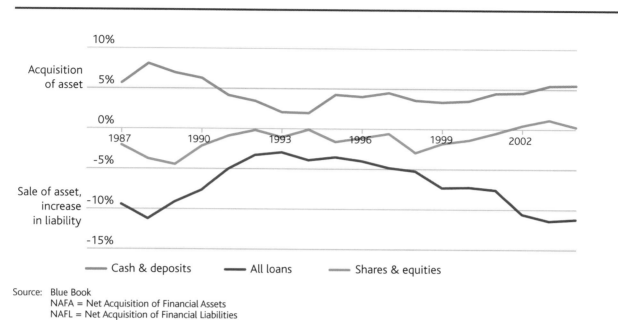

Source: Blue Book
NAFA = Net Acquisition of Financial Assets
NAFL = Net Acquisition of Financial Liabilities

Figure C.25 Non-pension financial assets and debt as a percentage of GDP: 1980-2004

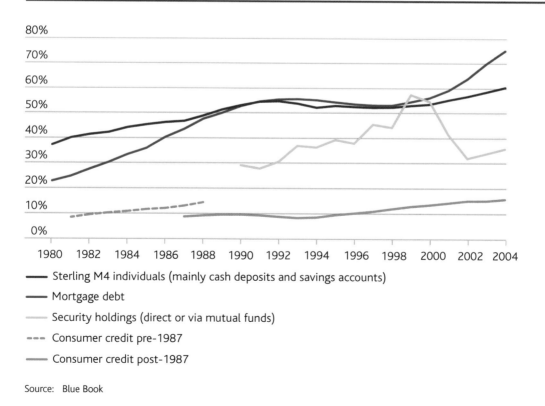

Source: Blue Book

The explanation of this phenomenon is integrally linked to the house price appreciation effect which will be considered in Section 5. As house prices rise relative to income, people choose to devote more of their working life earnings to the accumulation of housing assets, which they purchase with mortgage debt secured against the house value. But for most buyers of houses there is a seller from within the household sector.[12] That seller can be either decumulating housing assets during retirement, or selling an inherited house. In both cases the sale's proceeds result in cash receipts which to a significant extent at the aggregate level appear to be held in cash form rather than used to buy claims on corporate capital.

This phenomenon has important consequences both for the optimal design of pension policy and for any attempt to draw inferences for the adequacy of pension saving from the level of national aggregate savings. Thus:

■ As house prices rise (and if that rise is sustainable – see Section 6) it is possible for housing asset accumulation and decumulation to play an increasing role in lifecycle consumption smoothing. And the greater the extent that this smoothing is achieved via the accumulation and decumulation of housing assets, the lower may be the optimal level of income replacement rates which government pension policy should mandate or encourage.[13]

■ This effect may however be utterly invisible within any analysis of the national aggregate savings rate. House price appreciation can occur without any increase in the national savings rate (see Section 6). And the simultaneous growth of debt liabilities and cash assets by different groups **within** the household sector nets out at the total sector and total national level.

Overall therefore the key points to take from this analysis of household financial savings patterns are:

■ There is no evidence that declining levels of pension saving are being offset by increased accumulation of non-pension claims against corporate capital. Indeed the reverse is true. The UK household sector has been a steady liquidator of corporate capital claims held outside pension funds, an effect masked until 2000 by the equity price appreciation effect.

■ But increasing house prices are supporting increased **intra**-household sector flows, some households borrowing increasing proportions of income, while other households are holding increasing proportions of income in cash deposits. (The flow is intermediated via banks and building societies but is essentially a flow from one part of the household sector to another.)

---

[12] The exception is purchase of new built homes, where the seller is a house-builder (typically within the corporate sector).

[13] See Adair Turner "Political Choices and Macro-Economic Issues" LSE 8th March for a fuller exposition of this argument.

Figure C.26 Household gross saving, gross investment and net investment: 2002 £ billion

Gross saving	42.9	
+ Capital transfer	3.1	
- Capital investment	-50.0	
= NAFA	-3.9	
Capital investment	50.0 ⟵	of which 31.1 is in housing
- Capital consumption	35.6 ⟵	of which 20.0 is in housing
= Net investment	14.3 ⟵	of which 11.1 is in housing

Source: Blue Book

Note: NAFA = Net Aquisition of Financial Assets

6. Household saving in houses: capital investment and price appreciation

Figure C.8 set out the fact that the two fundamental forms of wealth which the household sector owns (and all of which is in some ultimate fashion owned by the household sector) are corporate capital and residential housing. Section 4 discussed the fact that the value of corporate capital has increased far more rapidly over the last 25 years than can be explained by saving invested in corporate capital either by the household sector or by the corporate sector on households' behalf. An analogous effect is found in residential housing. For the last several decades the value of residential housing has grown far more rapidly than can be explained by net investment in housing. Unlike with the corporate capital effect, this form of wealth increase without savings **may** continue into the future.

As Figure C.22 showed, the household sector had gross savings of £42.9 billion in 2002. More than 100% of this however was dedicated to investment within the household sector, predominantly in residential housing [Figure C.26]. This figure for housing investment, though labelled "in new houses" in national accounts, actually also covers major house improvement investments, such as conversions, conservatories and extensions. To calculate **net** effective investment in housing we have to allow for depreciation of the housing stock ("capital consumption") but also for the significant expenditures which households commit within current expenditure categories to offset this wear and tear [Figure C.27]. Taken altogether, the figures suggest that the household sector has invested a net £410 billion (in current money terms) in the housing stock it owns between 1989 and 2004.

This represents however, less than a third of the increase in the value of the housing stock over that period, with £930 billion of real value increase arising from real price appreciation (i.e. price rises above inflation unexplained by capital investment) [Figure C.28]. This "unexplained" wealth effect has been by far the largest source of household sector wealth accumulation over this period.

Just as with equity values in Figure C.7 so with housing [Figure C.29] we can define a set of the conditions under which no such pure price effects could occur, and under which therefore the real market value of housing would rise precisely in line with real net investment. To understand the circumstances under which these conditions might not exist, it is useful conceptually to split the value of housing into two elements [Figure C.30].

- The constructed house. By definition this will only rise in value as a result of net capital investment. Net capital investment as a percentage of income may tend to increase over time if housing amenity is a high income elasticity good: and may therefore form an increasing part of household gross savings. But it will be visible in national account measures of savings.

- The value of the land itself, and in particular of land which has specific locational characteristics which are strongly desired. This value will rise with rising income if land and in particular specific desired locations are in limited supply, and if specific positional characteristics are a high income elasticity good. If both conditions are true to a significant extent, the long-term trend can be for house prices to rise faster than average earnings.

These conditions do seem to apply in the UK (particularly in the more densely populated areas). Whether they are already fully (or more than fully) discounted in current house prices or whether they will continue to drive house prices faster than average earnings over the long-term is highly uncertain. But while there are good reasons for asserting that the unexplained equity price trend is very unlikely to apply in future (see Section 4 above), it is at least possible that the trend in house prices relative to average earnings could continue.

Figure C.27 Household gross and net investment in housing: 1989-2004, real 2005 £ billion

	1989	1990	1991	1992	1993	1994	1995	1996	1997	1998	1999	2000	2001	2002	2003	2004
Household gross capital investment in new houses	30.4	24.7	21.5	21.6	22.4	23.4	23.3	24.4	25.8	26.4	26.7	27.7	28.8	32.9	35.4	40.4
+ Maintenance and repair of dwelling	11.2	14.5	11.8	10.6	10.1	10.3	10.0	10.3	11.1	11.4	11.6	11.5	12.2	13.0	13.0	13.6
+ Goods and services for routine household maintenance	4.7	4.8	4.9	5.2	5.4	5.5	5.4	5.5	5.6	5.5	5.7	5.9	6.1	6.3	6.5	6.8
- Consumption of fixed capital	-13.1	-14.0	-14.0	-13.8	-14.0	-14.4	-15.0	-15.6	-16.1	-16.9	-18.2	-19.4	-20.4	-21.2	-21.5	-21.7
Total of maintenance and depreciation effects	2.8	5.2	2.7	2.0	1.5	1.4	0.5	0.2	0.6	0.1	-0.9	-2.0	-2.1	-1.8	-2.0	-1.3
Total net investment	33.1	29.9	24.3	23.6	23.9	24.8	23.8	24.6	26.3	26.5	25.8	25.7	26.7	31.1	33.5	39.1
Σ 1990 – 2004		29.9	54.2	77.8	101.7	126.6	150.4	175.0	201.3	227.9	253.7	279.4	306.1	337.2	370.7	409.8

Source: Blue Book

95

This increase in the value of houses does not however show up as an element within household sector or national saving. This is logical because an increase in house value unexplained by capital investment represents a windfall gain for all those who already own a house, but a matching windfall loss for those who do not yet own a house [Figure C.31]. This would be obvious if the effect were a one-off instantaneous event. It is solely because it has been spread over several decades that it appears that all people can gain from it: effectively each new cohort of house buyers for the last several decades has suffered a windfall loss to the previous generation, but then enjoyed a windfall gain at the expense of the following generation.

The fact that this increased wealth is quite correctly not counted within national savings, does not however mean that it is irrelevant to the adequacy of potential consumption in retirement resources. It obviously is in relation to those who enjoy a windfall gain, and who therefore have the potential to decumulate that gain e.g. via equity release or trading down in retirement. But even when comparing two steady state equilibria, one with low house prices relative to GDP and the other with high house prices, there is an important implication. The higher the value of houses relative to average earnings and GDP, the more that people may choose to devote savings during working life to house purchase, and the greater therefore will be housing assets available for decumulation, whether during their own retirement via equity release and trading down, or during the retirement of their inheritors, who will inherit housing assets in addition to those they have accumulated themselves.

Figure C.28 Net investment in housing and increasing value of housing: real 2005 £ billion

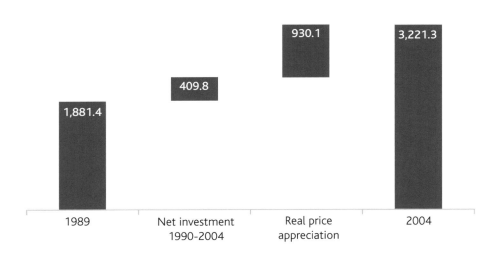

Figure C.29 Capital investment and price appreciation in the value of houses

- If land were constant in real prices, both in general and in specific locations (e.g. no change in the relative attractiveness of specific locations)...

- ... and if desirable new features (e.g. extensions) could always be added at construction price...

- ... and if "capital consumption" figure correctly estimates the expenditure required on repair and maintenance to keep real utility/value...

- ... then the real market value of housing would rise with real net investment.

Figure C.30 Two factors in house price appreciation

- Net capital investment in improvement in housing stock.

- Will occur with rising income if housing amenity is a positive income elasticity good.

- Real price appreciation of land, positional locations, unreplicable features etc.

- Will occur with rising income if
  - Land/positional locations are in limited supply.
  - Desire for land and positional aspects of housing are high income elasticity goods.

  If both factors are true to a significant extent (very limited supply, and high income elasticity) trend can be the prices rise faster than average earnings.

Figure C.31 Impact of one-off rise in the price of land

- Windfall gain to those who already own land/house:
  - Lower level of savings needed to achieve desired level of wealth.
  - Higher consumption in retirement possible if willing to run down wealth rather than bequeath.

- Windfall loss to those who do not yet own land/house:
  - Higher level of savings needed to achieve any given target level of housing amenity (or higher level of consumption spend on housing if rent rather than buy).

Thus we can establish the hypothesis set out in [Figure C.32]. The more that desired housing land is in scarce supply and the greater the income elasticity of demand for housing locational amenity, the greater the role that the acquisition and sale of housing will play in the process of inter-generational resource transfer, and the less therefore will be the need to achieve it via specifically defined pension savings. But this greater role of inter-generational resource transfer via the housing market will not register as an increase in national savings.

These considerations are clearly extremely important in the UK. The total value of residential housing as a percentage of GDP **may** be on a long-term upward trend (rather than simply oscillating over a cycle) [Figure C.33]. **Whatever** its trend, however the sheer size of the **stock** relative to GDP means that a large consumption resource transfer will occur via the purchase and sale of homes. And the proportion of the housing stock owned by the household sector (rather than by the government) has steadily increased over the last 20 years [Figure C.34]. Because of the distributional issues and risk issues discussed in Chapter 5 of the First Report, this cannot be seen as providing a complete answer to pension adequacy for all. But it is clearly a factor relevant to the optimal design of pension policy.

Figure C.32 Housing wealth and inter-generation resource transfer

If	Then	With Result That
■ Housing land is a scarce supply positional good, due to population density and/or zoning restrictions. AND ■ The desire for housing land/housing location amenity is strongly income elastic.	■ The land element of house prices will rise faster than average earnings for a period (and perhaps indefinitely). ■ And the value of the housing stock (including land) will rise faster than GDP.	The higher the level of house prices relative to average earnings, the greater is the inter-generational consumption resource transfer which will tend to be achieved via house purchase and sale.

Figure C.33 Gross residential housing value as a percentage of GDP: 1980-2004

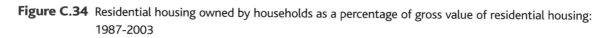

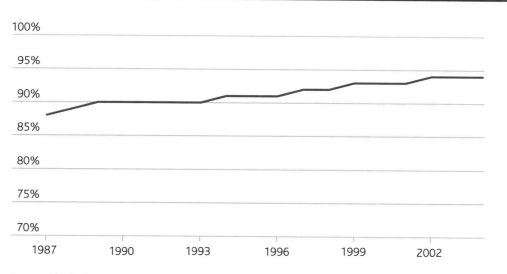

Source: Blue Book

Figure C.34 Residential housing owned by households as a percentage of gross value of residential housing:
1987-2003

Source: Blue Book

Pensions Commission research

APPENDIX D

Following publication of our First Report the Commission carried out research in five areas to gather evidence to inform our final recommendations. We have also drawn on other research conducted by government departments or other research/analytical bodies to supplement our evidence base.

The five areas we conducted research in were:

1. An understanding of individuals' attitudes towards the four options presented in the First Report.

2. Quantitative data from individuals to examine views on retirement planning, pensions adequacy and expectations of longevity.

3. Getting views from small firms on pension provision and their reactions to a range of compulsion scenarios and their elements.

4. Developing an awareness of the Independent Financial Adviser (IFA) market.

This Appendix focuses on each of these projects in turn outlining more details on the background and methodology used in each project, and highlighting key results and conclusions. The full reports for the two focus group projects, including all the discussion and research materials, are published on our website. In addition there is a short paper outlining the results of the macroeconomic modelling project.

1. Individuals' attitudinal research

(i) Background and methodology

The Commission's First Report stated that faced with the increasing proportion of the population aged over 65, society and individuals must make choices between four options:

■ pensioners will become poorer relative to the rest of society; or

■ taxes/National Insurance (NI) contributions devoted to pensions must rise; or

- savings must rise; or

- average retirement ages must rise.

We commissioned RS Consulting to undertake a series of 10 focus groups across England and Scotland during March 2005 to assess people's reactions to the four options we outlined in our First Report. Participants were recruited to reflect a variety of situations; the composition of the groups is outlined in Figure D.1. The research aimed to examine attitudes and expectations regarding retirement and reactions in detail to our four options.

Specifically, the research sought to discover:

- how people think about these issues as they face retirement planning;

- people's arguments for and against the four options;

- people's attitudes and preferences towards autonomy in saving for retirement;

- what people considered to be the most acceptable combination of the four options.

The qualitative methodology used was well suited to exploring the perceptions, opinions and expectations of groups in broadly similar circumstances according to their age, employment status, and potential lifetime income and location. Focus groups also allowed some of the motivations – both hopes and fears – underlying participants' views to be understood. Qualitative techniques such as focus groups do not, however, provide findings that are definitive or representative of the population. The results presented here should be interpreted with this caution in mind.

In addition to exploring perceptions, opinions and expectations, we also wanted to know more about the levels of awareness and understanding that people brought to their planning for retirement. To better understand levels of awareness and reactions to some key retirement-relevant facts, the groups were asked to consider stimulus material provided by the Pensions Commission, some of which was tailored to the circumstances of each group. Participants also completed short pre-and post-discussion questionnaires to get a better appreciation of their attitudes.

(ii) The retirement planning dilemma

The majority of participants expected to be fairly comfortable in retirement, but in contrast with these expectations, most people recognised that they were not currently saving enough to have the income they expected in retirement. Most people felt that saving for the future was becoming increasingly important and simultaneously more difficult. They recognised that the pension system was under strain due to an ageing population.

Figure D.1 Profile of participants in each group by predefined criteria

Age	Employment Status	Potential Lifetime Income	Location	Number of Participants	Gender: Male	Female
25-35	Full-time	Higher	Birmingham	7	4	3
25-35	Full-time	Lower	Long Eaton/Derby/Notts.	7	4	3
35-45	Full-time	Higher	London	7	4	3
35-45	Full-time	Lower	Long Eaton/Derby/Notts.	8	4	4
45-55	Full-time	Higher	Birmingham	7	4	3
45-55	Full-time	Lower	London	7	4	3
35-45	Self-employed	Higher	Barnet	7	4	3
35-45	Self-employed	Lower	Glasgow	7	4	3
25-45	Part-time/ unavailable for work	Higher	Barnet	7	Female only	
25-45	Part-time/ unavailable for work	Lower	Glasgow	7	Female only	

They were also aware that their own expectations for what constituted a comfortable retirement were higher than their parents' and grandparents' had been.

Despite their awareness that they ought to be "doing something", saving for the future was becoming increasingly difficult. Participants thought that the cost of living was increasing and that debt was increasingly widespread. Most contrasted the fixed demands of today with the uncertainties of the future. The combination of uncertainty about the future and concern about meeting current financial commitments led half to agree that they would prioritise having a good standard of living today rather than saving for retirement. Only a minority, those closest to retirement, were trying to address their uncertainties about what makes adequate preparation for retirement and how to achieve it.

Few participants expected the state pension to provide an adequate retirement income, and some expected nothing at all from the state. Participants thought that the adequacy of the state pension was in decline and that the trend would continue. The decline of the state pension, or uncertainty about its value, and the closure of generous occupational pensions led most participants to the uncomfortable conclusion that there was increasingly a need for people to look after themselves. Most people felt resigned to having to be more self-reliant in planning for retirement but only a few higher earning participants had plans in place and thought they knew how to achieve financial security in retirement.

Private pensions were, however, considered to be both risky and confusing, and this combination led, in some cases, to denial about the issues and to inaction. Participants considered private pensions to be unacceptably risky for a number of reasons including those that can be summarised under five headings: market risk, lack of liquidity, modest annuity values, the collapse of some schemes and charges of mis-selling. In addition to the risks, private pensions were also said to be difficult to understand. The majority claimed they lacked confidence in their ability to make decisions about pensions. The confusion that participants felt added to their sense that private pensions were unreliable.

Participants' lack of awareness of appropriate contribution levels and rates of return were consistent with what they described as an overall lack of understanding and knowledge of how pensions operate. Only an experienced minority had any understanding of appropriate contribution levels and growth rates. In particular, there was no evidence of understanding that contribution levels needed to be high enough to inflation-proof benefits or that fees could seriously erode returns. There was also little awareness of tax relief on contributions.

Investing in property was repeatedly raised as a "natural" solution to the retirement planning dilemma, although in reality only a minority had actually invested in property in addition to their own homes. To many participants investing in property rather than pensions had a number of advantages such as being easier to understand, and being perceived as providing greater returns and offering greater security.

(iii) Evaluation of four potential options for the future

As the initial stage of the discussion ended, but before the stimulus material about the four options had been presented and discussed, participants were asked to indicate their initial preferences. Participants were asked to allocate 20 points across the four options to reflect their preferred solution for society as a whole. This exercise was followed by detailed discussion of each option.

Following this in-depth discussion, participants were asked to allocate four points across four steps for each option, as described in Figure D.2. The results from this exercise are presented in Figure D.3. Presentation of the options was necessarily simplified to some extent to facilitate discussion. The exercise was conducted to:

■ establish preferred combinations and trade-offs once participants had explored all the issues; and

■ test acceptance of different levels of sacrifice.

Figure D.2 Description of combination exercise

Options	Starting position, as of today	1 Steps	2 Steps	3 Steps	4 Steps	Outcomes produced by taking up to 4 steps toward realising each option for change (based on the Commission's assumptions/best guesses)
A) Poorer pensioners	Today's pensioner income would be reduced by:	7.5%	15%	22.5%	30%	Pensioners would on average suffer about a 30% decline in their relative incomes in the next 20-30 years.
B) Increase basic rate tax	Today's basic tax rate of 22% would be increased to:	26%	30%	34%	38%	Taxes and/or National Insurance contributions devoted to pensions would rise taking the basic rate of income tax from 22% today to 38%.
C) Increase amount paid into pensions	The average pension contribution, currently around 7% of pay would be increased to:	11%	15%	19%	23%	Paying into private pensions would rise, increasing from around 7% of earnings today up to 23% in the next 20-30 years.
D) Later retirement	Average retirement age of 63 increased to:	64	66	68	70	The average age of retirement would have to rise for men from 64 up to 70, for women from 62 up to 70.

Figure D.3 Combination exercise: number of people allocating points to each option

Options	No change	1 Step	2 Steps	3 Steps	4 Steps
A) Poorer pensioners	61	8	1	0	0
B) Increase basic rate tax	18	39	13	0	0
C) Increase amount paid into pensions	3	21	31	7	8
D) Later retirement	27	23	16	2	2

Base: 70 participants answering

As the focus groups finished the initial assessment was repeated to see if attitudes had changed during the discussion.

Balancing sacrifices across the options illustrated in Figure D.2 appeared to force uncomfortable choices from participants and they seemed to be making the choices demanded of them according to a "lesser of evils" decision rule. The trade-off exercise showed that people favoured a combination of remedies in order to minimise the sacrifices that would be involved in moving very far in the direction of any one option. Having to pay more into a private pension, combined with some increase in tax/National Insurance, and along with voluntary extension of working life appeared to be the least painful combination of options.

A comparison of the "before" and "after" assessments showed that there was little change in participants' attitudes to each option, despite a lengthy discussion and exposure to the stimulus material [Figure D.4]. This surprising lack of movement in overall preferences demonstrates how the four options touch on deeply laid attitudes on issues of social justice, autonomy and the role of government in peoples' lives.

(iv) Detailed reactions: poorer pensioners

The option of having poorer pensioners in the future, relative to those in work, was the least acceptable choice in all three assessments, with little variation by participants' demographic characteristics. Participants said that this option was not a remedy to the problem; instead, it was seen as an unacceptable failure to adapt to changing circumstances and a sign of an uncivilised society. Therefore, a change in the pensions system to avoid pensioners becoming poorer was generally accepted as a matter of principle, although a few thought that the fear of being poor in old age could motivate people to save.

(v) Detailed reactions: increased saving

This option nearly always featured as an element of a combined solution, and often with greater emphasis placed upon it than upon any other option. It should be noted that despite allocating most points to this option, participants were clear that they viewed having to pay more into a pension or other savings as "the lesser of four evils". In fact, many initially misconstrued this option, thinking it called only for more voluntary saving.

Overall, respondents thought that having to pay more into pensions or other long-term savings offered greater personal control over retirement planning and that it was fairer, since people would be saving for themselves. Just as people liked the sense of personal responsibility they associated with this option they also understood that with greater responsibility would come greater risk.

Figure D.4 Average number of points allocated to each option (20 point exercise)

	Average number of points allocated	
	Step 1: Pre-discussion	Step 3: Post-discussion
Having to pay more into a pension or other savings	10	10
Increasing taxes/National Insurance	5	6
Work longer	3	3
Poorer pensioners	2	1

Base: 70 participants answering

Figure D.5 Compulsion scenario discussed with employees

A personal pension with a total level of contributions (from employer and employee) of around 10% of earnings.

The pensions would be run in the same way as current personal pension schemes are run:

■ Pension contracts taken out by individuals with insurance companies, banks, building societies etc

■ The money paid in is invested in shares, bonds, property and perhaps other things

■ The amount of pension income depends on:
 – the total amount paid in
 – the rate of growth achieved by investing the money paid in, e.g. the performance of the stock market during the time that payments are made, minus the fees charged to manage the investments
 – the age at which the individual retires

Participants were asked for their views on one specific example of a compulsory pension saving scheme using personal pensions [Figure D.5]. Note that as this research was conducted while we were considering and developing our recommendations it was not possible to get participants' views on our final recommendations about the type of scheme and level of contributions.

Participants' most significant objection to this example lay in the lack of guarantees: how could the government compel people to save without providing a minimum pension guarantee? Many thought that government should not enforce saving without sharing the risk. Compulsion itself was at odds with the wish for choice and individual control that most participants had initially associated with the "saving more" option.

Participants also argued that compelling people to save was too rigid and claimed it would be detrimental to their own financial well-being, especially their ability to meet current financial obligations. People also thought compulsion would be very hard on people on low incomes. It might also be inappropriate to force some to save. Overall, participants thought that compulsion would only be acceptable if benefits were guaranteed, at least to a minimum level, and clear statements of returns were provided at regular intervals.

Despite strong objections, many could still see that compulsion might have some advantages. Participants thought that compulsion would ensure that people made the correct level of contributions and reduce the likelihood that many would fail to save enough. Without compulsion to save, some said, the system would remain essentially unchanged, since everybody today had the possibility of starting a pension but many did not. Additionally, taking money out at source would make the loss of income less noticeable; it would simplify the process, and in the end people would get used to it.

Participants thought that only a transitional approach to introducing compulsion would be fair. Many participants felt that compulsion alone was too draconian and argued that other measures could be used to encourage greater saving, usually in the form of more education and knowledge. Some participants also mentioned the desirability of a "consolidated forecast" that would give clear information regarding an individual's overall retirement prospects. By informing everyone of what they will, or will not, receive, people would be encouraged to look after themselves. Finally, participants thought that pensions themselves could be made more attractive by:

- giving greater security and predictability with simple illustrations and guarantees;

- providing better tax breaks, although the majority were unaware of existing tax incentives;

- allowing flexible payment options, so people could stop paying for a while;

- giving ownership rights to the individual so pensions could be moved easily from job to job;

- making pensions available through a truly independent channel, since IFAs were not trusted.

But despite these suggestions for alternatives to compulsion, participants' comments gave no grounds for concluding that encouraging people to pay more into private pensions or other savings without compulsion would overcome the barriers to saving that they had already mentioned. There did appear to be some contradiction between participants wanting to make their own decisions, but also wanting to be told what to do because they did not always feel they could make the right decisions.

Participants' initial reaction to the idea of a compulsory employer contribution was very positive. Most participants soon reasoned that they would pay for this in other ways and recognised that the negative impact would be stronger in smaller firms. Furthermore, participants' reactions provided little evidence that the employer would get much credit from employees for a compulsory pension contribution. Some still reasoned, however, that employers' contributions would act as a sweetener if employees were compelled to contribute because they would feel that part of the financial burden of compulsory contributions was being met by their employer.

Participants were questioned on their knowledge and understanding of the State Second Pension (S2P) or its predecessor, the State Earnings Related Pension Scheme (SERPS), to see if the existence of this form of compulsion in the current pension system influenced their attitudes. No-one in any of the groups had heard of S2P, although some had heard of SERPS, mainly through letters advising them recently to opt back into the State Second Pension. Only a small minority of those who knew of SERPS actually understood what it referred to or how it operated. Overall, information about S2P/SERPS had no impact on attitudes except to heighten impressions of the complexity and uncertainty of pensions.

(vi) Detailed reactions: increasing taxes/NI contributions

Most people thought that increasing taxes/NI contributions had a role to play in a combined solution, although a less significant one than having to pay into a private pension. For most, the logic behind increasing taxes/NI contributions to some extent was clear. These participants thought that the government could manage the money well and because government is accountable to society, it would have a clear interest in doing so. The other perceived advantage of this option was that everyone would be assured of a fair and adequate pension, thus relieving individuals of the burden of having to make their own arrangements. Participants also reasoned that not only would they themselves be assured of an adequate pension, but also the "deserving poor" and those unable to help themselves would also receive sufficient support in retirement. Participants saw fairness as one of the advantages over compulsion, which they did not think would necessarily benefit all fairly.

The principle of NI was generally considered to be sound by participants because it aimed to raise taxes for specific socially motivated purposes, and in ring-fencing contributions, it provided at least some safeguards that the intended benefits would be delivered. On a practical level, many reasoned that taking money at source had advantages: if you never received it, you could not spend it and would miss it less. Participants saw the appeal of not having to make active decisions and put effort into making private arrangements. Despite being able to see advantages to this option, participants also expressed fear and concern about the costs involved and the level of benefits that might be received, for example, that showed ambivalence in their attitudes to government involvement. As a result, participants demanded that increased taxes/NI contributions should be accompanied by guarantees of ring-fencing and clarification of the pension pay-outs people could expect to receive.

(vii) Detailed reactions: working longer

The possibility of having to work longer was initially assumed to mean that everyone would have to work until the age of 70, probably as a result of media reports that were current at the time. On this basis many rejected the idea outright. Upon realising that this was not the case attitudes towards working longer became more positive, provided the decision to work longer was voluntary and flexible. It should be noted that during the discussion it was made clear that participants were not being asked to consider increasing the State Pension Age (SPA).

Reactions to working longer were still mixed: all could see benefits and drawbacks. Many thought that keeping active and busy in old age improved the quality of life and could also provide a way of topping up retirement income after other commitments were met. Equally, however, participants expressed resistance to the idea of working longer for a number of reasons. Participants expected their 60s and 70s to be a time when they could enjoy retirement. They did not wish to work through retirement into "old age". People seemed to view retirement as the period that follows working, when life can be enjoyed while people are fit and healthy. Retirement itself precedes old age, which begins when health deteriorates.

All participants appreciated that some people would be unable to work longer, even if they wanted to. Circumstances surrounding working and retirement were thought to be highly individual, leading to a strong desire for choice in all elements associated with working longer. Working longer would be acceptable if it were optional, many thought, and so long as it was not the result of increasing the SPA. Participants felt that they should be allowed to continue working if they wished, and that decisions on this issue were best made as people approached retirement age, rather than far in advance and for a fixed term. Many thought that working longer would become more attractive if people were allowed greater flexibility, such as part-time working and flexible hours. It was suggested that people who chose to work longer should still be able to claim pension benefits, in full or part, according to their choice.

During the discussions, participants were presented with information showing trends in average life expectancy and average time spent in retirement. The life expectancy figures did not come as a surprise to most participants, who had already recognised that society is ageing, but the number of years spent in retirement came as a shock to many. The length of retirement had rarely been considered by participants or accurately estimated. Consequently participants had not thought much about the length of their retirement or estimated in a realistic way the funding needed for a long retirement. For some the information about the length of retirement increased their willingness to consider working beyond 65, provided the decision remained optional.

It is worth noting that in focus groups conducted by the Institute for Public Policy Research (IPPR) when participants were presented with longevity data similar to the material we used, in some cases there was outright refusal to believe that people are living longer and are healthier. In short many in the groups were disinclined to take the information put forward at face value. Attitudes ranged from surprise, through to healthy questioning and scepticism, and to outright rejection and disbelief.

(viii) Conclusions

Seven main themes emerged from the research:

- There was general agreement that pensions and achieving financial security in retirement are problematic, on a personal level and for society as a whole. There was also general agreement that something needs to be done, but acceptance of painful change was lacking. There may be the start of a consensus, though, that the pensions system needs to change to avoid future generations of poorer pensioners.

- There was resignation about state provision and some feeling that it would become inadequate. Expectations of state provision were heavily discounted by uncertainty about entitlements, the basic mechanics of how pensions work, and many other matters. Despite knowing that they would have to do more to prepare for retirement, most said that they did not know how to help themselves in ways they thought would be effective. Participants said they lacked the funds, the necessary knowledge and a sense of urgency to be able to act upon their instinct to be more self-reliant.

- Looking to the future, participants would envisage changes in policies affecting pensions that they thought would be constructive. For instance, transparency in the form of linking savings and benefits would give people a sense of control and greater ability to make long-term plans. Guarantees would help to achieve predictability, fairness and security. Ring-fencing would be required to protect public funds collected to provide for retirement income from being diverted for other purposes. A consistent policy regime would ensure continuity for individuals, with some choice and flexibility allowed for personal circumstances.

- A combined solution was favoured by nearly all when choices were forced between the four options. Increasing savings into a private pension met people's wish for rewards commensurate with input, and for autonomy. Despite the fact that compulsion was unappealing, there was no evidence that alternatives would encourage significant numbers to save voluntarily. Increasing taxes/NI contributions was seen as a way to balance the risks associated with personal pensions. A solution that also involved increasing taxes/NI contributions and possibly working longer was considered to be the best for society as a whole.

■ Everybody would support greater choice about working longer, but no one would make that decision far in advance. Flexibility, such as working part-time, would make working longer more attractive. Many said that those who choose to work longer should not lose out financially compared to those who do not.

■ An age-based transitional approach to change in the pensions system was seen as more appropriate than a "Big Bang". Most said it would be unfair to enforce a new system on people who were half way through their working lives and had made plans based on the current situation. The gradual lifting of the SPA for women had been successful in that it was widely accepted as fair and reasonable. This approach to change might be a reference point for other changes to the pension system.

■ No solution will be acceptable unless people have the necessary financial literacy and information to understand the issues involved. Inaction and a sense of paralysis feed on lack of understanding and expectations that can be unrealistically optimistic or pessimistic. Participants in this research agreed that education is also needed to explain why the system is under such pressure, to dispel myths and to show why painful solutions are necessary.

2. National Statistics Omnibus survey

Background

In addition to our qualitative research the Pensions Commission wanted quantitative data on individuals' views on retirement plans, expectations of retirement income, awareness of longevity and savings behaviour. We were able to place a short module of questions in the April 2005 National Statistics Omnibus survey, with two additional questions included in the May survey so that they were asked outside the pre-election period.

This section outlines the following results:

i. Methodology

ii. Knowledge and attitudes

iii. Saving

iv. Sources of retirement income

v. Income aimed for in retirement

vi. "Minimum" and "comfortable" levels of retirement income

vii. Replacement rates

viii.   Expected retirement ages

ix.   Expectations about length of retirement and longevity

x.   Confidence in the pensions system

xi.   Conclusions

This Appendix cannot include all of the potential analysis from the module, but includes a number of the key findings. The questionnaires used are included at the end of this Appendix.

(i) Methodology

Interviews were conducted with approximately 1,200 adult individuals aged 16 or over in private households in Great Britain. All interviews were carried out face-to-face by members of the general field force of interviewers trained to carry out National Statistics surveys. The response rate for April was 69%, with a similar result for May.

All the questions in the April module were asked of those defined as "working age" that is, being of working age if aged below State Pension Age (SPA) and not retired, or aged over SPA and in employment. This definition was used in previous Omnibus modules investigating pension issues and has been used again for consistency.

(ii) Knowledge and attitudes

The initial questions of the April module were aimed at introducing the respondent to the theme of pensions and retirement. A number of these questions were previously included in a shorter ONS Omnibus module on behalf of the Pensions Commission in March 2004, and in past research conducted by the Department for Work and Pensions (DWP). The remaining questions explored whether people are saving for retirement, how much income they are aiming to receive in retirement and how long they expect to spend in retirement.

Previous research has indicated that people find pensions in general confusing and complicated. Since 2000 there has been a significant decline in the percentage of the population reporting to have at least a reasonable knowledge of pensions issues [Figure D.6]. In 2005, men were more likely than women to report a good knowledge of pensions and less likely to report no knowledge.

Since 2000 there has been a significant decline in the percentage of people who have given a lot of thought to making arrangements for an income in their retirement [Figure D.7]. Our research found that nearly two-thirds (63%) of working age respondents have never tried to work out how much they will need to save for retirement. There was great variation by age with younger respondents unsurprisingly less likely to have attempted this.

In the May module we also asked people of working age who should be mainly responsible for ensuring that people "have enough money to live on" in retirement. Overall, 55% said the government should be mainly responsible, which is a significant increase since we last asked the question. And there was a significant shift downwards in the percentage of people stating that the individual and their family should be mainly responsible [Figure D.8].

A possible explanation for this change in overall attitudes could be due to this particular question being asked immediately following a general election. Pensions issues have been highlighted in the media for a while and may also be at the forefront of individual's minds. It will be important to see if this shift in attitude around responsibility is a one-off as a result of the recent attention pensions issues have been receiving or the start of a long-term trend.

Few respondents thought that employers should be mainly responsible for ensuring people have enough to live on in retirement. Those aged 25-44 were more likely to say that the individual and their family should be mainly responsible, while older people were more likely to say the government should be mainly responsible. This could reflect that older people may feel it is too late for them to take steps themselves to provide retirement income, and so may feel more reliant on the government, or it may reflect differences between generations. Forty per cent of men reported that they thought the individual and their family should be mainly responsible compared with 34% of women. This difference could reflect the reduced opportunities that women currently have to build up a private pension in their own right. These results were also

Figure D.6 Self-reported knowledge on pensions issues

	2000	2002	2004	2005
			Column percentages	
I have a good knowledge of pensions issues	13%	13%	12%	12%
I have a reasonable, basic knowledge of pensions	40%	37%	32%	35%
My knowledge of pensions is patchy	28%	29%	31%	31%
I know little or nothing about pensions issues	18%	20%	22%	20%
Don't know	1%	1%	3%	2%
Base (n)	1,304	1,223	1,231	875

Source: Pensions Commission modules 2004 and 2005, Pensions 2002, Pensions 2000

Figure D.7 Thought given to arrangements for an income in retirement

	2000	2002	2004	2005
			Column percentages	
A lot of thought	35%	31%	31%	26%
Some thought	36%	39%	37%	36%
Very little thought	17%	20%	21%	23%
Not thought about it at all	12%	10%	11%	15%
Base (n)	1,304	1,222	1,226	868

Source: Pensions Commission modules 2004 and 2005, Pensions 2002, Pensions 2000

Figure D.8 Responsibility for ensuring that people have enough money to live on in retirement

	2000	2002	2004	2005
			Column percentages	
Mainly the government	42%	44%	43%	55%
Mainly a person's employer	4%	7%	6%	4%
Mainly the person themselves and their family	50%	46%	45%	37%
Don't know/No opinion/None of these	4%	2%	5%	3%
Base (n)	1,304	1,222	1,231	855

Source: Pensions Commission modules 2004 and 2005, Pensions 2002, Pensions 2000

reflected in the focus groups of individuals described earlier where it was felt the responsibility mainly lies with the government or the individual themselves and less with the employer.

(iii) Saving

This next section takes a look at the extent to which working age individuals save for retirement. There are a number of reasons why individuals choose not to save, we explored the reasons why and looked at the characteristics of these people. Only four out of ten working age respondents said that they are currently contributing to a pension. There is little variation between men and women [Figure D.9]. As an alternative or in addition to saving for retirement in a pension, only 21% of respondents said they save money each month specifically for their retirement in a form that is not in a private pension.

Attitudes towards current standards of living will affect whether individuals save specifically for retirement. Our research found that around half (52%) of the respondents tend to agree or strongly agree that they would rather live well now than save for retirement [Figure D.10]. Again there was little variation between these attitudes for men and women. Of those who strongly agree with having a good standard of living today instead of saving for retirement, 80% said they are not currently contributing to a pension.

We asked all respondents who were not currently contributing to a pension the reasons for this. Figure D.11 illustrates the top five specific reasons given for not saving in a pension. The predominant reason chosen is that respondents do not think they earn enough to be able to save, followed by not being able to afford to do so. There were also a number of respondents who gave "other" for their reason for not currently contributing to a pension even though they had a fairly comprehensive list to choose from.

For each reason stated in Figure D.11, there is variation in the distribution by the level of current income. Of those respondents who said they do not earn enough to save, almost 80% have a current gross income of less than £12,480. People who said they cannot afford to save as they have other financial commitments are more likely to have an income between £5,200 and £20,799 [Figure D.12].

Six out of ten working age respondents thought they should be saving more, specifically for retirement. Perhaps surprisingly there is little variation seen in this attitude for those with current pension membership and those without. Although more respondents with current pension membership thought they were saving the right amount compared to those without [Figure D.13]. Overall only 1% of respondents thought they should be saving less.

Figure D.9 Current pension membership, by sex (self-reported)

	Column percentages		
	Men	Women	All
Occupational pension	32%	30%	31%
Personal or Stakeholder	9%	6%	8%
Neither	59%	65%	62%
Base (n)	411	465	876

Note: Respondents were only asked about current pension membership, not about previous pension participation.

Figure D.10 Extent of agreement or disagreement with statement "I'd rather make sure that I had a good standard of living today than put aside money for my retirement"

	Column percentages		
	Men	Women	All
Strongly agree	14%	15%	14%
Tend to agree	38%	38%	38%
Tend to disagree	34%	32%	33%
Strongly disagree	8%	9%	9%
Don't know	6%	6%	6%
Base (n)	411	465	876

Figure D.11 Top five specific reasons why individuals are not currently contributing to a pension

Don't earn enough	38%
Can't afford to/too many debts, bills, financial commitments	24%
Not working at the moment	19%
Too early to start a pension	12%
Don't know enough about pensions/complexity of issues	11%
Base: all with no current occupational, personal or Stakeholder pension (n)	451

Note: This was a multi-coded question where respondents could select as many responses that applied to their situation so the total will not sum to 100%.

(iv) Sources of retirement income

An individual can rely on a number of sources for an income in retirement. Our survey found that 71% of all working age respondents reported that they expect some type of pension to be their main source of income, and almost one-third (32%) expect the main source to be an occupational pension [Figure D.14]. As anticipated there was a relationship between current pension membership and the expected main source of income. Those currently contributing to a pension were much more likely to report that they expect a pension to be their main source of income in retirement.

In comparison to previous Omnibus modules, which included a question on expected source of income in a slightly different format, there has been a decrease in the percentage of respondents expecting their main source to be their own Basic State Pension (BSP) and an increase in the percentage expecting their main source to be "other". Figure D.14 shows that of those with no current pension, 27% expect to rely on "other" sources for their main income. When looking into this group in more detail, 34% expect this to be non-pension state benefits. These figures need to be treated with caution as it is possible when answering the new style question (m373_13) that some respondents assumed the "own pension" option referred only to a private pension.

As other research has shown, women are more likely than men to expect to be dependent on their partner's income in retirement. Overall, 22% of women expect their main source of income to be from their spouse or partner. Of those expecting their main source of income to be from their partner, 97% were women. Of those women expecting to rely on their partner, the majority anticipated this income to be from a private pension [Figure D.15].

Figure D.16 illustrates the distribution of the expected main source of non-pension income in retirement. Of respondents expecting to rely on non-pension sources, 20% expected their income to be from non-pension state benefits. As mentioned previously these figures need to be treated with caution.

As in other research, our survey suggested that some, but not a high percentage, expected property to be their main source of income. Our findings from the individual focus groups suggested that people saw it as a "natural" solution to fund their retirement but only a minority had actually invested in property for this purpose. Our survey results found only 5% of respondents expected their main income source to be property [Figure D.14]. When looking only at those who expect their main source to be non-pension income, this percentage increases to 18%, still a relatively small minority. Ten per cent of these respondents expect to down-size (some people in the focus groups had thought about this as a means to fund their retirement income). In comparison to previous research, there is a difference in the percentage of individuals expecting their main source to be their own earnings with a larger percentage expecting to be earning (20%).

Figure D.12 Top five specific reasons for not currently contributing to a pension by gross individual income band

Row percentages

	Current income					
	Less than £5,200	£5,200– £12,479	£12,480– £20,799	£20,800 – £33,799	£33,800+	Base (n)
Don't earn enough	47%	33%	16%	2%	2%	134
Can't afford to/too many debts, bills, financial commitments	18%	37%	33%	9%	3%	109
Not working at the moment	57%	36%	7%	0%	0%	63
Too early to start a pension	48%	18%	33%	0%	1%	44
Don't know enough about pensions/complexity of issues	18%	36%	39%	4%	2%	31

Figure D.13 Attitude towards amount currently being saved specifically for retirement by current pension membership

	Column percentages		
	Pension	No pension	All
Should save more	62%	60%	61%
Should save less	2%	1%	1%
Saving right amount	31%	12%	19%
Don't know	5%	13%	10%
No income at present	0%	14%	9%
Base (n)	352	524	876

Note: Pension category includes all current members of occupational, personal or Stakeholder Pensions. Respondents were only asked about current pension membership, not about previous pension participation.

Figure D.14 Expected main source of retirement income by current pension status

	Column percentages		
Expected main source of income	**Pension**	**No pension**	**All**
Own state pensions	7%	20%	14%
Own occupational pension	60%	13%	32%
Own personal or Stakeholder pension	13%	13%	13%
Partner's state pensions	0%	1%	1%
Partner's occupational pension	5%	8%	7%
Partner's personal or Stakeholder pension	2%	3%	3%
Property	3%	7%	5%
Other savings & investments	5%	7%	6%
Other	5%	27%	18%
Pension – don't know type	0%	1%	1%
All pension sources	**87%**	**59%**	**71%**
All non-pension sources	**13%**	**41%**	**29%**
Base (n)	341	457	798

Note: Pension category includes all current members of occupational, personal or Stakeholder Pensions.
Respondents were only asked about current pension membership, not about previous pension participation.
The Pensions Commission definition of "other" includes own or spouse/partner's earnings, inheritance, profit from selling own business,
state non-pension benefits, sale of possessions, income from family, and other.

Figure D.15 Distribution of main source of retirement income for women expecting to rely on their partner

Partner's state pensions	7%
Partner's occupational pension	59%
Partner's personal or Stakeholder pension	23%
Partner's earnings	9%
Partner's pension – don't know type	2%
Base (all women expecting their main income source to be reliant on their partner) (n)	85

Figure D.16 Expected main source of non-pension income where pension income is not main source of retirement income

(Non-pension) savings and investments	**20%**
Savings accounts	13%
Stocks, shares, unit trusts	3%
Endowment/life assurance	2%
Other insurance	1%
Annuity	0%
Property	**18%**
Rent from property	8%
Profit from selling property and moving to a less expensive one	10%
Earnings from paid employment	**20%**
Own	16%
Partner's	3%
Other sources	**42%**
Inheritance	9%
Profit from selling own business	6%
State benefits (non-pension)	20%
Income/allowance from family	1%
Sale of possessions	2%
Other	5%
Base (all expecting non-pension sources of retirement income) (n)	226

Note: Totals may not sum to 100% due to rounding.

Some individuals may be expecting more than one main source of retirement income. We asked respondents to select their second main source (if any) from the same list as the main source. Twenty two per cent of respondents do not expect a second source of income in retirement [Figure D.17].

When looking only at those who do expect a second source, the majority expected this to be from either other saving and investments or the "other" category. Almost one-third of respondents (31%) who classified their second income source as "other" expected to have their own earnings. Almost as many people expected an income from an inheritance to be their second income source [Figure D.18].

(v) Income aimed for in retirement

The income an individual will receive in retirement is dependent on many factors and circumstances during their working life. We knew that asking specifically what level of income people expect to get in retirement would be difficult and that a number of respondents would not know what their income in retirement would be, particularly those who are younger and so retirement is a long way off. Our survey found almost half (47%) of the respondents had no idea what their income in retirement would be and this did vary by age as expected. Seventy-seven per cent of those aged 16-24 had no idea compared to 22% aged 55-64.

Our approach therefore was to ask respondents to think about the income in retirement they are aiming for and to indicate this by selecting a statement from a show-card describing this in terms of standard of living. We wanted to compare income aimed for in retirement and behaviour and attitudes towards saving for retirement.

An individual's current living standards and perception of current income will have an influence on what they are aiming to get in retirement. When asking respondents to describe the level of income they are aiming to receive in retirement, 38% aimed to have enough to treat themselves about every week and 19% aimed to have enough to be able to afford luxuries [Figure D.19].

Around two-thirds (67%) of respondents who were currently contributing to a pension were aiming to have at least enough to afford expenses and treat themselves every week in retirement. In contrast, 51% of respondents with no current pension were also aiming for the same level of retirement income [Figure D.20].

When looking at this question in more detail, respondents aiming to have "enough to have a treat every month" in retirement were more likely to agree with the statement that they would rather have a good standard of living today than save for retirement. Whereas individuals aiming for a higher level of retirement income were more likely to disagree with this statement. Figure D.21 illustrates this relationship.

Figure D.17 Expected second source of retirement income by current pension status

Expected second source of income	Column percentages		
	Pension	No pension	All
Own state pensions	12%	9%	10%
Own occupational pension	10%	6%	8%
Own personal or Stakeholder pension	8%	8%	8%
Partner's state pensions	2%	2%	2%
Partner's occupational pension	13%	5%	8%
Partner's personal or Stakeholder pension	3%	2%	2%
Property	8%	7%	7%
Other savings & investments	16%	16%	16%
Other	15%	17%	16%
Pension – don't know type	0%	1%	1%
No other source	13%	28%	22%
All pension sources	**49%**	**32%**	**39%**
All non-pension sources	**38%**	**40%**	**39%**
Base (n)	317	411	728

Note: Pension category includes all current members of occupational, personal or Stakeholder Pensions.
Respondents were only asked about current pension membership, not about previous pension participation.
The Pensions Commission definition of "other" includes own or spouse/partner's earnings, inheritance, profit from selling own business, state non-pension benefits, sale of possessions, income from family, and other.

Figure D.18 Breakdown of "other" expected second source of income in retirement

Own earnings	31%
Inheritance/income from inheritance	27%
Profit from selling own business	8%
State benefits other than state pension	18%
Sale of possessions	0%
Income or allowance from family	1%
Other source of income	11%
Spouse/partner's earnings	4%
Base (all expecting "other" as a second source of income) (n)	111

Figure D.19 Income aimed for in retirement

Plenty of money to afford food, housing, living expenses and luxuries	19%
Enough to afford basic food, housing and living expenses and to treat self about every week	38%
Enough to afford basic food, housing and living expenses and to treat self every month or so	23%
Enough to afford basic food, housing and living expenses	10%
Not enough to afford basic food, housing and living expenses	2%
Don't know	8%
Base (n)	876

Figure D.20 Income aimed for in retirement by current pension membership

	Column percentages		
	Pension	No Pension	All
Plenty of money to afford food, housing, living expenses and luxuries	20%	18%	19%
Enough to afford basic food, housing and living expenses and to treat self about every week	47%	33%	38%
Enough to afford basic food, housing and living expenses and to treat self every month or so	24%	22%	23%
Enough to afford basic food, housing and living expenses	4%	14%	10%
Not enough to afford basic food, housing and living expenses	1%	3%	2%
Don't know	5%	11%	8%
Base (n)	352	524	876

Note: Respondents were only asked about current pension membership, not about previous participation. Pension category includes all current members of occupational, personal or Stakeholder Pensions.

Figure D.21 Income aimed for in retirement by extent of agreement or disagreement with statement "I'd rather make sure that I had a good standard of living today than put aside money for my retirement"

	Row percentages					
	Good standard of living today rather than save for retirement					
Aim for retirement income	Strongly agree	Tend to agree	Tend to disagree	Strongly disagree	Don't know	Base (n)
Plenty of money to afford food, housing, living expenses and luxuries	10%	38%	35%	14%	4%	151
Enough to afford basic food, housing and living expenses and to treat self about every week	11%	37%	38%	9%	5%	336
Enough to afford basic food, housing and living expenses and to treat self every month or so	15%	45%	31%	7%	2%	206
Enough to afford basic food, housing and living expenses	24%	36%	25%	8%	7%	94

(vi) "Minimum" and "comfortable" levels of retirement income

Even though some respondents may not have given their retirement income much thought, we wanted to look at what levels of income individuals thought they would need and how realistic these expectations are in terms of their expected income sources. Again, this is a difficult area to study for a number of reasons, so we decided to ask people what their absolute minimum level of income needed would be, and what a more comfortable level needed would be, if they were retired today. We related this to the qualitative measures used as outlined in section (v). Answers were captured in £25 bands, based on individual weekly income after tax. We do not know whether individuals answered this question on a household basis rather than an individual basis as requested.

For analysis purposes we excluded those who we have assumed would receive enough income from the state (BSP, SERPS/S2P, Pension Credit, Housing Benefit and Council Tax Benefit) to have a high replacement rate (income in retirement relative to their current income). This group included individuals with an annual gross income less than £5,200 which is in line with the assumptions made in our group modelling published in the First Report.

The amount respondents said they would need as a "minimum" in retirement if they were retired today did vary by current income. Lower earners were more likely to state they need a higher level of income in retirement than their current income. As current income increases so does the percentage within each current income band where the "minimum" is less than their current gross income [Figure D.22].

The Guarantee Credit element of Pension Credit for an individual in 2004/05 is £109.45 per week. Ninety-four per cent of respondents said they would need substantially more than what the state currently provides as a minimum. This suggests that individuals would need to make savings during their working life so they would be able to have the additional income in retirement that they said they would need as a "minimum".

Figure D.23 compares what respondents said they would need as a "minimum" and "comfortable" level of income in retirement. To illustrate this analysis, the mid-point of each £25 is shown in Figure D.23. There is a clear difference between the two levels with the median increasing from the £212 to £237 band to the £312 to £337 per week band.

On an individual basis for most people earning £5,200 or more there is a difference of less than £100 between their "minimum" and "comfortable" level. Indeed for 14% of respondents there was no difference at all [Figure D.24]. But as Figure D.23 shows for most income groups the typical difference is around £100 per week. At the median this makes "comfortable" income 45% higher than "minimum" income.

Figure D.22 Comparison of current income and "minimum" income level needed in retirement if retired today

| | Current gross income (£ per week) | | | | | Column percentages |
"Minimum" net income in retirement	£100 – £160	£161 – £259	£260 – £359	£360 – £499	£500+	All
Less than £149	27%	15%	15%	12%	5%	13%
£150 - £249	39%	48%	50%	34%	24%	38%
£250 - £349	12%	22%	22%	31%	31%	25%
£350 - £499	7%	7%	9%	10%	16%	11%
£500+	1%	2%	2%	7%	21%	9%
Don't know	13%	7%	2%	5%	3%	5%
Base (n)	83	147	121	113	190	654

Note: Individuals with a current gross income less than £5,200 per year have been excluded from analysis. The question on minimum retirement income was asked with the objective of collecting individual net income, and current income is on a gross individual basis. The numbers highlighted represent the percentage of respondents whose current gross income and minimum net income in retirement are in a similar band.

Figure D.23 Cumulative distribution of comparison of "minimum" and "comfortable" levels of net income in retirement

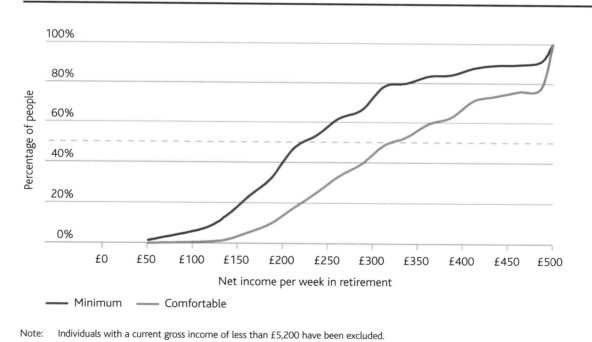

Note: Individuals with a current gross income of less than £5,200 have been excluded.

The average of each £25 band is shown

We explored further those in the £5,200 - £12,479 and £20,800 - £33,799 categories for current gross income. The "comfortable" level of income for the lower income group was only a little higher than the "minimum" for the higher income group [Figure D.25]. The difference in the median values between the "minimum" and "comfortable" levels for the lower earners was smaller than for the higher earners (although the percentage differences are both near 40%).

Respondents in the higher income group were more likely to have a difference of between £50 to £200 per week between their "minimum" and "comfortable" levels of income in retirement. The majority of respondents in the lower income group had a difference of up to £100 per week in retirement [Figure D.26]. About the same percentage of people in both income bands do not think there is a difference between their "minimum" and "comfortable" levels of retirement income.

Figure D.27 illustrates that there is a relationship between the amount an individual said they would need in retirement as a "minimum" and what they expect their main source of retirement income to be. The majority of individuals who said they would need either £250-£399 or £400+ per week as a "minimum", expect their main source to be their own occupational pension while those with a lower "minimum" income level were more likely to expect a state pension as their main source.

(vii) Replacement rates

A key area of interest for the Pensions Commission is individual replacement rates – the income received at the point of retirement as a percentage of income prior to retirement. We calculated a broad replacement rate using the £25 categories from the valid answers to our "minimum" and "comfortable" levels of retirement income questions ("don't knows" were excluded). The replacement rate takes the mid-point of the net income in retirement band and is divided by the mid-point of the individual's current gross income band. As before, we have excluded those with a current gross income of less than £5,200 from our analysis.

As net income is lower than gross income this means that the replacement rates, when comparing across current income levels, are lower than if calculated on a gross basis. But the extent of this underestimate will depend on the amount of taxes paid at each income level. Typically replacement rates calculated in the way normally applied (gross income in retirement as a percentage of gross income when in work) would be about a tenth higher than those calculated below (net income in retirement as a percentage of current gross income).

Figures D.28 and D.29 show the distribution of replacement rates across all income bands for the population for "minimum" and "comfortable" levels of retirement income respectively. There is a clear shift in the replacement rates when comparing the "minimum" and "comfortable" levels of income. Generally those in lower income bands said they need a higher replacement rate in

Figure D.24 Distribution of difference between "minimum" and "comfortable" levels of income in retirement

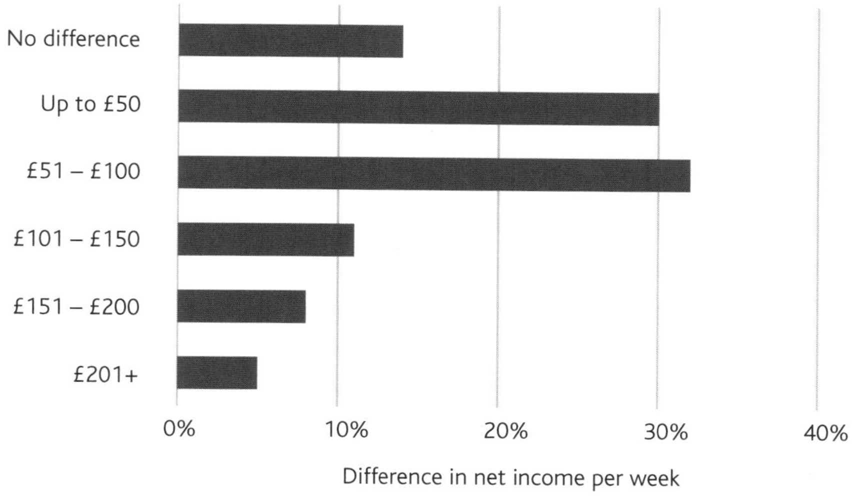

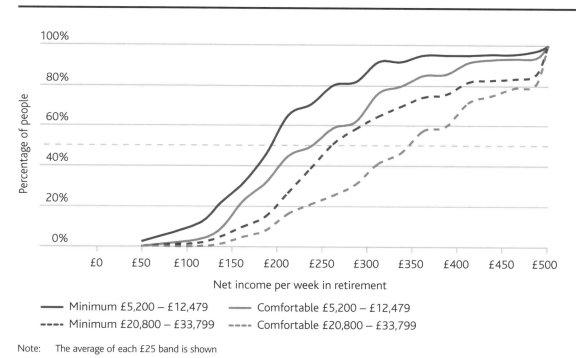

Difference in net income per week

Note: Individuals with a current gross income of less than £5,200 have been excluded.

Figure D.25 Cumulative distribution of comparison of "minimum" and "comfortable" levels of net income in retirement by current gross income band

Net income per week in retirement

—— Minimum £5,200 – £12,479   —— Comfortable £5,200 – £12,479
---- Minimum £20,800 – £33,799   ---- Comfortable £20,800 – £33,799

Note: The average of each £25 band is shown

Figure D.26 Distribution of difference between "minimum" and "comfortable" levels of income in retirement by current gross income band

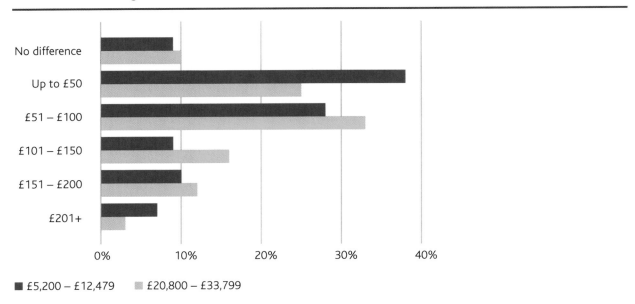

Figure D.27 "Minimum" income per week in retirement by expected main source of income: pension based income only

					Row percentages
"Minimum" income per week	Own state pension	Own occupational	Own personal or Stakeholder	Partner's pension	Base (n)
Up to £149	35%	26%	25%	14%	86
£150 - £249	22%	46%	19%	14%	220
£250 - £399	17%	52%	17%	13%	154
£400+	7%	56%	20%	17%	75

Note: Only respondents whose expected main source of income in retirement is either their own or partner's pension have been included in the analysis.
Due to small sample sizes, the main source of partner's pension has been combined for state, occupational or personal or Stakeholder Pension.
Respondents who said "pension, don't know which kind" have been excluded due to small sample numbers.

Figure D.28 Distribution of replacement rates for "minimum" income in retirement by current gross income band

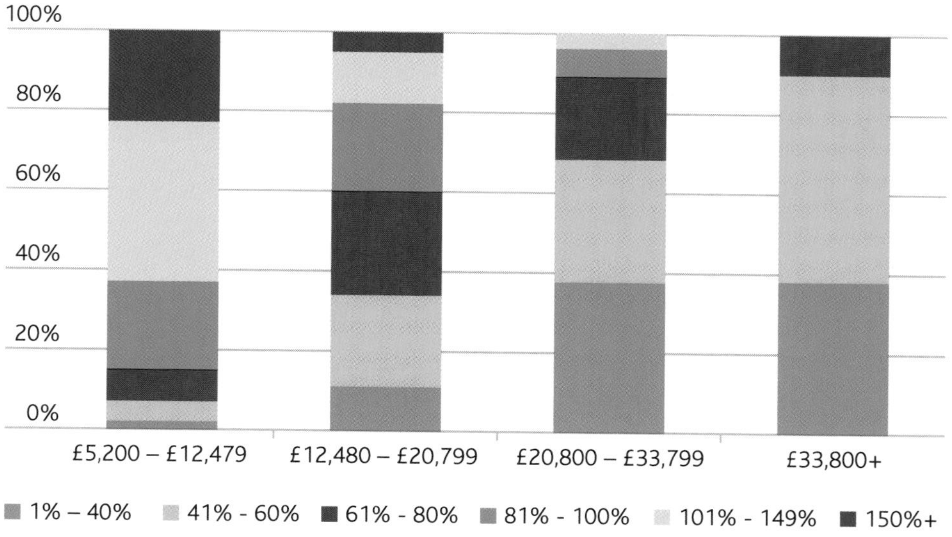

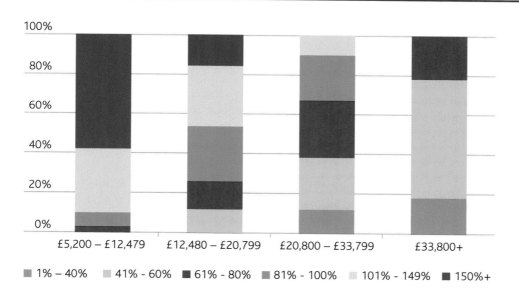

Note: The derived replacement rates are calculated by dividing net individual income in retirement by current gross income.

Figure D.29 Distribution of replacement rates for "comfortable" income in retirement by current gross income band

Note: The derived replacement rates are calculated by dividing net individual income in retirement by current gross income.

retirement, often higher than their current income, that is more than 100%. Whereas most of those in the higher income bands said they would need less than their current income.

In the group modelling work in our First Report (Chapter 4, Figure 4.11) we used benchmark replacement rates which varied according to earnings band. A direct comparison between both sets of results is not possible, but a broad comparison can be made. In our group modelling we assumed a replacement rate of 67% for someone on median earnings. From our survey results if we consider someone with median income so in the £20,800-£33,799 gross income band the median "minimum" replacement rate is 50%. For the same income group the median "comfortable" replacement rate increases to 72%. So our group modelling estimate lies between the "minimum" and "comfortable" levels of retirement income needed. Within each income group there is a lot of variation between the "minimum" and "comfortable" replacement rates.

(viii) Expected retirement ages

We asked respondents who are either currently in employment or thought they would be in employment in the future to state the age at which they expect to retire.

The median expected age of retirement among respondents is 62. Almost half (46%) of the men expect to retire at 65 followed by the same percentage expecting to retire before age 65. As found in previous research, the majority of people did not expect to retire after age 65 [Figure D.30].

Between 2010 and 2020 the State Pension Age (SPA) for women will change from 60 to 65 years. The following analysis divides the women in the sample into three groups depending on their age at the time of the survey and when their SPA will be. The majority of respondents lie in the group where their SPA will be 65 [Figure D.31]. Over half (59%) of these women expect to retire before they will be entitled to collect their state pension. The women in the other two groups generally expect to retire at or after their SPA but the sample sizes are small. Previous research has highlighted that some younger women are not even aware of the upcoming change in SPA. This lack of awareness could be the reason behind our results, rather than individuals making a conscious decision to retire before SPA.

As shown in Figures D.30 and D.31, for both men and women a number of individuals expect to retire before they will be able to receive the state pension. It is important to look at the relationship between when individuals expect to retire, when their SPA is and what their main expected source of income in retirement will be. As highlighted we are not sure if the results for women regarding their retirement age are due to their lack of awareness of the planned change or a conscious decision. For this reason, the following analysis will only focus on men.

Figure D.30 Expected retirement ages, by sex

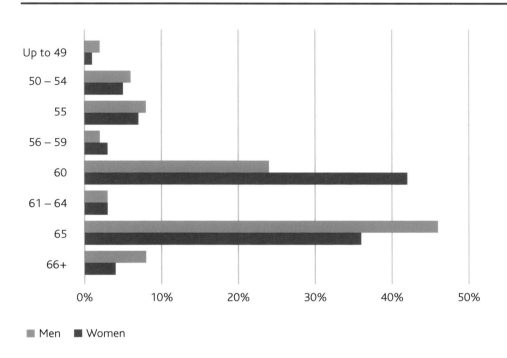

■ Men ■ Women

Figure D.31 Expected retirement ages for women with different State Pension Age

Expected retirement age	SPA = 60	SPA = 65	Column percentages SPA = 60 - 65	All
Up to 49	0%	1%	0%	1%
50 - 54	0%	6%	0%	5%
55	0%	9%	0%	7%
56 - 59	4%	3%	0%	3%
60	46%	40%	55%	42%
61 - 64	13%	0%	11%	3%
65	34%	36%	29%	36%
66+	4%	4%	5%	4%
Base (n)	48	294	34	376

Note: The numbers highlighted represent the percentage of respondents whose expected retirement age is the same as their SPA.

Men who are currently contributing to a private pension are more likely to expect to retire before their SPA [Figure D.32].

Even though the sample size is small for the number of men who said they expect to rely on state provision for their main income source, the results suggest a relationship between expected retirement age and expected main income source [Figure D.33]. About a quarter (23%) who expect their main source to be from the state expected to retire before the SPA compared to a half (50%) of others. Anyone who expects to retire before the SPA will need to have an income source in their own right or from their partner between when they stop earning and when they become entitled to receive a state pension.

(ix) Expectations about length of retirement and longevity

We asked the respondents who gave a retirement age to state how many years they expected to spend in retirement. There was an 89% response rate to this question. Women were more likely not to respond than men and almost half of the women who did not respond were aged between 16 and 29 reflecting that it is difficult to answer when looking further into the future.

How long an individual expects to spend in retirement is an important factor when looking into how much they need to save specifically for retirement. Fifty per cent of respondents anticipated spending between 20 and 24 years in retirement [Figure D.34]. There is no difference in the median expected length of retirement between men and women. However, as found in previous DWP research, women were more likely than men to expect to spend 20 years or more in retirement (60% to 49%).

For both sexes, individuals who expect to retire before their SPA are more likely to anticipate spending 25 years or more in retirement. For those who expect to retire after SPA over half of respondents anticipate spending fewer than 14 years in retirement [Figure D.35]. However we do need to treat the results for those expecting to retire after SPA with caution due to the small sample numbers.

We wanted to explore people's expectations of their longevity and how they compared to the official forecasts, but as this could be a sensitive subject for some, we have tried to capture this indirectly by looking at planned age of retirement and expected length of retirement.

Where both questions were answered, an approximation of the individual's expectation of life has been calculated by taking the age they said they expect to retire, and adding this to the mid-point of the years expected to be spent in retirement. Any respondent who stated "don't know" for either of these questions was excluded from the analysis. The highest category for expected length of retirement is open-ended at "25 years or more". For the purposes of this analysis we used a value of 30 years to add to the expected retirement age for individuals expecting to spend 25 years or more in retirement. The overall results might change if a different value were chosen. The official figures used

Figure D.32 Expected retirement age and current pension participation: men

	Column percentages		
Expected retirement age	**Pension**	**No pension**	**All**
Below SPA	50%	42%	45%
At SPA	42%	50%	46%
After SPA	9%	8%	8%
Base (n)	171	183	354

Note: Respondents were only asked about current pension membership, not about previous pension participation.
Pension category includes all current members of occupational, personal or Stakeholder Pensions

Figure D.33 Expected retirement age and expected main source of retirement income: men

	Column percentages		
Expected retirement age	**State provision**	**Non-state provision**	**All**
Below SPA	23%	50%	30%
At SPA	71%	41%	58%
After SPA	6%	9%	11%
Base (n)	52	280	332

Note: State provision includes own or partner's BSP, own or partner's SERPS/S2P and state benefits other than pension. Non-state provision includes all other expected main sources of retirement income.

Figure D.34 Expected length of retirement, by sex

	Column percentages		
	Men	**Women**	**All**
Less than 5 years	2%	1%	1%
5 - 9 years	6%	5%	6%
10 - 14 years	15%	12%	13%
15 - 19 years	17%	15%	16%
20 - 24 years	22%	27%	24%
25 years or more	27%	33%	30%
Don't know	11%	9%	10%
Base (n)	354	376	730

as a comparison are the Government Actuary's Department (GAD) 2003-based principal projection of cohort life expectancy at age 65. The 2003-based projection was used as this was the latest data available at the time of the survey. Each individual was given a life expectancy at age 65 based on the year they would reach 65.

Figure D.36 outlines for men and women by current age the GAD average estimate for the respective age band, and the difference between the derived individual estimate and the official estimate. By comparing the derived individual's expectation of life to the GAD data we can determine whether an individual is likely to be under or overestimating their longevity. For both sexes, there is variation in the differences between all age groups. On average women are more likely than men to underestimate their life expectancy. Unsurprisingly the younger respondents have the highest average underestimates with women aged 16-25 years reporting an underestimate of almost nine years. If we had used the 2004-based figures the average underestimation for both sexes and all age groups would be higher.

There are many factors which can influence how an individual perceives how long they will spend in retirement and hence their longevity. These include alcohol consumption, whether they smoke and their general health. Respondents were asked to comment on their general health, and due to small sample numbers of respondents in the "fair", "bad" or "very bad" categories we have grouped these together. Almost half (49%) reported that their health is very good, followed by 39% reporting good health with little variation between men and women [Figure D.37]. This indicates that individuals are not underestimating how long they will spend in retirement due to reporting being in poor health.

GAD does not calculate average life expectancy by health status. But each individual in our sample had a value for their derived estimate of longevity, and also their own value of the GAD projected estimate. Therefore we could recategorise the groups based on health status and compare the average individual and GAD estimates for each group. The results indicate that individuals reporting a relatively worse current health status are more likely to have a lower derived expectation of life [Figure D.38] which could indicate they are making a rational assessment.

A number of studies have investigated how an individual's expectation of their longevity compares to official projections. A study by Nottingham University found that on average individuals in Great Britain underestimate their longevity by 4.62 years (for men) and 5.95 years (for women) compared with the estimates from the GAD data. The results from our survey are consistent and suggest that individuals in Great Britain do underestimate their longevity. On average men underestimate by 4.2 years and 6.9 years for women. Our results will differ from those in other research because of the different approaches taken. Unlike the Nottingham study we did not explore in more detail other relevant factors such as smoking status.

Figure D.35 Expected length of retirement by expected retirement age and sex

					Column percentages	
Expected length		Men			Women	
of retirement	Before SPA	At SPA	After SPA	Before SPA	At SPA	After SPA
Less than 5 years	0%	1%	10%	1%	0%	0%
5 - 9 years	3%	8%	13%	4%	5%	24%
10 - 14 years	13%	14%	32%	9%	13%	27%
15 - 19 years	9%	26%	15%	17%	16%	17%
20 - 24 years	21%	25%	8%	22%	30%	31%
25 years or more	41%	17%	7%	41%	25%	0%
Don't know	13%	9%	14%	8%	11%	0%
Base (n)	155	166	33	169	114	11

Note: Only women whose SPA will be 65 have been included in this analysis due to small sample sizes for the other groups of women.

Figure D.36 Comparison of average derived individual estimates and GAD forecasts, by sex

Current age Men	Derived individual's average estimate	Average 2003-based GAD estimate	Average 2004-based GAD estimate	Derived estimate minus GAD 2003-based	Derived estimate minus GAD 2004-based
16 - 25	81.1	86.7	88.5	-5.6	-7.4
26 - 35	81.4	86.3	87.6	-4.9	-6.2
36 - 45	82.2	85.8	86.7	-3.6	-4.5
46 - 55	81.9	85.2	85.9	-3.3	-4.0
56 - 65	81.7	84.6	85.1	-2.9	-3.4

Difference in derived individual's estimate and GAD 2003-based				Mean	Median
All working aged men 16 - 65 years				-4.2	-3.9

Current age Women	Derived individual's average estimate	Average 2003-based GAD estimate	Average 2004-based GAD estimate	Derived estimate minus GAD 2003-based	Derived estimate minus GAD 2004-based
16 - 25	80.7	89.4	91.0	-8.7	-10.3
26 - 35	81.4	89.0	90.1	-7.6	-8.7
36 - 45	82.6	88.6	89.2	-6.0	-6.6
46 - 55	81.3	88.1	88.4	-6.8	-7.1
56 - 65	83.6	87.5	87.7	-3.9	-4.1

Difference in derived individual's estimate and GAD 2003-based				Mean	Median
All working aged women 16 - 65 years				-6.85	-6.5

Source: GAD 2003-based and 2004-based cohort expectancy of life, GB

Note: Expectation of life at 65 is used on the basis that answers about expected length of retirement would be given assuming survival to retirement age.

(x) Confidence in the pensions system

We asked people in the May module what changes they thought would improve their confidence in the pensions system. Respondents could choose up to three measures from a given list of options. Overall, almost half of respondents thought that a simpler pensions system would improve their confidence, and this was closely followed by the option of guaranteeing that contributions would not be lost [Figure D.39]. These two issues were also highlighted in our focus group discussions. The provision of clearer information about both state and private pensions was also supported by around a third of respondents.

Women in particular highlighted the need for better information about state pensions, and the provision of a guarantee that contributions would not be lost. More men than women highlighted the issue of better protection for Defined Benefit (DB) schemes, which could reflect higher participation in these schemes by men.

Those approaching SPA were more likely to highlight the need for better information on state pensions, than younger age groups. Those aged 25 to 44 older were more likely to choose the option of the provision of a guarantee that contributions would not be lost. It could be that the experience of some of this group, for example, endowment mortgages and pensions scandals could be influencing their responses. They were also less likely to choose the option of receiving free advice from the Government. Again, they may feel that it is too late for them to take on board advice at this stage in their working lives. Overall, younger people were more likely to say that they had no opinion on this issue, which probably reflects a general lack of knowledge and awareness by young people of pensions issues.

(xi) Conclusions

This research has highlighted a number of issues:

■ Individual's attitudes to pensions, expectations, saving for retirement and longevity were varied across the population. There has been a significant decline in the percentage of the working age population who said that they have a "good" or "reasonable" knowledge of pensions issues. There has also been a decline in the percentage giving "a lot" or "some" thought to arrangements for an income in retirement. In the last year there has been a significant shift in who is seen to be mainly responsible for providing enough money in retirement, from the individual to the government.

Figure D.37 Distribution of general health, by sex

	Men	Women	All
		Column percentages	
	Men	**Women**	**All**
Very good health	46%	52%	49%
Good health	41%	37%	39%
Fair to very bad health	13%	12%	12%
Base (n)	313	340	653

Note: Due to small sample numbers of respondents who said their general health was "fair", "bad" or "very bad" have been grouped together.

Figure D.38 Comparison of average derived individual estimates and GAD 2003-based estimates, by sex and general health status

Health status	Derived individual's average estimate	Average 2003-based GAD estimate	Derived estimate minus GAD 2003-based
Men			
Very good health	82.4	86.0	-3.6
Good health	81.7	85.7	-4.0
Fair - very bad health	78.9	85.7	-6.8
All	81.7	85.8	-4.2
Women			
Very good health	82.2	88.7	-6.5
Good health	81.5	88.6	-7.2
Fair - very bad health	81.2	88.5	-7.3
All	81.8	88.7	-6.9

Source: Pensions Commission analysis on GAD 2003-based cohort expectation of life data, GB

Note: Due to small sample numbers of respondents who said their general health was "fair", "bad" or "very bad" they have been grouped together. GAD does not publish estimates on a health basis. The average is re-calculated for the particular health group.

■ Our research found that over half (61%) of respondents thought that they should be saving more for retirement with only 1% who said that they should save less. The majority of respondents expected their main source of retirement income to come from pensions of one kind or another. The others divide into five roughly equal groups between other investment income, property, earnings, non-pension state benefits and other sources (of which half are inheritance). Around one-fifth did not expect to receive a second main source of income in retirement.

■ There was a clear difference between the levels of income that individuals would need as a "minimum" or to be "comfortable". Half of the respondents said they would need a net individual weekly income of at least £237-£262 as a "minimum" in retirement to afford only basic food, housing and living expenses. Half said they would need at least £337-£362 to be "comfortable". These levels tended to increase with respondent's current income, but there was a very wide spread in suggested levels even within income groups: people's views of what constitutes an adequate retirement income vary considerably.

■ When comparing the replacement rates with those suggested as benchmarks in our First Report [Chapter 4, Figure 4.11], there is no evidence that our benchmarks were over-stating people's expectations. Those figures suggest that the benchmark of a 67% gross replacement rate for those with median earnings lies between the median replacement rate for "minimum" and "comfortable" levels of retirement income needed for individuals with a gross income of £20,780 to £33,799. However, our benchmark for those with low incomes of 80% is well below the median replacement rate that people in this income group said they needed.

■ Despite the planned increase in women's SPA there was very little difference between younger and older women in the spread of ages at which they expect to retire. Very few men or women expect to retire after the SPA. Our research found that the majority of respondents expected to spend at least 20 years in retirement. When combining expected retirement age with expected length of retirement, the findings confirm recent research from Nottingham University which suggested that people tend to underestimate their own expected longevity. In comparison to the GAD 2003-based projection, women tended to underestimate their longevity by 6.9 years on average and men by 4.2 years. The extent of the underestimation is greater if the recently published 2004-based figures are used.

■ Our research found that when asked what would most improve their confidence in the pensions system, almost half said a simpler pensions system would do so, and over 40% said a system that guaranteed that their contributions would not be lost.

Figure D.39 Which of the following would most improve your confidence in the pensions system?

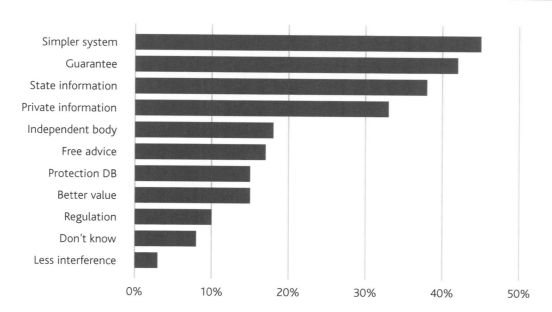

Note

Individuals were asked to choose up to 3 options. The options individuals could choose from were asked in the order as follows:

- Simpler, less complex pensions system;
- Clearer information about the State pension and my entitlement;
- Clearer information about private pensions and what I neeed to save and can expect to receive;
- Free individual advice paid for by the Government;
- Better value private pensions;
- A guarantee that you would not lose the value of the contributions that you have put into a money purchase pension;
- Independent body to run the pensions system in people's interests;
- Better regulation of financial service companies;
- Better protection for employer-sponsored (defined benefit) pension schemes;
- Less interference by Government;
- Don't know/no opinion (spontaneous only).

3. Small firms focus groups and DWP financial intermediary research

(i) Background and methodology

From the analysis in our First Report we were aware that pension provision in small firms was low, and indeed that the requirement on employers to establish a Stakeholder Pension scheme excluded firms with fewer than five employees. Therefore any recommendations that we made in relation to employers would be likely to affect small firms and the smallest firms in particular. We were therefore keen to undertake a piece of research to understand the views of small firms more clearly. The research was undertaken by Durham Business School on behalf of the Pensions Commission between May and July 2005.

The primary aims of the research were to establish how various options for change in the pension system, particularly options for introducing compulsion, would be received by small businesses and how such changes would affect these businesses. The specification for the research defined the following areas of interest:

- The implications for small firms of extending compulsion, and the main aspects of concern for small and medium enterprises (SMEs): for example, administrative burden, payroll costs, competitiveness, and thresholds.

- The administrative/regulatory burdens associated with different forms of compulsion, and the ways in which these could be ameliorated, including who administers the scheme, tax and NI relief arrangements.

- The position taken by those operating Stakeholder Pension schemes, and the potential impacts upon them of compulsion.

- Comparative impacts of introducing a scheme from scratch versus the extension of an existing one, including benefits and dis-benefits of outsourcing payroll functions including pensions.

- Employers' preferences and views relating to the four options identified by the Commission to deal with the future issues: poorer pensioners, higher taxes, higher savings, higher average age of retirement.

The research specification also required that the research should elicit small businesses' views on four holistic change scenarios.

The brief for the project specified that it should be based around 12 focus group discussions with owners or senior managers of small businesses from a variety of business sectors. This approach allowed for in-depth exploration of key issues and testing of individuals' responses as these are discussed within groups.

Figure D.40 Location of focus groups

Group number	Locality	Number of participants
1	Norwich	7
2	London	10
3	Cardiff	8
4	Birmingham	9
5	Paddington	9
6	Southampton	8
7	Trowbridge	6
8	Hull	11
9	Durham	6
10	Digbeth	14
11	Perry Barr	10
12	Lichfield	8
Total		106

Each group session included three core activities: a pre-discussion questionnaire, a group discussion and a post-discussion questionnaire. The questionnaires were used to provide background data on the respondents' businesses and responses to specific options for change. The group discussions were designed to solicit more considered responses to the issues being discussed and an understanding of the thinking that underpinned these responses. The discussions were facilitated using a semi-structured topic guide and open questions followed by prompts as necessary.

As part of a broader research programme, this project was not intended to involve a large-scale, nationally representative survey of small businesses. Rather the intention was to construct a sample that would capture the ways in which small firms would generally respond to the options for change being considered, and to identify effects that would be commonly experienced throughout the small business sector.

The research was not intended to evaluate the appropriateness or potential effectiveness of any of the options for change being considered. Rather, it was concerned to acquire a small business perspective on these options and so the findings are basically descriptive. The research was limited to considering specific possible changes to pension provision. It did not consider the impact of working longer or increasing taxation or the trade-offs between the four options identified in our First Report. The scenarios put to participants were designed to elicit responses to a wide range of possible pension reforms.

It is also important to be clear that the findings reflect the immediate, necessarily less than fully considered, responses to a range of complex issues. It is likely that on reflection some participants may well reconsider and generally soften their positions on the various options for change considered.

The sample was constructed to include participants with different experiences of pension provision across a range of business sizes, sectors and regions, of different ages, and with varying growth performances and aspirations. In total, the project involved 12 completed focus groups and a total of 106 participants [Figure D.40].

(ii) Responsibility, choice and compulsion

While most participants readily accepted that there is a rationale for change, most were less clear about where the responsibility for action lies. They were, however, quite clear on one point; virtually none of the participants believed that employers have any significant responsibility in this area. They were also almost unanimous in arguing that there is no benefit to employers from providing enhanced pensions for their staff. Group participants consistently maintained that employees generally perceive little real value in having a pension and that providing a pension does not provide any benefits in terms of recruitment or retention.

Participants' views on whether primary responsibility lies with the government or individuals were mixed. They expressed uncertainty and, to some extent, views were inconsistent and contradictory. Most respondents argued that individuals have a clear responsibility to provide for their own retirement.

In principle, almost all participants considered individual choice to be important and most were unsympathetic to government intervention and regulation both generally and specifically in this area. However, when the issue of choice was subsequently considered in greater depth, positions became less clear. In more detailed discussion of the various options for change put to the groups, most participants apparently placed considerable weight on flexibility; certainly this was one of the most common reasons given for their individual preferences. However, analysis of the discussions suggests that, in part at least, this position reflected the inherent potential that flexible systems have to facilitate employer non-engagement rather than concerns about personal freedoms. Most groups recognised that there are potential tensions between allowing for choice and flexibility and the complexity of the system. Most participants favoured simplicity even if this meant some loss of choice.

Most groups were generally unsympathetic to the notion of compulsion. However, if an element of compulsion was to be introduced, most participants were clear that this should focus on individuals; few favoured the introduction of any form of compulsion for employers. These perceptions persisted throughout the sessions despite the fact that in subsequent discussions there was a widespread assumption that the potential to enhance voluntarist arrangements may well be limited.

Objections to the introduction of compulsion took several forms. First, there was a widespread view that it was inappropriate in principle-government should not intervene on what were perceived to be essentially the concerns of individuals and employers. Second, there was a relatively general concern that the government could not formulate and deliver an effective policy in this area, a view that was compounded by very deep concerns about private pension providers. Third, there were a range of concerns regarding the costs and impacts that compulsory new arrangements may have on small businesses.

Most participants in the study favoured measures that would make current voluntarist arrangements more attractive and thus more effective. Suggestions in this area focused on two themes: education and incentives.

The possibility of shifting from the current "opt-in" arrangements for pensions to an "opt-out" system based on auto-enrolment was generally seen as an acceptable and potentially effective policy option; not least because it was seen as an appropriate compromise solution that stopped short of increased compulsion. However, many participants suggested that their knowledge of their employees led them to believe that the opt-out rate would be relatively high. Some participants were concerned that such a system would necessarily be accompanied by inducements, possibly including employer contributions, to discourage opt-out.

(iii) Administrative burden

The groups expressed relatively little concern about the administrative burdens that the options for change being considered would have on their businesses. Any administrative burden that might be incurred was generally regarded as likely to be no more than a relatively small cost to the business. Because such increases were generally seen as likely to be less costly to the business than potential increases in employer contributions, they were widely regarded as a secondary issue.

Suggestions that any new pension arrangements might be administered through existing systems, such as PAYE or National Insurance, were generally well received. In part, this reflected a view that any reduction of administrative burden on employers was positive. To a greater extent, however, preferences for a state-administered system appear to have reflected very negative perceptions of private pension providers. A significant number of discussants tended to conflate the administration of schemes with their operation. From this perspective, state-administered schemes were at least seen as being safer than private pensions. Similarly, the option for a "clearing house" for pension contributions was seen as being potentially positive, but of little real significance.

(iv) Employer contributions

The small businesses included in this study saw the possibility of an increased obligation to contribute to employees' pensions as the single most important and concerning issue amongst all the options for change reviewed in the discussions. In very general terms, participants believed that a situation requiring an employer contribution of 5% of earnings for most, if not all, employees would be highly problematic, but possibly one that they could cope with. Almost all argued that an employer contribution of 10% would have profound effects on the viability of their businesses.

Questionnaire responses suggest that approximately a quarter of the respondents were sympathetic to some level of employer contribution. This proportion corresponds quite closely with the proportion of respondents already making contributions of some kind. Whilst this was not generally evident from the group discussions, it seems likely that these responses reflect a perception that extended compulsion to make employer contributions would create some competitive advantage for these businesses. Therefore, it is likely that the respondents sympathetic to an increased obligation to make employer contributions were generally those that believed that such an obligation would have relatively little impact on their businesses.

A significant proportion of participants argued that if they were faced with contributions of 5% they would reconsider their growth objectives and staffing policies; some suggested that they would forego planned growth to avoid making such contributions. Some also argued that they would actively seek to avoid making such payments through strategies such as contracting-out work or using more casual labour. There was a clear view that if employer contributions were required for most staff, many small businesses would seek to recover this added expense back by making effective reductions in employees' salaries.

There was little evidence that participants' views on these issues softened during more in-depth discussion. Almost all participants believed that an expanded obligation to make employer contributions would impact negatively on their competitiveness, even where the obligation was universal. Few discussants recognised any benefits for employers from making contributions.

(v) Thresholds

Discussants were generally in favour of thresholds and exemptions. That is, they were sympathetic to any arrangement that would potentially reduce employers' obligations to contribute to employees' pensions. Most groups argued there is little point in individuals on low incomes being in a pension scheme; they have little, if any, spare income, and the contributions they might reasonably afford are too low to be meaningful. There was a widely held view that all employees should be in a pension scheme as soon as they begin work; the principal argument for this being that it is important to normalise the idea of being in, and contributing to, a pension scheme. Few groups spontaneously suggested a threshold related to time in post.

Perhaps unsurprisingly given the high proportion of micro and small businesses within the sample, exempting businesses below a minimum size was seen to be very significant and clearly the most important of the various possibilities considered. Most groups suggested that the burdens associated with many of the options for change were likely to fall disproportionately on small businesses. A very high proportion of participants assumed that current exemptions for businesses with fewer than five employees should and would be retained. Micro-businesses were concerned by the prospect of any new obligation to provide, administer or contribute to employee pensions. These views appear to reflect both apprehension, stemming from a general lack of knowledge of pension schemes and their administration, and concerns about additional staff costs.

A limited number of respondents volunteered the unprompted suggestion that the age of the business is important because established businesses are generally more able to cope with change and increased costs than newer ones, the implication being that some exemptions should be granted to new businesses.

A number of groups made the point that the potential burdens involved in extending employers' responsibilities would affect businesses in different sectors disproportionately; with the most severe effects falling on labour intensive, low wage sectors because wage costs represent a high proportion of overall cost for these businesses. Some respondents pointed out that there was little opportunity to pass on additional costs in their sector.

(vi) The four scenarios

When this research was being developed the Pensions Commission were considering a range of possible options and ideas for pension reform. It was not possible to consider all the potential options in the research and so we developed four specific options for discussion [Figure D.41]. The scenarios had some key features that were discussed in the focus groups, and we necessarily had to simplify the details in order to facilitate discussion. The scenarios focused on the elements that would directly affect employers. It is worth noting that there was not a scenario with exactly the same features as our final recommendation. In particular, the contribution levels discussed were significantly higher than those we have recommended in our preferred option.

The four scenarios were systematically considered in each of the focus groups. Participants were asked to identify elements that they liked and disliked, to suggest how the individual scenarios would affect their businesses, to identify any reasons why each scenario would not work in practice and to suggest how they each might be improved.

A number of participants found the scenarios complex, and a minority were reluctant to comment on options that they felt they did not have time to consider fully. A number of participants were clear that in identifying preferences for particular scenarios they were choosing the "least bad" option.

Figure D.41 The four scenarios

Orange Scenario: Compulsory employer contributions and administration
- All employees have to join a pension scheme that is organised by the employer with a private pension provider, unless individuals are members of a suitable personal pension scheme.
- All employees have to make a contribution of at least 5% of earnings and employers have to contribute 5% for all employees.
- Employers have to organise their own scheme and payments to it.
- For employees not in the employer's scheme the employer has to arrange payments, and make contributions to the pension providers nominated by the employees.
- Applies to all employees aged 21 and over, earning at least £12,100 a year, and who have been with the employer for at least 6 months.
- Contributions are in addition to NI contributions and contracted-out rebates.
- New arrangement would only apply to people who are not already in a pension scheme with some minimum standard, assumed for now to be 10% total contributions.

Yellow Scenario: Compulsory employer contributions minimised administration
- All employees have to be members of a new national pension scheme run through the NI system, unless individuals are members of a suitable alternative pension scheme.
- Employers do not have to run their own pension scheme.
- Employees have to make a contribution of at least 5% of earnings.
- Employers have to contribute 5% for all employees.
- Contributions are made through the PAYE system to the national scheme as currently happens if an employee is contracted-in. A clearing house is established via the PAYE system to co-ordinate payments to personal pensions.
- Applies to all employees aged 21 and over, earning at least £12,100 a year, and who have been with the employer for at least 6 months.
- Contributions are in addition to NI contributions and contracted-out rebates.
- New arrangement would only apply to people who are not already in a pension scheme with some minimum standard, assumed for now to be 10% total contributions.

Blue Scenario: Voluntary employer role and contributions, compulsory membership
- All employees have to be a member of a private pension scheme of their choice, i.e. it does not necessarily have to be provided by the employer. Employees have to make a contribution of at least 10% of earnings, payment of which to the provider is organised by the employer through a clearing house.
- Employers can choose to set up their own alternative pension scheme if they want to.
- Employers can choose to make contributions if they want to. If employers do contribute individuals' contributions can be reduced.
- Applies to all employees who are aged 21 and over, earning at least £12,100 a year, and who have been with the employer for at least 6 months.
- Contributions are in addition to NI contributions and contracted-out rebates.
- New arrangement would only apply to people who are not already in a pension scheme with some minimum standard, assumed for now to be 10% total contributions.

Figure D.41 Continued

Pink Scenario: Automatic enrolment minimised administration

- All employees are automatically enrolled into a new national pension scheme run through the NI system, unless individuals are members of a suitable alternative pension scheme.
- If employees opt out of this system they do not have to do anything else as an alternative. If they do join an alternative scheme they can choose to make contributions at a lower rate.
- Employees who are members of the national scheme have to make a contribution of at least 10% of earnings.
- Employers can choose to make a contribution. If employers do contribute, individuals' contributions can be reduced. Contributions are made through the PAYE system as currently happens if an employee is contracted-in. A clearing house is established via the PAYE system to co-ordinate payments to personal pensions.
- Applies to all employees who are aged 21 and over, earning at least £12,100 a year, and who have been with the employer for at least 6 months.
- Contributions are in addition to NI contributions and contracted-out rebates.
- New arrangement would only apply to people who are not already in a pension scheme with some minimum standard, assumed for now to be 10% total contributions.

Figure D.42 Most and least preferred scenarios

	Most preferred	Least preferred
Orange	4%	45%
Yellow	12%	10%
Blue	51%	13%
Pink	34%	32%

Base: Most preferred = 79, Least preferred = 78

In practice, most participants were concerned to choose scenarios that they believed would have least impact on their businesses, rather than because of their positive features. However, data from the post-discussion questionnaires and the group discussions provided relatively clear findings and did point to some individual elements that were generally well received.

About half of participants favoured the blue scenario. A third favoured the pink scenario. There was little if any support for the remaining two scenarios [Figure D.42].

The main perceived positive features of the blue scenario were:

- voluntary employer contributions;

- employer choice about having own scheme or not;

- relatively straightforward administration;

- scenario is relatively simple overall.

The main perceived positive features of the pink scenario were:

- voluntary employer contributions;

- employer choice about having own scheme;

- minimised administration;

- automatic employee enrolment and opt-out.

The distinguishing feature of both of these options is that they allow the employers to choose not to contribute to employees' pensions. Discussion of the scenarios in the group sessions suggested that businesses were fundamentally concerned by this factor and that it was this that determined their preferences. Employers' ability to choose whether to have their own scheme was seen as an important secondary consideration – in part because of concerns over the implications for the business of a scheme failing. The relatively modest administrative burdens associated with these two scenarios were also seen as positive features. The added attraction of the blue scenario appears to be its relative simplicity.

Nearly half of respondents least preferred the orange scenario and a third least preferred the pink, almost exactly the same proportion as most preferred it. The results for the pink scenario were somewhat incongruous in that it was both the second most preferred and the second least preferred.

The main perceived negative features of the orange scenario were:

- the compulsory 5% employer contribution;

- the compulsory minimum 5% employee contribution (in relation to low-wage employees);

- potential administrative burden involved in dealing with multiple pension providers.

The main perceived negative features of the pink scenario were:

- perceived lack of effectiveness – most respondents assumed that a high level of opt-out would make this scenario ineffective in practice;

- uncertainty about the nature of the proposed "national scheme".

The reasons given for disliking scenarios were generally the inverse of those for preferring others; a deep antipathy to employer contributions and to a lesser extent concerns about administrative burden. It was also clear that preferences for particular scenarios were deeply influenced by perceptions of the impacts they would have on the participants' businesses.

(vii) Effects on Small and Medium Enterprises (SME) performance and behaviour

Of all the potential impacts of the specific options for change considered in the groups, participants were only really concerned by those arising from any increased obligation to make contributions to employee pensions. Other potential impacts, including those associated with additional administrative burdens, were generally regarded as unwelcome but probably not that significant for the operation and profitability of small businesses.

Almost all participants argued that an increased obligation to contribute to employees' pensions would profoundly affect the viability of their businesses, impacting on their competitiveness and profitability. Few groups accepted that a general obligation, applying to all employers, would produce a level playing field and thus not be likely to have a great impact on competitiveness. Participants in almost all the groups argued that the various options for change would have a greater effect on small businesses than it would on larger firms.

Although the findings reported here relate to the immediate, and necessarily less than fully considered responses of the group participants, and so may well exaggerate respondents' negative perceptions and suggested responses to new policy, it seems likely that:

- a general level of hostility would persist;

- some businesses would be profoundly affected; and

- some businesses, at least, would seek to resist any new obligations.

(viii) Increasing acceptance and buy-in amongst SMEs

Participants in each of the group discussions were asked what could be done to make the various options for change more attractive to them as small business owners and what changes could be made to ameliorate the negative impacts of these options on their businesses. Largely because they were so fundamentally concerned by the possibility of being obliged to contribute to employees' pensions, most perceived relatively little value in any such measures.

Overall, there was little belief that any thresholds or exemptions included in new arrangements would be more than relatively insignificant palliatives. That said, participants were generally in favour of any measures that would potentially reduce their exposure to new responsibilities and most were supportive of thresholds that might reduce their obligations and costs. Most micro business owners were particularly concerned by the prospect of new responsibilities and costs.

Several participants pointed out that a key part of the disproportionate impact of new regulation on small businesses relates to establishment costs that are not necessarily lower for small firms than large ones. The implication of this was that some form of financial assistance to help small businesses cope with change would be well received.

Participants in the groups almost invariably thought that some of the options for change being considered were complex and would be difficult to operate in practice. Most suggested that although arrangements with high levels of flexibility and choice might be desirable in principle, they may well be unpopular and impractical if this made them overly complex.

It was clear that at least some small businesses lack adequate knowledge and understanding of pension issues and most groups did feel that appropriate information and support to help SMEs cope with changes would be useful.

Most of the groups suggested that any new arrangements should be introduced progressively and most discussants assumed that some phasing-in would be involved. One suggestion made in a number of groups was that if employer contributions were to be made compulsory, a gradual increase in the level of contributions, rising at say 1% per year up to the required level, would be very helpful.

(ix) Conclusions

It is important to be clear that the findings from this research are not only based on a small and not necessarily representative sample of small businesses, but also that they reflect immediate, and less than fully considered responses to a range of often complex issues that were mostly considered out of the context in which they may occur. Therefore for some of the findings at least, it may be more appropriate to focus on the inclination and tenor of the responses rather than the depth of the impacts anticipated by the participants.

The researchers' interpretation of the discussions held with SMEs during the study is that these businesses are only really concerned with the potential costs that any changes in the pension system might impose on their businesses. Although they recognise that there is a range of broad considerations and imperatives related to pensions, these are not seen as being a concern of small businesses or as secondary and relatively inconsequential issues. Irrespective of their ideological and ethical positions, participants' responses and preferences were almost invariably determined by their perceptions of the direct impacts they believed the options for change would have on their businesses.

Small businesses were generally convinced of the case for development of the pension system. However, they have deeply negative perceptions of private pension providers and were sceptical of the government's motives for reform and its ability to deliver a more appropriate and effective system.

There was little sympathy for introducing additional compulsion into the pension system – almost all participants in the study preferred using education and inducements to make the established voluntarist arrangements more effective by increasing their attractiveness to individuals, although they doubted this would work. Most participants favoured approaches based on flexibility and choice and preferred systems that included a range of exemptions and thresholds – largely because this would allow non-engagement. Almost all the micro-businesses included in the study were profoundly concerned by the prospect of any obligation to provide, administer or contribute to pension schemes.

Most businesses were relatively untroubled by the prospect of any increased administrative burden. They were, however, profoundly concerned by the prospect of an increased obligation on the part of employers to contribute to employees' pensions. Although larger businesses tended to be more willing than micro and small businesses to accept that they could cope with possible new obligations in this area, the data suggest that they are equally unsympathetic to such options.

Most participants argued that some of the options for change considered, particularly those involving the imposition of additional costs on small businesses, would not only be highly unpopular, but also likely to have a range of negative effects on SMEs. Although many participants believed that they probably could cope with the options for change considered, many argued that some of these options might well compromise the profitability and growth potential of their businesses. Some participants suggested that they would revise their growth aspirations, and some claimed that they might seek to avoid meeting new obligations – a strategy that could result in distortions to the labour market. It was also widely claimed that some of the options for change would have differentiated impacts across the highly heterogeneous SME sector.

(x) DWP Micro-employer research

It is worth noting that DWP recently published a small-scale qualitative research project with micro-employers, those employing fewer than five employees, focusing on their attitudes towards pensions. The research found very little evidence of any pension provision, information or advice being given to employees of micro-employers. Participants felt little, if any, responsibility for their staff's pensions or much of a sense that their business might benefit from providing pensions or guidance to staff on pensions. Indeed, participants usually believed that their staff would prefer higher wages over pension contributions.

Participants doubted that much could be done with workplace information to improve the situation of their employees. The discussions did, however, suggest that there was considerable appetite for strong measures that would improve the credibility of private pensions' investment for both the small business owner and their employees. Despite the suggestions for improving the current pensions system, from what they knew of their employees, some participants believed that some form of compulsion was the only way to increase saving and counteract current resistance and/or inertia. However, participants were only willing to consider the idea of compelling the employee to save. Compulsion for micro-employers to pay into employees' pensions was rejected because they did not feel that they had a responsibility in this area, and because they felt the extra cost would be too much of a burden on their businesses.

So, in terms of general attitudes to pension provision and possible options for improving pension saving, there were some similar points of view expressed in both the Pensions Commission research and the DWP research.

4. Independent Financial Advisers' survey

(i) Background

Following publication of our First Report, we wanted to learn more about how Independent Financial Advisers (IFAs) provided pensions advice to those on low to average earnings. A number of questions were of interest:

- How important is this customer group to IFAs, compared to those on higher earnings?

- Are means-testing and the introduction of the Pension Credit seen as a potential barrier to saving to this group?

- Do IFAs take the Pension Credit, or the impact of tax credits, into account when providing advice?

Sesame, a major network of IFAs, agreed to help us explore these issues. We developed a short questionnaire that was distributed to IFAs attending a series of regional events, organised by Sesame, during February and March 2005. (The questionnaire is included at the end of this Appendix for reference.) Attendees were asked to complete the questionnaire and return it to the organisers at the end of the day. Of almost 2,500 attendees we

Figure D.43 Estimated distribution of business

	0-19%	20-39%	40-59%	60-79%	80-100%
Pension savings	61%	30%	6%	2%	1%
Annuities	82%	15%	3%	0%	0%
Investments	40%	34%	17%	6%	3%
Protection products	25%	49%	19%	6%	1%
Mortgages	49%	29%	15%	6%	0%

received 416 responses, a crude response rate of 17%, which did vary significantly across events. Subsequently Sesame emailed a link to the questionnaire to its members, in order to give the attendees a second chance to respond to the survey, but we received just one additional reply. We are grateful for Sesame's help in distributing the questionnaires and inputting the data received.

Given the approach taken we do need to consider how representative our analysis is. For a start we need to ask ourselves how representative Sesame members are of IFAs as a whole. Then given the low response rate, which is in the region one might expect for a postal survey, we need to bear in mind that those who did respond may have different characteristics and views than those who did not respond. In both cases we are unable to quantify the effect on representativeness, so we cannot say that the results presented here are representative of all IFAs, or even all Sesame members. However, the results do give an indication of IFA views. We should also bear in mind that the results are based on a "snapshot" response to the issues raised in the questionnaire. This survey was not able to explore the issues in great detail.

(ii) Characteristics of respondents and their customer base

The members of our sample were less likely to have only one registered individual within the firm than overall Sesame membership and more likely to have four or more. And almost half of respondents were aged 50 or over. For most respondents pension and annuity products formed only a small proportion of their business, while investment and protection products were more important [Figure D.43]. If pension business is not so important to respondents we might want to bear in mind how this would affect their knowledge of the issues under investigation.

Respondents were asked about the composition of their customer base in terms of annual earnings levels. Low earners were not a significant part of the customer base of these IFAs [Figure D.44]. Again this should be remembered when considering the results from the rest of the survey.

If low earners were not a significant part of the customer base, IFAs may have responded to the other questions on a more theoretical basis, than based on their day-to-day activity.

Respondents were also asked about the importance of different types of customers to them, taking account of the products they were looking for and whether they were small business owners or employees [Figure D.45]. Customers seen as being of high importance by a majority of respondents include those requiring protection products, those seeking to invest a lump sum and those approaching retirement. Self-employed individuals seeking to set up their own personal pension were seen as important, but small firms seeking to set up Group Personal Pensions (GPPs) on behalf of their employees were not. In comparison, employees earning less than £25,000 per year were generally seen as an unimportant customer group across different product types, while those earning more than £25,000 per year were seen as being of high importance by around a third of respondents.

(iii) Profitability

Respondents were asked to consider a number of statements relating to the selling of pensions for employees earning less than £15,000 per year, and for those earning between £15,000 and £25,000 per year, and state whether they agreed or disagreed with them. In particular the statements focused on issues of profitability and incentives to save [Figure D.46].

Half of the respondents strongly disagreed with the statement "Individuals in this group can be served profitably given commission rates and likely premiums" in reference to employees earning less than £15,000, compared with only 16% in reference to individuals earning between £15,000 and £25,000. Therefore the respondents do not believe that those with low earnings can be profitable for them.

Half of the respondents agreed with the statement "Only if I am able to take the transfer of a large existing pension pot is this group profitable" in reference to those earning less than £15,000 compared with 42% in reference to those earnings between £15,000 and £25,000. Therefore the respondents see lower earners as profitable if they transfer a pension pot, but in reality how many low earners will be in this position to make them attractive to an IFA?

(iv) Incentives to save

Only 12% of respondents agreed with the statement "The design of the state system means that the returns to saving for people in this group are good" in reference to individuals earning less than £15,000 compared with 27% in reference to those earning between £15,000 and £25,000.

A third of the respondents agreed with the statement "Tax reliefs and tax free lump sums create good incentives for people in this group to save" in reference to individuals earning less than £15,000 compared with more than

Figure D.44 Estimated composition of customer base: percentage of respondents

Annual earnings	Less than 10%	10%-19%	20%-29%	30%-39%	40%-49%	50% or more
£15,000 or less	71%[1]	17%	8%	3%	0%	1%
£15,000-£24,999	12%	29%	27%	20%	8%	4%
£25,000-£39,999	4%	11%	21%	37%	20%	7%
£40,000 or more	20%	24%	16%	14%	8%	19%

Note: [1] i.e. means that 71% of respondents said that people earning £15,000 or less accounted for less than 10% of their customer base.

Figure D.45 Importance of different types of customers

	High importance	Medium importance	Low importance	Unimportant/ not targeted
People approaching retirement	60%	30%	7%	3%
People wanting a mortgage	50%	20%	12%	19%
People looking to invest regular sums of money	25%	41%	30%	4%
People looking to invest a lump sum	69%	24%	6%	0%
People requiring protection products	68%	26%	6%	0%
Small business owners or self-employed people wanting a personal pension	30%	41%	26%	3%
Small business owners wanting to set up a Stakeholder/Group Personal Pension scheme	17%	29%	37%	17%
Employees earning less than £25,000 per year for savings or investments products	10%	32%	39%	19%
Employees earning less than £25,000 per year for personal pensions	12%	34%	37%	17%
Employees earning less than £25,000 per year for Group Personal Pensions	13%	27%	36%	24%
Employees earning £25,000 or more per year for savings or investments products	35%	48%	14%	3%
Employees earning £25,000 or more per year for personal pensions	35%	46%	16%	4%
Employees earning £25,000 or more per year for Group Personal Pensions	29%	36%	23%	12%

Figure D.46 Responses to attitudinal statements, by annual earnings band

	Strongly agree	Agree	Disagree	Strongly disagree	Depends on personal circumstances	Don't know
Individuals in this group can be served profitably given commission rates and likely premiums.						
<£15,000	1%	10%	30%	49%	7%	3%
£15,000-£25,000	3%	31%	39%	16%	8%	2%
Only if I am able to take the transfer of a large existing pension pot is this group profitable.						
<£15,000	14%	52%	17%	3%	9%	6%
£15,000-£25,000	11%	42%	28%	2%	12%	6%
The design of the state system means that the returns to saving for people in this group are good.						
<£15,000	1%	12%	45%	32%	5%	5%
£15,000-£25,000	2%	27%	45%	14%	7%	6%
Tax reliefs and tax free lump sums create good incentives for people in this group to save.						
<£15,000	5%	35%	35%	18%	4%	2%
£15,000-£25,000	6%	55%	28%	7%	3%	2%
If I advise people in this group, and means-testing reduces their entitlement to future state benefits, I could be accused of mis-selling.						
<£15,000	30%	49%	10%	3%	4%	5%
£15,000-£25,000	18%	43%	24%	3%	5%	6%
The tax credit system creates good incentives for people in this group to save.						
<£15,000	2%	11%	45%	29%	5%	9%
£15,000-£25,000	2%	21%	47%	16%	6%	8%

half in reference to individuals earning between £15,000 and £25,000. So the respondents do not believe that tax reliefs are a good incentive for lower earners.

Half of the respondents agreed with the statement "If I advise people in this group, and means-testing reduces their entitlement to future state benefits, I could be accused of mis-selling" in reference to individuals earning less than £15,000, and another 30% agreed strongly with the statement, compared with 43% agreeing in reference to individuals earning between £15,000 and £25,000. So it seems that respondents are concerned about the potential for mis-selling because of the impact of means-testing, but again remember that in practice the IFAs may not be advising many low earners.

Only 11% of respondents agreed with the statement "The tax credit system creates good incentives for people in this group to save" in reference to individuals earning less than £15,000 compared with 21% in reference to those earning between £15,000 and £25,000. So it seems that respondents are unclear about the impact of tax credits on pension contributions. As we showed in our First Report, the returns to saving for some of those receiving the Child or Working Tax Credits can be better than for those not receiving this tax credit. This is because tax credits are given on income after pension contributions, so an increase in contributions of £100 will lead to an increase of £65 in tax credits making the cost to the individual only £35.

Respondents were asked specifically what effect on the incentives for private pension saving there was for an individual receiving tax credits. Only 5% of respondents answered that being on the taper for these credits makes the incentives for such individuals more attractive, while 44% thought it made them less attractive. Again, it seems that respondents do not know the benefits of the tax credit system in relation to pension contributions. The majority of respondents also reported that for Working Tax Credit, Pension Credit and Housing Benefit recipients, or future recipients, they would be less likely to advise them to buy a private pension. But remember that in practice the IFAs may not be advising many low earners, so on a day-to-day basis this issue may not be relevant for them.

(v) Conclusions

Our survey found that respondents do not consider those earning less than £25,000 to be an important part of their business. It appears that means-testing is one factor in this, but lack of profitability is more significant. The questions we asked on incentives to save for people with low earnings suggested that the respondents were not aware of the incentives available from the tax credit system.

(vi) DWP financial intermediary research

DWP recently published research it had commissioned to investigate the role played by a variety of financial intermediaries in the provision of advice about saving for retirement. Within this objective, the study sought to increase understanding about whether income-related benefits affect that advice. The research involved depth interviews with 45 financial intermediaries who provide advice to the public at a local level. A further 11 interviews were held with senior staff working at the headquarters of pension providers.

The clients of the financial intermediaries included very few people on lower incomes, who did not tend to approach them for advice. Indeed, it was noted by the authors that the decline in direct sales forces has led to a more restricted access to advice for people on low or moderate incomes. It was clear that the IFAs did not market their services to people on lower incomes because the commission they could earn was too low to make it worthwhile – their customer base tended to be people with middle to high incomes.

The research found very little evidence to suggest that Pension Credit made financial intermediaries reluctant to provide savings advice to people on lower incomes. Nor did the financial intermediaries themselves think it played an important part in clients' decisions regarding saving for retirement. Financial intermediaries rarely discussed Pension Credit with their clients. None of those interviewed raised any fears about mis-selling in the context of Pension Credit.

There was a difference in views between financial intermediaries working at a local level and the senior headquarters staff. Headquarters staff were far more knowledgeable about state pension provision than those on the ground. Headquarters staff perceived that the Pension Credit can potentially create disincentives to save, but they did not think this was the main reason why people on low incomes did not take out personal pensions. Indeed the main barrier to people making private pension provision was identified by financial intermediaries as lack of consumer confidence in long-term savings, in pension providers and in advisers, resulting in inertia on the part of individuals, so that few people actively seek advice about saving and retirement. Affordability was also highlighted as an issue as well as a perceived lack of understanding among the general public about pensions and how they work.

Some of these results backed up the results of our own Sesame research, but there were also some differences. This is to be expected as the DWP research was able to discuss issues more widely using its qualitative approach. This approach meant that that given the nature of the topic they could explore and understand the process of giving advice more thoroughly than we could in the time available.

National Statistics Omnibus Survey April 2005 Module 373

ASK IF: working age

M373_1

Showcard C373_1
Which of the statements on this card best describes how knowledgeable you feel about pensions issues?
Code one only

(1)	good	I have a good knowledge of pensions issues
(2)	basic	I have a reasonable, basic knowledge of pensions – I know how they work generally but do not understand the details
(3)	poor	My knowledge of pensions is very patchy – I know a bit about what concerns me but no more
(4)	nothing	I know little or nothing about pensions issues
(5)	dontk	Don't know (spontaneous only)

ASK IF: working age

M373_2

How much thought have you given to making arrangements for an income when you retire. Would you say that you have given it...
Running prompt

(1)	lot	a lot of thought
(2)	some	some thought
(3)	little	or a little thought
(4)	notho	Not thought about it at all (spontaneous only)

ASK IF: working age
AND: M373_2 <> notho

M373_3M

Showcard C373_3M
Have you ever tried to work out how much you need to save for retirement?
Code all that apply

(1)	own	Yes – I have done this on my own or with help from family/friends
(2)	advice	Yes – with the help of a professional adviser, for example an independent financial adviser or pension provider representative
(3)	comput	Yes – on my own using the Internet or other computer software
(4)	unable	Yes – but I was unable to work it out
(5)	notry	No – I have not tried to do this

ASK IF: working age

AND: (QMainJb.Stat = Emp) AND (QILO.Wrking = Yes)

M373_4

Showcard C373_4

Looking at this card, please tell me which type of organisation you work for?

(1)	priv	Private firm or company
(2)	charity	Charity or trust
(3)	nation	Nationalised industry / public corporation
(4)	LA	Local authority / local education authority
(5)	health	Health authority / NHS hospital / hospital trust
(6)	gov	Central government / civil service / armed forces
(7)	other	Other type of organisation

ASK IF: working age

AND: (QMainJb.Stat = Emp) AND (QILO.Wrking = Yes)

M373_5

Showcard C373_5

Some employers provide an occupational pension or superannuation scheme that all, or some, of their employees can join. Please look at this card and tell me which of these applies to you.

Note: This refers only to the respondent's current situation. If they have a pension from a previous job it is not included here.

Code one only

(1)	current	My employer provides an occupational pension or superannuation scheme for all, or some, employees, and I am currently a member of the scheme
(2)	notin	My employer provides an occupational pension or superannuation scheme for all, or some, employees, but I am not a member of the scheme
(3)	notprov	My employer does not provide an occupational pension or superannuation scheme for any employees
(4)	dontk	Don't know (spontaneous only)

ASK IF: working age

AND: (QMainJb.Stat = Emp) AND (QILO.Wrking = Yes)

AND: M373_5 = current

M373_6

Showcard C373_6

What type of occupational pension are you currently a member of?

(1)	final	Final salary
(2)	salary	Salary related
(3)	average	Career average
(4)	DB	Defined Benefit
(5)	purchase	Money purchase
(6)	DC	Defined Contribution
(7)	other	Hybrid of the above types
(8)	dontk	Don't know (spontaneous only)

ASK IF: working age

AND: M373_5 <> current

M373_7

Do you have a private pension plan, including a Stakeholder pension, that you, or your employer, are currently contributing to?

(1)	yes	Yes
(2)	no	No
(3)	dontk	Don't know

ASK IF: working age
AND: M373_7 = No

M373_8M

Showcard C373_8M
May I just check, why are you not currently contributing to a pension?
Code all that apply

(1)	earn	Don't earn enough
(2)	afford	Can't afford to / too many debts, bills or financial commitments
(3)	otherpl	I am relying on other sources of income / I already have adequate pension provision
(4)	nojob	Not working at the moment
(5)	early	Too early to start a pension
(6)	late	Too late to start a pension
(7)	interest	Not interested
(8)	ignore	Don't know enough about pensions / complexity of issues
(9)	inelig	I am not eligible to join my employer's scheme
(10)	otherin	Other investments offer a better return
(11)	state	State pension will provide enough
(12)	other	Other reason
(13)	dontk	Don't know (spontaneous only)

ASK IF: working age

M373_9

Showcard C373_9
Do you save some money each month for your retirement that is not in a private or occupational pension of some sort? Which of these best describes your situation?

(1)	yes	Yes
(2)	afford	No – I can't afford to save every month
(3)	saveoth	No – I choose not to save for my retirement at the moment, but I do save for other reasons
(4)	nosave	No – I choose not to save for my retirement or any other reason at the moment

ASK IF: working age (question text depends on whether respondent currently saving or not)

M373_10

'Although you are not currently saving for your retirement, do you think you should be saving...' or
'Taking into account whatever pensions or long-term savings you have specifically for retirement, do you think you should be saving...'

Running prompt		
(1)	more	more for your retirement than you do at the moment
(2)	less	less for your retirement than you do at the moment
(3)	right	or are you saving the right amount for your retirement
(4)	dontk	Don't know (spontaneous only)
(5)	noinc	No income at present (spontaneous only)

ASK IF: working age
AND: QILO.DVILO3a <> InEmp
M373_11

Can I just check, do you expect to be in paid employment in the future?

(1)	yes	Yes
(2)	no	No
(3)	dontk	Don't know

ASK IF: working age
AND: (M373_11 = Yes) OR (QILO.DVILO3a = InEmp)
M373_12

At what age do you expect to retire?

ASK IF: working age

M373_13

Showcard C373_13
I'd now like to ask you about your income in retirement.
What do you expect to be your main source of income in retirement?
Code one only

(1)	ownstate	Own pension (see next screen)
(2)	ownearn	Own earnings
(3)	spouse	Spouse's money from pension, savings or earnings (see next screen)
(4)	endow	Endowment / life assurance policy
(5)	insure	Other insurance policy
(6)	shares	Stocks, shares or unit trusts
(7)	saving	Savings accounts
(8)	inheri	Inheritance / income from inheritance
(9)	annuity	Income from annuity
(10)	rent	Rent from property (including subletting)
(11)	profit	The profit from selling property and moving to a less expensive property
(12)	profbus	The profit from selling my own business
(13)	equity	Equity release scheme
(14)	state	State benefits (other than state pension)
(15)	sale	Sale of possessions
(16)	allow	Income or allowance from family or children
(17)	other	Other source of income
(18)	dontk	Don't know (spontaneous only)

ASK IF: working age

AND: M373_13 = ownstate

M373_13a

Showcard C373_13a
What kind of pension would this be?

(1)	basic	Own basic state pension
(2)	SERPS	Own SERPS / S2P
(3)	employ	Own employer's pension
(4)	person	Own personal pension / annuity bought from personal pension
(5)	stake	Own stakeholder pension
(6)	credit	Own Pension Credit

ASK IF: working age

AND: M373_13 = spouse

M373_13b

Showcard C373_13b
What kind of income would this be?

(1)	basic	Spouse or partner's basic state pension
(2)	SERPS	Spouse or partner's SERPS / S2P
(3)	employ	Spouse or partner's employer's pension
(4)	person	Spouse or partner's personal pension / annuity bought from personal pension
(5)	stake	Spouse or partner's stakeholder pension
(6)	credit	Spouse or partner's Pension Credit
(7)	earn	Spouse or partner's earnings from paid work
(8)	exspouse	Ex-spouse's pension

ASK IF: working age
AND: M373_13 <> dontk

M373_15

Showcard C373_13
Do you expect to have another major source of income in retirement? If so, what?
Code one only

(1)	ownstate	Own pension (see next screen)
(2)	ownearn	Own earnings
(3)	spouse	Spouse's money from pension, savings or earnings (see next screen)
(4)	endow	Endowment / life assurance policy
(5)	insure	Other insurance policy
(6)	shares	Stocks, shares or unit trusts
(7)	saving	Savings accounts
(8)	inheri	Inheritance / income from inheritance
(9)	annuity	Income from annuity
(10)	rent	Rent from property (including subletting)
(11)	profit	The profit from selling property and moving to a less expensive property
(12)	profbus	The profit from selling my own business
(13)	equity	Equity release scheme
(14)	state	State benefits (other than state pension)
(15)	sale	Sale of possessions
(16)	allow	Income or allowance from family or children
(17)	other	Other source of income
(18)	noother	Do not expect to have another major source of income (spontaneous only)
(19)	dontk	Don't know (spontaneous only)

ASK IF: working age
AND: M373_15 = ownstate

M373_15a

Showcard C373_13a
What kind of pension would this be?

(1)	basic	Own basic state pension
(2)	SERPS	Own SERPS / S2P
(3)	employ	Own employer's pension
(4)	person	Own personal pension / annuity bought from personal pension
(5)	stake	Own stakeholder pension
(6)	credit	Own Pension Credit

ASK IF: working age
AND: M373_15 = spouse

M373_15b

Showcard C373_13b
What kind of income would this be?

(1)	basic	Spouse or partner's basic state pension
(2)	SERPS	Spouse or partner's SERPS / S2P
(3)	employ	Spouse or partner's employer's pension
(4)	person	Spouse or partner's personal pension / annuity bought from personal pension
(5)	stake	Spouse or partner's stakeholder pension
(6)	credit	Spouse or partner's Pension Credit
(7)	earn	Spouse or partner's earnings from paid work
(8)	exspouse	Ex-spouse's pension

ASK IF: working age

M373_16

Showcard C373_16
I'd now like you to think about how much your income in retirement will be.
Which of the statements on this card best describes your knowledge of how much your income in retirement will be?

(1)	good	I have a good idea of what my income in retirement will be
(2)	reason	I have a reasonable knowledge of what my income in retirement will be
(3)	vague	I know vaguely what my income in retirement will be, but no more than that
(4)	noidea	I have no idea what my income in retirement will be
(5)	dontk	Don't know (spontaneous only)

ASK IF: working age

M373_17

Showcard C373_17
Which of the statements on this card best reflects the income you are aiming to get in retirement from pensions, and any other sources of retirement income?
'Living expenses' means costs such as utility bills, council tax, transport, clothes, etc.

(1)	plenty	I will have plenty of money to afford food, housing, living expenses and luxuries.
(2)	comfort	I will have enough to afford basic food, housing and living expenses and will be able to treat myself about every week. I will be comfortable.
(3)	basic1	I will have enough to afford basic food, housing and living expenses and will be able to treat myself every month or so.
(4)	basic2	I will only have enough to afford basic food, housing and living expenses.
(5)	ntenough	I will not have enough to afford basic food, housing and living expenses.
(6)	dontk	Don't know (spontaneous only)

ASK IF: working age

M373_18

Showcard C373_18

If you were retired today, how much money, after tax, do you think you personally would need as an absolute minimum each week to live on. By this I mean how much would you need to afford basic food, housing and living expenses with no regular treats?

(1)	less100	Less than £100
(2)	f100t124	£100 to £124
(3)	f125t149	£125 to £149
(4)	f150t174	£150 to £174
(5)	f175t199	£175 to £199
(6)	f200t224	£200 to £224
(7)	f225t249	£225 to £249
(8)	f250t274	£250 to £274
(9)	f275t299	£275 to £299
(10)	f300t324	£300 to £324
(11)	f325t349	£325 to £349
(12)	f350t374	£350 to £374
(13)	f375t399	£375 to £399
(14)	f400t424	£400 to £424
(15)	f425t449	£425 to £449
(16)	f450t474	£450 to £474
(17)	f476t499	£475 to £499
(18)	over500	£500 or over
(19)	dontk	Don't know (spontaneous only)

ASK IF: working age

M373_19

Showcard C373_18
You just described how much money you would need as a minimum. If you were retired today, how much money, after tax, do you think you personally would need each week to have enough to live on to live comfortably. That is, to afford basic food, housing and living expenses and treat yourself about every week?

(1)	less100	Less than £100
(2)	f100t124	£100 to £124
(3)	f125t149	£125 to £149
(4)	f150t174	£150 to £174
(5)	f175t199	£175 to £199
(6)	f200t224	£200 to £224
(7)	f225t249	£225 to £249
(8)	f250t274	£250 to £274
(9)	f275t299	£275 to £299
(10)	f300t324	£300 to £324
(11)	f325t349	£325 to £349
(12)	f350t374	£350 to £374
(13)	f375t399	£375 to £399
(14)	f400t424	£400 to £424
(15)	f425t449	£425 to £449
(16)	f450t474	£450 to £474
(17)	f476t499	£475 to £499
(18)	over500	£500 or over
(19)	dontk	Don't know (spontaneous only)

ASK IF: working age
AND: ((M373_12 = RESPONSE) AND (M373_12 <> REFUSAL)) AND (M373_12 <> DONTKNOW)
M373_20

Showcard C373_20
How many years of retirement do you expect to have?

(1)	Less5	Less than 5 years
(2)	f5t9	5 to 9 years
(3)	f10t14	10 to 14 years
(4)	f15t19	15 to 19 years
(5)	f20t24	20 to 24 years
(6)	over25	25 years or more
(7)	dontk	Don't know (spontaneous only)

ASK IF: working age
AND: QSETUP.RAGE > 24
M373_21

In the past five years, have your plans for retirement changed in any way?

(1)	yes	Yes
(2)	no	No
(3)	dontk	Don't know
(4)	noplan	No plans for retirement at the moment (spontaneous only)

ASK IF: working age
AND: M373_21 = Yes
M373_22M

Showcard C373_22M
From the options on this card, please say which you have done?
Code all that apply

(1)	later	Planning to retire later
(2)	earlier	Planning to retire earlier
(3)	increase	Increased pension contributions
(4)	decrease	Decreased pension contributions
(5)	start	Started a pension
(6)	incother	Increased other savings / investments for retirement
(7)	property	Bought property in the UK as an investment
(8)	mortgage	Made plans to pay off mortgage and debts
(9)	abroad	Now plan to move abroad on retirement
(10)	other	Other change to plans

ASK IF: working age
M373_23

Showcard C373_23
Please tell me how strongly you agree or disagree with the following statement.
I'd rather make sure that I had a good standard of living today than put aside money for my retirement.

(1)	strag	Strongly agree
(2)	ag	Tend to agree
(3)	disag	Tend to disagree
(4)	strdisa	Strongly disagree
(5)	dontk	Don't know / no opinion (spontaneous only)

National Statistics Omnibus Survey May 2005 Module 373

ASK ALWAYS:

M373_25

Showcard J1
Please say from this card who you think should be mainly responsible for ensuring that people have enough money to live on in retirement?

(1)	govt	The Government
(2)	employ	A person's employer
(3)	self	The person themselves and their family
(4)	dontk	Don't know (spontaneous only)

ASK ALWAYS:

M373_26M

Showcard J2
There is currently a lot of debate and discussion about the pensions system and a number of people have put forward ideas to make it better.
Which of the following would most improve your confidence in the pensions system?
Code up to three

(1)	simple	Simpler, less complex pensions system
(2)	stateinf	Clearer information about the State pension and my entitlement
(3)	privinf	Clearer information about private pensions and what I need to save and can expect to receive
(4)	freead	Free individual advice paid for by the Government
(5)	value	Better value private pensions
(6)	guaran	A guarantee that you would not lose the value of the contributions that you have put into a money purchase pension
(7)	indep	Independent body to run the pensions system in people's interests
(8)	regul	Better regulation of financial service companies
(9)	protect	Better protection for employer-sponsored (Defined Benefit) pension schemes
(10)	interfe	Less interference by Government
(11)	dontk	Don't know / no opinion (spontaneous only)

Survey of Sesame IFAS

The Pensions Commission has been asked by the Government to review the regime for UK private pensions and long-term savings. It published its first report in October 2004.

Patrick Gale has agreed that Sesame will help the Commission in canvassing views from advisers on a range of savings issues. These views will help the Commission develop its recommendations in the coming months.

Please complete this questionnaire and leave it on your chair for collection. Your individual views will be kept confidential. Aggregated results will be used for analysis.

1. How many registered individuals are there in your firm? (please tick one box)

   One ☐   2-3 ☐   4 or more ☐

2. What is the estimated split of your individual business across the following categories, on a percentage basis?

   Pensions Savings Products ☐   Pensions Annuities & Drawdown ☐   Investment ☐   Protection ☐   Mortgage ☐

3. Which age group are you? (please tick one box)

   20-29 ☐   30-39 ☐   40-49 ☐   50+ ☐

4. How important do you think these types of customers are to your business? (please tick one box in each row)

	High importance	Medium importance	Low importance	Unimportant/ not targeted
People approaching retirement	☐	☐	☐	☐
People wanting a mortgage	☐	☐	☐	☐
People looking to invest regular sums of money	☐	☐	☐	☐
People looking to invest a lump sum	☐	☐	☐	☐
People requiring protection products	☐	☐	☐	☐
Small business owners or self-employed people wanting a personal pension	☐	☐	☐	☐
Small business owners wanting to set up a stakeholder/ group personal pension scheme	☐	☐	☐	☐
Employees earning less than £25,000 per year for savings or investment products	☐	☐	☐	☐
Employees earning less than £25,000 per year for personal pensions	☐	☐	☐	☐
Employees earning less than £25,000 per year for group personal pensions	☐	☐	☐	☐
Employees earning £25,000 or more per year for savings or investment products	☐	☐	☐	☐
Employees earning £25,000 or more per year for personal pensions	☐	☐	☐	☐
Employees earning £25,000 or more per year for group personal pensions	☐	☐	☐	☐

5. **What percentage of your current customer base has annual earnings in the following bands?**
(please tick one box in each row)

	Less than 10%	10-19%	20-29%	30-39%	40-49%	50% or more
Less than £15,000	☐	☐	☐	☐	☐	☐
£15,000 - £24,999	☐	☐	☐	☐	☐	☐
£25,000 - £39,999	☐	☐	☐	☐	☐	☐
£40,000 or more	☐	☐	☐	☐	☐	☐

6. **Thinking of pensions sold individually to employees earning less than £15,000 per year**, how far do you agree or disagree with the following statements? (please tick one box in each row)

	Strongly agree	Agree	Disagree	Strongly disagree	Depends on personal circumstance	Don't know
Individuals in this group can be served profitably given commission rates and likely premiums.	☐	☐	☐	☐	☐	☐
The design of the state system means that the returns to saving for people in this group are good.	☐	☐	☐	☐	☐	☐
Tax reliefs and tax free lump sums create good incentives for people in this group to save.	☐	☐	☐	☐	☐	☐
If I advise people in this group, and means-testing reduces their entitlement to future state benefits, I could be accused of mis-selling.	☐	☐	☐	☐	☐	☐
The tax credit system creates good incentives for people in this group to save.	☐	☐	☐	☐	☐	☐
Only if I am able to take the transfer of a large existing pension pot is this group profitable.	☐	☐	☐	☐	☐	☐

7. Thinking of pensions sold individually to employees earning between **£15,000 and £25,000 per year**, how far do you agree or disagree with the following statements? (please tick one box in each row)

	Strongly agree	Agree	Disagree	Strongly disagree	Depends on personal circumstance	Don't know
Individuals in this group can be served profitably given commission rates and likely premiums.	☐	☐	☐	☐	☐	☐
The design of the state system means that the returns to saving for people in this group are good.	☐	☐	☐	☐	☐	☐
Tax reliefs and tax free lump sums create good incentives for people in this group to save.	☐	☐	☐	☐	☐	☐
If I advise people in this group, and means-testing reduces their entitlement to future state benefits, I could be accused of mis-selling.	☐	☐	☐	☐	☐	☐
The tax credit system creates good incentives for people in this group to save.	☐	☐	☐	☐	☐	☐
Only if I am able to take the transfer of a large existing pension pot is this group profitable.	☐	☐	☐	☐	☐	☐

8. If a client is on the taper for either Working Tax Credit or Child Tax Credit what effect does this have on their incentives for private pension savings?

Makes more attractive ☐   Has no effect ☐   Makes less attractive ☐   Don't know ☐

9. If a client is currently in receipt of or **may in future** be eligible for the following credits/benefits, would you be more or less likely to advise them to buy a private pension? (please tick one box in each row)

	More likely	No effect	Less likely	Don't know
Working Tax Credit/Child Tax Credit	☐	☐	☐	☐
Pension Credit	☐	☐	☐	☐
Housing Benefit	☐	☐	☐	☐

Thank you for completing this questionnaire. Please leave it on your chair for collection.

Uncertainties in life expectancy projections

Chapter 1 of this report includes a discussion of population projections and dependency ratios. One of the key factors affecting these projections is the assumption for life expectancy. But the future path of life expectancy is uncertain. This Appendix examines the extent of that uncertainty. It is drawn from a lecture the Chairman of the Pensions Commission gave at Cass Business School in April 2005. At that time the most up to date Government Actuary's Department (GAD) estimates of life expectancies were the 2003-based projections. The lecture therefore analysed uncertainty around these projections. This Appendix does the same, and then shows how the new 2004-based projection fits within the uncertainty range we proposed around the 2003-based projection.

The Appendix covers 5 issues:

1. Background to the life expectancy projections

2. How uncertain are projections of life expectancy?

3. Comparison of the Pensions Commission's hypothetical range of uncertainty and GAD's 2004-based principal projection

4. Latest developments from the Continuous Mortality Investigation (CMI)

5. Conclusions and recommendations

1. Background to the life expectancy projections

There is uncertainty over the average life expectancy of entire age cohorts. Figure E.1 sets out how the GAD estimates of life expectancy for a man aged 65 have developed in the past 50 years and GAD's principal projections (as at 2003) for the next 50. (Although the analysis presented in this Appendix focuses mainly on life expectancy for men, similar trends and issues exist for women.) As Figure E.1 shows, GAD's principal projections have changed radically in the past, with major upward revisions between the 1983-based and 2003-based projections.

The future path of life expectancy will depend upon the future path of age-specific mortality rates. GAD projections depend on mortality rate assumptions. To understand uncertainty in life expectancy, we therefore need to understand how wide a reasonable range of assumptions relating to mortality rate developments might be, and how these would translate into life expectancy uncertainty.

Figure E.2 sets out how life expectancy at 65 would evolve if mortality for men over 65 declined from now on at 1%, 2% or 3% per year. It illustrates that there is uncertainty even as to the life expectancy of today's 65 year olds, but that that uncertainty rapidly increases as we look further into the future. Figure E.3 shows the historic record of mortality rate declines in the UK for older age groups over the last 50 years. Across the whole 50 year period, mortality rate declines have tended to be in the 1-2% per year range, but in the 1990s declines of 2-3% have been observed for men aged between 60 and 90 and for women aged between 60 and 80.

Figure E.4 shows how the GAD 2003-based principal projection fitted within alternative future assumptions for mortality rate decline. For a few years the 2003-based principal projection is close to the 2% line, but it then diverges down to the 1% line, falling just below it by 2050. This reflects GAD's assumption in its 2003-based projections that mortality rate declines would gradually decelerate (halving every 25 years), thus producing a long-term projection with a "limit to life" of the average man of about 22 years beyond age 65. [GAD's new assumptions for the 2004-based principal projection are discussed in Section 3.]

2. How uncertain are projections of life expectancy?

The question then is: how uncertain should we consider this principal projection? And how indeed, do we set about estimating the degree of uncertainty? At least two approaches are possible.

One is to consider alternative expert points of view about future potential medical advances and about whether a biologically given "limit to life" exists. Lectures at the Cass Business School in Spring 2005 set out the two sides in the debate.[1] On one side Professor Jay Olshansky and others suggest that life expectancy could level off or even decrease in the 21st century given factors

---

[1] See *The Uncertain Future of Longevity*, Watson Wyatt/Cass Business School Public Lectures on Longevity, March 2005.

such as the rise in obesity levels and the potential effects of infectious diseases. This school of thought believes that there is an absolute limit to how far life expectancy can go on rising. On the other hand, experts such as Professor James Vaupel suggest that life expectancy is set to continue to increase at a rapid rate. He reports that there is no indication that a change in the trend of increasing life expectancy is in sight.

Figure E.5 is a reasonable representation of their philosophies, Vaupel arguing that life expectancy at birth and at 65 is likely to continue rising by roughly one year every four years, Olshansky arguing that life expectancy in developed countries will soon level off. But of course these are simply two positions: the fact that they exist gives us no basis for assuming that more extreme positions are impossible (and indeed there are some scientists who predict an accelerating rather than merely constant rate of improvement, with major breakthroughs in genetic science). And the fact that these two points of view exist gives us no basis for using their views to define a specific confidence level.

An alternative approach is to try to use past variations in forecasts as a basis for stochastic analysis, applying forecast changes/errors to the future principal projection to produce a distribution of future possibilities. This was the approach used to generate the fan chart that Mervyn King discussed in his lecture "What Fates Impose" [Figure E.6]. The fan chart was intended simply to highlight the importance of the issue. But it poses the question: is it actually possible to calculate confidence intervals of future life expectancy projections in a mathematical fashion? Are we dealing with mathematically modellable risk or inherent uncertainty?

To consider that question the Pensions Commission and GAD have together conducted analysis of how uncertainties in mortality rate projections might drive variability in life expectancy projections. We began by assuming that our degree of uncertainty about future mortality rates would increase the further away the forecast year is. And we hypothesised an error rate function geometric in form, i.e. error rate of 1% per year compounding [Figure E.7]. If this is the potential uncertainty function looking forward, male life expectancy at 65 today could lie anywhere between 17.7 and 20.5 years compared with the principal projection estimate of 19 years. But by 2040 the range could be 17.2-26.7 years around a base case of 21.3 years.

We then analysed the errors/changes to forecast which have actually emerged between GAD's 1983 and 2003-based projections [Figure E.8]. For years prior to 2003 we are comparing the 1983 forecast with an actual result: for years after 2003 we are comparing the 1983 forecast with the 2003-based forecast. Interestingly, the errors and changes do follow the hypothesised pattern of increasing uncertainty over time, but with somewhat higher error rates than our simple +/-n% model above would suggest. Looking forward from 1983 to 2014, estimates of mortality rates for men aged 65 and 75 were 46% and 43% higher than the rates we now forecast.

Figure E.1 Male cohort life expectancy at 65

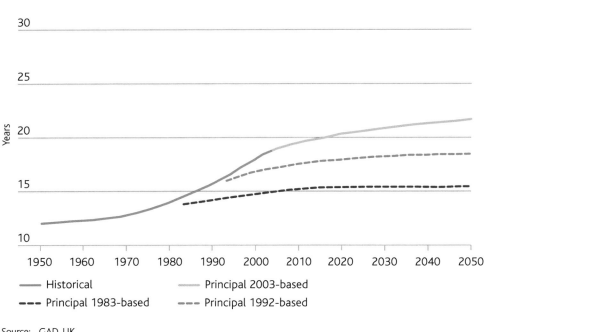

Source: GAD, UK

Figure E.2 Male cohort life expectancy at 65: impact of future mortality rate declines

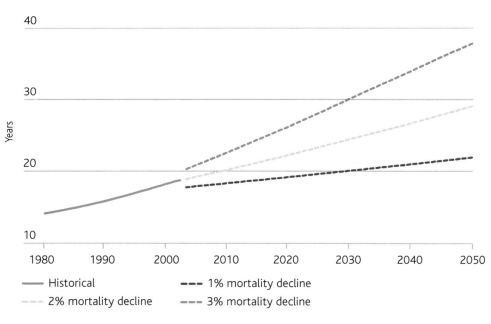

Source: GAD, UK

Note: Mortality declines are annual figures i.e. a 2% decline indicates a 2% reduction in mortality every year.

Figure E.3 Past mortality declines at older ages

Age	Male						Female					
	1950s	1960s	1970s	1980s	1990s	Average 1950-2002	1950s	1960s	1970s	1980s	1990s	Average 1950-2002
60-70	0.4%	1.0%	1.2%	2.8%	2.7%	1.6%	1.5%	0.6%	0.4%	1.7%	2.4%	1.3%
70-80	0.2%	0.0%	1.6%	1.8%	3.1%	1.4%	1.3%	1.1%	1.3%	1.1%	2.3%	1.4%
80-90	0.7%	0.6%	0.6%	1.6%	2.0%	1.1%	1.4%	1.3%	1.4%	1.6%	1.3%	1.4%
90+	1.3%	0.6%	0.6%	1.0%	0.7%	0.9%	0.9%	1.1%	0.7%	1.7%	0.1%	0.9%

Source: GAD, England and Wales

Notes: 1950s' improvement compares age-specific mortality rates averaged over 1960-62 with those averaged over 1950-52.
A similar method is used for other time periods.

Figure E.4 Male cohort life expectancy at 65: mortality declines and the GAD 2003-based principal projection

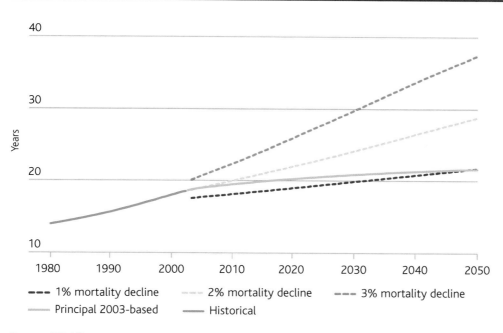

Source: GAD, UK

Note: Mortality declines are annual figures i.e. a 2% decline indicates a 2% reduction in mortality every year.

Figure E.5 Male cohort life expectancy at 65: optimists and pessimists

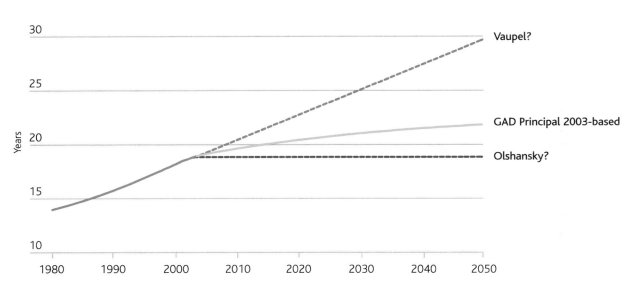

Source: GAD and Pensions Commission estimates, UK

Figure E.6 Female period life expectancy at birth: range of uncertainty

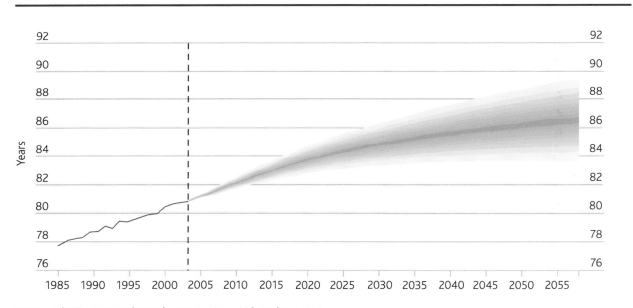

Source: *What Fates Impose*, lecture by Mervyn King, British Academy, 2004

Figure E.7 Error rates in mortality and life expectancy projections: model results

If mortality rate errors, as a percentage of forecast mortality rates, were

1 year ahead	+/-1
2 years ahead	+2.01/-1.99
3 years ahead	+3.03/-2.97
20 years ahead	+22/-18
n years ahead	$+[(1.01)^n -1] * 100/$ $-[1-(0.99)^n] * 100$

Then life expectancy forecast errors would be

Mean male life expectancy at 65 forecast for

	2005	2020	2040
Lower mortality	20.5	23.5	26.7
Base case	19.0	20.3	21.3
Higher mortality	17.7	17.8	17.2

Source: GAD, UK

Figure E.8 Actual past differences in mortality rate forecasts

Mortality rates forecast/measured in year

	1984	1985	1986	...	1994	...	2004	...	2014
	Actual vs 1983 forecast						2003 forecast vs 1983 forecast		
Male at age 65	-8%	-0%	-3%	...	-17%	...	-41%	...	-46%
Male at age 75	-4%	-1%	-4%	...	-17%	...	-28%	...	-43%
Male at age 85	+2%	+3%	+1%	...	-6%	...	-12%	...	-24%

Source: GAD, UK

Finally we use the actual error rate profile looking forward from 1983 to estimate the range of uncertainty looking forward from 2003. Figure E.9 shows the results, which illustrate:

■ If the errors/changes which have already emerged since the 1983 forecast define the maximum error possible looking forward one year, two years, three years, n years etc;

■ And if this error potential is symmetric;

■ Then male life expectancy at 65 today could lie in a range 17.6-19.9 years, but by 2033 it could be within a range 16.3-26.5 years.

It is vital, however, to interpret these mathematical estimates of the range of uncertainty correctly. There are four points to consider:

■ First, we are dealing with inherent uncertainty not risk. We are not sampling a definitively existing underlying universe. Nor are we even observing a sequence of changing actual variables over time. We are simply comparing our forecast made in one year with our forecast made in another. The Commission therefore tends to the conclusion that we have here no real basis for making a mathematically precise estimate of confidence ranges. Using confidence interval statements to communicate expert judgements may still be valuable, but solely as a communication device.

■ Second, we cannot be certain that the maximum error rate potential is revealed by the 1983-2003 comparison. We know that our estimate of the male 65 year old mortality rate in 2014 has fallen by 46% in the 20 years between 1983 and 2003. But it could perhaps fall still more by the time we get to 2014. For any year more than 20 years in the future there is no reason to believe that changes to the forecast between 1983 and 2003 define the maximum possible error, even if past performance carries implications for the future.

■ Third, we need to think through whether the error potential looking forward is symmetric around the base case or asymmetric. When the Commission concluded this analysis we suspected that the range was asymmetric around the 2003-based principal projection. In the past 20 years of course the errors have been all one way. That does not necessarily imply that they will be one way in the future: our principal projection may now be a best average expectation. But note that the symmetrical application of uncertainty in Figure E.9 implies a lower bound that predicts actual falls in life expectancy, while the range of scientific and medical dispute is predominantly between stability and further increases. And note that the 2003-based principal projection already assumed a limit to life, albeit over a longer term than was assumed in 1983. The Commission's judgement was that around the 2003-based principal projection we were more likely to see errors that increased life expectancy than decreased it.

Figure E.9 Male cohort life expectancy at 65: estimates of uncertainty

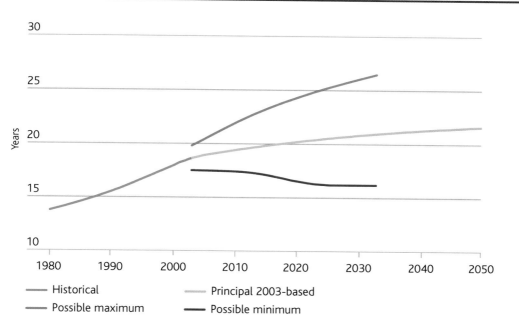

Source: GAD and Pensions Commission estimates, UK

Note: Figure shows the uncertainty in 2003-based forecasts if already apparent 1983 errors/changes are the maximum possible and if error potential is symmetrical.

- But finally, the Commission suspects that over the next 20 years we are unlikely to see the emergence of errors quite as large as emerged within the first 20 years after 1983. Between 1983 and 2003 the principal projection was changed from a very strong version to a weaker version of the limit-to-life hypothesis. And errors as large and in the same direction as emerged between 1983 and 2003 would now, looking forward, imply actual acceleration of mortality rate declines and life expectancy increases, not just a continuation of the trend. The Commission's judgement was therefore that the 2003-based principal projection was likely to prove more accurate over the next 20 years than the principal projection did between 1983 and 2003. But beyond the next 20 years, compared with a base case that assumes a rapidly decelerating mortality rate decline, there is no reason to believe that errors could not be as large as they were in the past.

Taking these considerations together, a reasonable judgement on uncertainty **might** be as shown in Figure E.10, with a somewhat predictable development over the next 10-15 years or so, but with increasing uncertainty thereafter, and with male life expectancy at 65 in 2050 anywhere from 20 to 29 years. As a judgement one might say that this range defines a 90% confidence interval. But a judgement is all that would be, since the Commission believes that no mathematically precise definition of risk is possible.

3. Comparison of the Pensions Commission's hypothetical range of uncertainty and GAD's 2004-based principal projection

Since the analysis outlined above was undertaken, GAD has changed the mortality assumption used in the principal projection. The new projections assume that mortality rates at each age will converge to a common rate of improvement of 1% a year at 2029 and continue to improve at that constant rate thereafter. In the 2003-based projections, the rate of improvement was assumed to halve every subsequent 25 years, that is from 1% a year by 2028 to 0.5% a year by 2053. As a result of the new more optimistic long-term assumptions, life expectancy forecasts, for both men and women, have increased significantly.

Figure E.11 shows how the new 2004-based principal projection fits within the results of our previous analysis. The 2004-based projection is now closer to the middle of our range of uncertainty than the previous projection, providing support for our hypothesis that the uncertainty range around the 2003-based projection was asymmetric.

Figure E.10 Male cohort life expectancy at 65: range of possible uncertainty

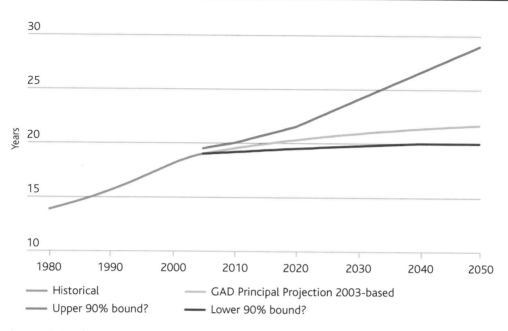

Source: GAD and Pensions Commission estimates, UK

Figure E.11 Male cohort life expectancy at 65: range of possible uncertainty around 2004-based principal projection

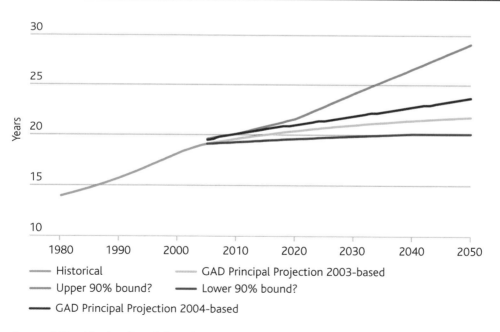

Source: GAD and Pensions Commission estimates, UK

4. Latest developments from the Continuous Mortality Investigation (CMI)

The Continuous Mortality Investigation (CMI) is the largest single research project organised by the UK actuarial profession. It has been accumulating and analysing data on mortality and morbidity risks arising under life assurance, annuity and pension business for over 80 years. In September 2005 it published proposed new mortality tables (the "00 series" tables) for pensioners in receipt of private pensions, a subset of the total population. The new tables, based on data from the four year period 1999-2002, show mortality rates around 30% lower than those in the previous tables (the "92 series" tables, which were based on data for 1991-94) for both males and females in their late 60s. This represents an improvement rate of over 4% per year in mortality. Mortality rates at older ages have also improved, but less dramatically.

At the same time the CMI presented to the profession its latest thinking on how to take account of uncertainty in future mortality. It stressed the uncertainty surrounding any projections of future mortality. It does not therefore propose to publish a single projection of future mortality, or even a single methodology for doing this, alongside the new tables. Instead it stresses that actuaries and other professionals using mortality projections must consider a range of scenarios to reflect the uncertainty in the projections.

It illustrates this uncertainty with an example based on a simple extrapolation of the recent trends in CMI mortality rates. On these assumptions, a 65 year old man may now expect to live on average until he is 86 years and seven months – an increase of 3.5 years since the previous tables were published. But even if recent trends continue and the model used remains valid, the CMI argues that the range of uncertainty could stretch from 85.5 to 88 years. New trends, or the recognition of trends that have not been identified, could invalidate the model and result in figures outside this range. The CMI thus believes that the range of uncertainty about the life expectancy of a 65 year old **today** is wider than our hypothetical range suggested.

The work of the CMI is continuing. But it notes that there are no magic answers when it comes to projecting future mortality. Its proposed stochastic methodologies should not be seen as a means of supplying definitive answers to questions that have strong subjective elements. This is in line with our own conclusion that there is large inherent uncertainty in future estimates of life expectancy, and that while stochastic techniques can be used to illustrate that uncertainty, they cannot give us quantitatively precise measures of the confidence ranges of future projections.

5. Conclusions and recommendations

Both our work with GAD and that of the CMI have illustrated the large uncertainty involved in estimates of life expectancy: these are considerable even when estimating the life expectancy of a 65 year old man or women today: but the uncertainties increase dramatically as we look into the future. Two sets of recommendations follow:

- Official publications which set out estimates of projected life expectancy should ideally provide not only the best mean estimate, but also the range of possible results which could arise from alternative reasonable assumptions. The GAD publications already include high and low variants: these should be given wider publicity.

- Pension systems (state and private) must be resilient in the face not only of rising life expectancy, but of large uncertainty over how rapid the rise will be. This implies that pre-retirement longevity risk should be shifted from the pension provider to the individual, either via linking future pensionable ages to future presently unknown increases in life expectancy, or by moving to 'Notional Defined Contribution' systems of the sort described in Chapter 1 Section 5.

Pensions Commission modelling

In addition to the models described in our First Report we have used several new models to inform our decisions, this Appendix provides details of these models:

1. Pensim2

2. Stylised individuals

3. Tax relief

4. The cost of pension provision model

5. National Pension Savings Scheme: employer costs

6. National Pension Savings Scheme: macroeconomics

We cover each in detail in this appendix, explaining the modelling techniques used in our findings.

1. Pensim2

As noted in Appendix A of our first report, the Department for Work and Pensions (DWP) has for the past few years been building and validating a dynamic micro-simulation model called Pensim2. This is a highly sophisticated model which attempts to mimic the evolution of both private and state pension accumulation and decumulation between now and 2050. We have used Pensim2 to help inform our recommendations for the UK private and state pension systems. In particular we use Pensim2 to estimate the cost of state pension reforms, the number of individuals on Pension Credit and the impact of the proposed National Pension Savings Scheme on private pension incomes.

This section explains the inputs to Pensim2, and how Pensim2 works. It is divided into five parts:

i.   Introduction to Pensim2

ii. Explaining dynamic micro-simulation

iii. Creation of Pensim2 "base-data"

iv. Simulation and calibration

v.   Using the model: a caution in interpreting results

(i) Introduction to Pensim2

Pensim2 is a dynamic micro-simulation model built by the DWP to help inform the analysis of pensioner incomes in the long-run. Rather than looking only at average incomes, or the income of stylised individuals, it estimates the income of every member of a representative sample of future pensioners, and thus the distribution of incomes across the population, for each year up to 2050. The model is designed as a tool for policy simulation, allowing the user to carry out scenario analysis in order to gauge the likely long-term impact of different policy regimes or of different macroeconomic or demographic scenarios on pensioner incomes.

(ii) Explaining dynamic micro-simulation

Pensim2 is a dynamic micro-simulation model. This means that that it models at the individual level, over a number of time periods taking into account the implications of events that occurred in the previous time period for events in the current period. It starts with a set of synthetic individuals who are representative of the GB population in 2001. It then simulates the occurrence of a wide range of events in 2002, 2003, 2004 etc to 2050 which affect their eventual pension income. These events include, job change, marriage, the birth of children, retirement and death. Dynamic micro-simulation models are particularly useful for policy analysis:

■ When the effects of a policy change affect individuals in diverse ways and hence the consequences of a proposal are not well summarised by the effect on an "average" individual or in aggregate.

■ Where the distribution of income affects the outcome of a policy e.g. means-tested benefits.

■ Where the distributional effects of policy changes are themselves of interest e.g. do the rich or the poor benefit most from an increase in the Basic State Pension?

■ When the effects of policy changes take a long time to build up.

(iii) Creation of Pensim2 base-data [Figure F.1]

The starting data or "base-data" for Pensim2 is a representative sample of the GB household population in 2001. In order properly to simulate pensions at the individual level, the model requires information in the base-data about the current status of individuals and households and historical information such as pension contributions, earnings, and work histories. Unfortunately, no single source of data currently meets these requirements. Generally speaking, DWP's administrative data contain good longitudinal information, but not enough information on contextual variables (such as education), which can be found in survey data. Therefore for Pensim2 a synthetic data set has been constructed from three separate sources to make use of both administrative

Figure F.1 Creation of Pensim2 "base-data"

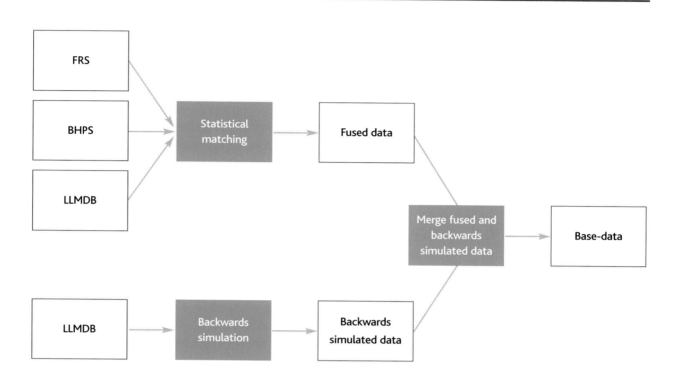

and survey data. The Family Resources Survey (FRS), the British Household Panel Survey (BHPS) and the Lifetime Labour Market Data Base (LLMDB2) (a 1% sample of the National Insurance Recording System) are fused together using statistical matching.

In order to predict future private pension incomes, Pensim2 requires full work and pension contributions histories for those individuals who will retire in the future. This information cannot be obtained (directly or indirectly) from any existing data source, so contribution histories in the base-data have to be simulated (this is known as the backwards-simulation).

For the simulation of past private pension rights two groups have to be distinguished: the group of individuals above pension age in the base year; and the group of individuals below pension age. Members of the first group are already in receipt of income from private pensions, and they are assumed not to accrue any further rights. For these people information on private pension incomes is taken directly from the FRS.

For individuals below pension age the situation is more complicated, as we have very little information about the private pension rights that they have already built up. Therefore we carry out a backwards simulation to construct contribution records for these people. For members of the oldest cohort below pension age in the base data, those aged 64 in 2001, this implies that records have to be constructed stretching back to 1953, the year in which these individuals reached 16.

The backwards simulation constructs a series of episodes spent contributing to private pension schemes for each individual. The simulation makes use of information from the LLMDB2, to identify episodes where the individual was contracted-out from 1978 onwards and uses cross sectional data from the Government Actuary's Department (GAD) survey and the General Household Survey (GHS) alongside a random assignment mechanism to create contracted in and pre-1978 episodes. An earnings equation and simple allocation of scheme rules is used to determine the rights accrued from each episode.

State Pension contribution histories for those yet to retire are obtained from the LLMDB2.

(iv) Simulation and calibration

Conceptually Pensim2 works by "rolling forward" this base-data until 2050, using micro-econometric equations to simulate the future values of variables on the dataset. In simple terms the simulation operates using equations to give the probabilities of a series of different life events occurring. For example probabilities are calculated for whether or not an individual works, changes job, joins a pension scheme, dies etc. Figure F.2 depicts the order that these life events occur for each year in Pensim2. The predicted probabilities generated by these equations are compared to random numbers drawn for

Figure F.2 Order of process in Pensim2

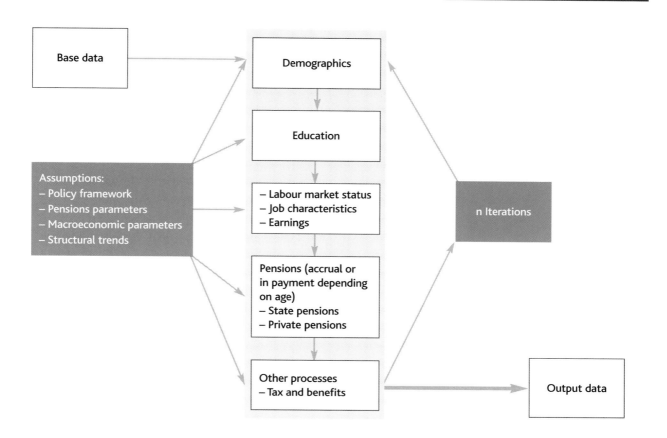

each member of the sample. Those individuals with a random number less than the probability are selected to have the event in question occur.

By the end of the simulation a large dataset has been created containing synthetic life histories for each member of the sample. These life histories contain all the information required to calculate pension entitlements for every member of the sample for every year from the base year to 2050. The model automatically calculates the pension incomes (state and private) for those who have retired.

Sometimes one might wish to ensure that the outcomes of particular parts of the simulation are consistent with those suggested by other sources (for example ensuring that the number of individuals who die in the simulation in any given year is consistent with the number forecast by GAD). In this instance the model can be calibrated, or aligned, to hit the required total. Pensim2 uses external alignment for a number of variables in the simulation (e.g. mortality and fertility rates, the employment rate, average earnings).

(v) Using the model: a caution in interpreting results

Any estimate of figures 50 years into the future is subject to a wide range of uncertainty. For example, we can assume that inflation will stay around 2.5%, yet we cannot know this will happen. So Pensim2 is only giving a picture of the future under a set of assumptions. The model's results will be very different if, for example, we assume that current rates of pension membership stay the same, increase, or decline. The model cannot help us to make a judgement about which scenario is more likely, but will show us the implications of each. Because of the sensitivity of results to the assumptions used, conclusions drawn from the model will generally be more robust when comparing alternative scenarios than when using any particular scenario as a "prediction" of the future. Where we have used Pensim2 to indicate forecast spending our estimates should be considered as indicating broad trends. As with published official estimates they will tend to vary from year-to-year with different assumptions and information e.g. life expectancy. Pensim2 is not a behavioural model, i.e. individual decisions do not respond to changes in policy, unless the user explicitly changes the input assumptions. This has implications for our analysis, for example in our analysis of state pension costs we keep private saving behaviour constant between scenarios; in reality we might expect options that entail stronger/weaker savings incentives to lead to greater/lower pension saving behaviour.

We would have liked to have presented sensitivity analysis on all the policy scenarios we have considered to show the uncertainties involved, but have been unable to do so due to time pressures. We recommend that Government and other producers of long-term projections, e.g. to 2050, on pensions policy should be careful to emphasise the uncertainty inherent in such analysis and ideally should present sensitivity analysis.

Pensim2 is just one of a range of analytical tools that we have used for the report. Like any model it has its limitations and so we have taken the approach of drawing on the whole suite of models and data at our disposal when addressing analytical questions. Rather than being used in isolation, Pensim2 is usually employed in combination with these other analytical tools to provide the most appropriate output.

2. Stylised individuals modelling

(i) Purpose of the modelling

In the First Report we presented the evolution of the state system based on hypothetical individuals who had constant earnings (relative to average earnings) over time. While this is a useful, simple approach it ignores that individuals have a variety of different employment patterns and earnings profiles. As pensions income depends on the earnings history and savings behaviour of each individual assuming constant earnings profiles over-simplifies the impact of the evolution of the system.

Therefore in this report we have created a set of stylised individuals, who are not meant to represent the whole range of working lives, but give an insight into the possible paths and how different savings levels could impact on their retirement income. This work is meant to complement the more simple constant earning models, as well as Pensim2 which simulates the whole population, which we have also used in this report.

(ii) Methodology

The stylised individuals are not meant to be a representative cross-section of the working age population with each individual being typical of a group of people. Instead they have been created to be indicative of certain stylised employment histories and associated earnings patterns. We have attempted to vary the age at which people start and end their working life, whether they have career breaks during working life and their earnings levels and profiles over time. The different individuals have been created drawing on a variety of reports and data sources which have looked at earnings profiles over time. Figure F.3 sets out the characteristics of the individuals and Figure F.4 is a graphical representation of their earnings levels in relation to full-time median earnings.

Using the stylised career history and earnings profile we calculate their pension income for the individual. We model their state pension income which is based on either earnings or eligibility for credits or Home Responsibilities Protection while out of work. We also model private saving into a pension: the pension assumed is a Defined Contribution scheme with only contributions from the individuals and we assume that the entire pot is annuitised at State Pension Age (SPA).

Figure F.3 Characteristics of the stylised individuals

Name	Age started employment	Age left employment	Labour market status	Sex
Constant median	21	SPA	Employed	Male
High earner	21	SPA	Employed	Male
Long-term illness	16	50	Employed then moves onto Incapacity Benefit	Male
In and out of employment	16	60	Employed with spells of unemployment	Male
Mid-career self-employed	16-30 45-SPA employed, 30-45 self employed	SPA	Employed from 16-30 and 46-SPA Self-employed from 30-45	Male
End-career self-employed	21	SPA	Self-employed from age 50 Same earnings as high earner	Male
Early retiree	21	50	Employed then takes early retirement	Male
Late entrant	30	SPA	Employed	Male
Mid-career leaver Early long-term carer	21	28	Employed until has children and does not return to paid employment	Female
Caring responsibilities	21	SPA	Employed with career break for child between 28 and 39	Female
Low earner	16	SPA	Employed	Female
Career break	16	SPA	Employed with career break from 26 to 33 and works part-time from 33 to 40	Female
Graduate mother	21	SPA	Employed, takes a two year career break from 29-31 and a three year career break from 34-37	Female
Early leaver – carer	16	50	Employed then leaves paid employment at 50 because of caring responsibilities, but not eligible for credits	Female

Source: Pensions Commission

Note: We have modeled SPA increasing in line with life expectancy [as explained in Figure 6.6 in the Main Report].

Figure F.4 Earnings levels for the stylised individuals

Male

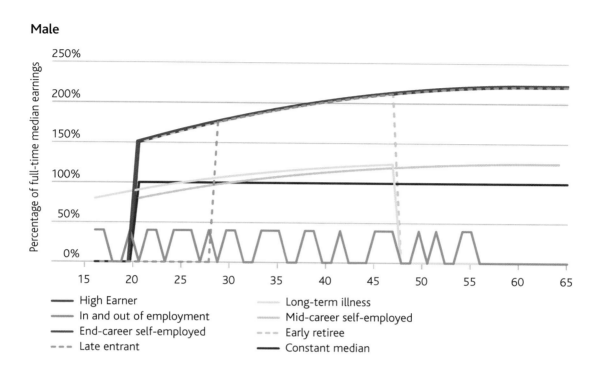

- —— High Earner
- —— In and out of employment
- —— End-career self-employed
- --- Late entrant
- —— Long-term illness
- ······ Mid-career self-employed
- --- Early retiree
- —— Constant median

Female

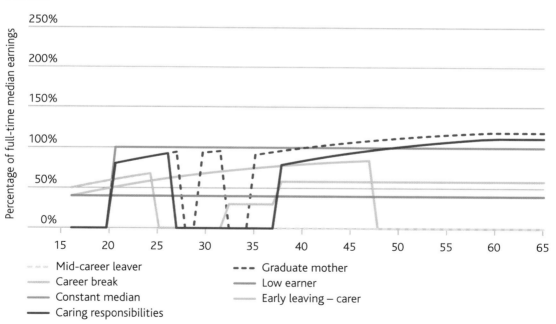

- ---- Mid-career leaver
- —— Career break
- —— Constant median
- —— Caring responsibilities
- ---- Graduate mother
- —— Low earner
- —— Early leaving – carer

Source: Pensions Commission analysis

We assume that an individual will start saving once they reach a given age (here we assume 30) in any year that their earnings are above £5,000 per year (in 2004 earnings terms), and that they save a proportion of their income above this level. The annuity that is purchased is assumed to be an index-linked single life annuity and we have adjusted annuity rates over time to account for the increase in life expectancy.

The model is flexible to change in any parameter in the pension system. We have modelled a "no change" scenario where current indexation arrangements are continued indefinitely. We have also modelled the two main policy alternatives presented in the report, that is the Enhanced State Pension where the Basic State Pension (BSP) increases to the value of the Guarantee Credit by 2030 and accrual of State Second Pension (S2P) ceases in 2010, and the Pensions Commission's preferred option of the two-tier flat-rate system where the BSP is linked to earnings and the Upper Earnings Limit (UEL) is fixed in cash terms from 2010 (for purposes of S2P accrual) and the Savings Credit threshold increases faster than earnings to keep the real value of the maximum Savings Credit fixed at its 2010 value. For modelling purposes we have assumed that SPA will rise to 68 by 2050 and a universal accruals basis for entitlement to the BSP.

In order to model the evolution of the system we have focused on individuals who reach the age of 65 in 2010, 2030 and 2050 at SPA, 75 and 85. To simplify the presentation of results we have looked at the pension income produced as a percentage of median earnings at that date. To examine the impact of savings on outcomes, we have looked at three savings scenarios for each individual:

- No saving

- Medium saving: 8% of earnings above £5,000

- High saving: 16% of earnings above £5,000

(iii) Results

Figure F.5 sets out the outcomes for each of the stylised individuals at 75, as this is midway through retirement, for each of the policy scenarios by whether they have savings (at the 8% level) or not. The charts showing the position at SPA and 85 for all savings levels are available on the Pensions Commission website (www.pensionscommission.org.uk).

The results for the constant median earner, high earner, low pay and career break individuals are presented in Chapter 6 in main report.

Figure F.5 Pension income for the stylised individuals at age 75 according to savings level; policy option and year they reached 65

Figure F.5.a Constant Median Earner

Medium Saving

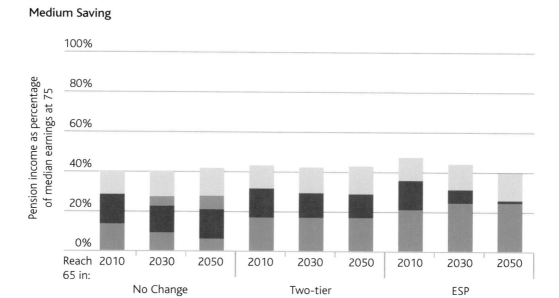

No Saving

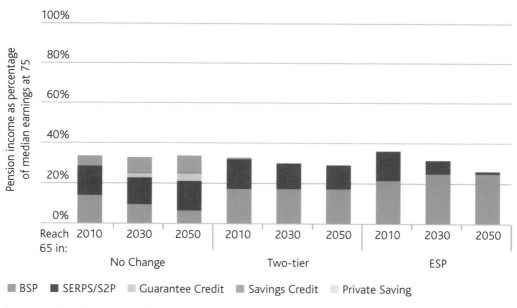

■ BSP ■ SERPS/S2P ■ Guarantee Credit ■ Savings Credit ■ Private Saving

Source: Pensions Commission analysis

Note: Figure F.5 covers pages 203-216.

All assumes working life as set out in Figure F.3 and F.4.
All assumes SPA at 65 in 2030 and 68 in 2050.
All assume 3.5% real rate of return on saving and 0.3% AMC saving 8% of earnings.

Figure F.5.b High earner

Medium Saving

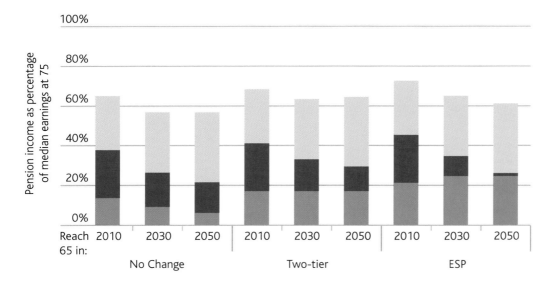

No Saving

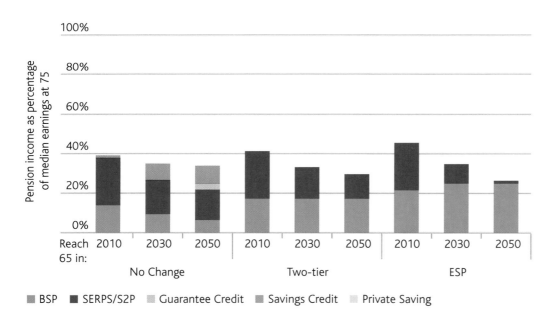

■ BSP ■ SERPS/S2P ▨ Guarantee Credit ▨ Savings Credit ▨ Private Saving

Figure F.5.c Long-term illness

Medium Saving

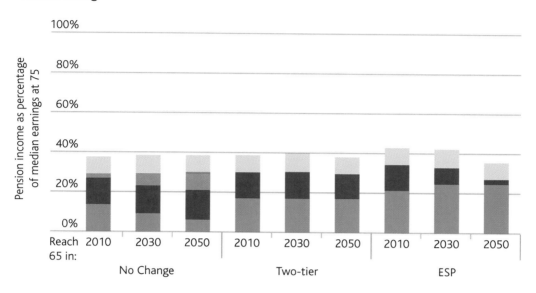

No Saving

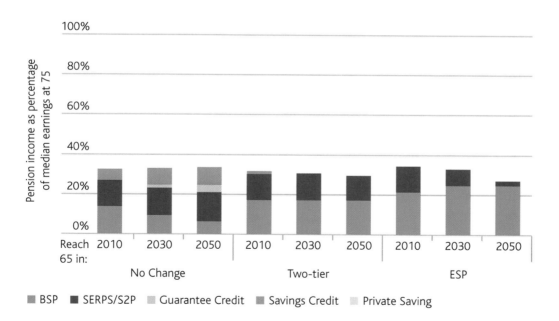

■ BSP   ■ SERPS/S2P   ■ Guarantee Credit   ■ Savings Credit   ■ Private Saving

Figure F.5.d In and out of employment

Medium Saving

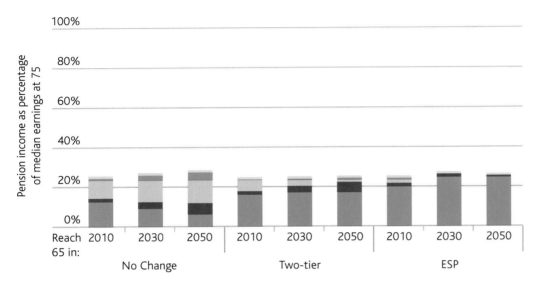

No Saving

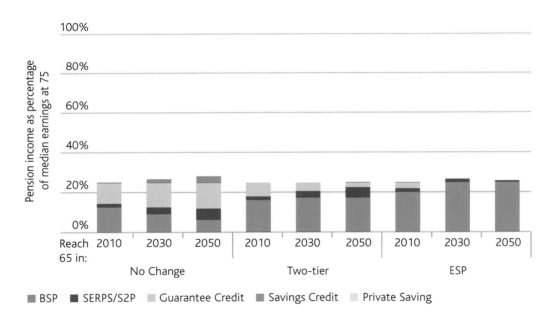

■ BSP ■ SERPS/S2P ▨ Guarantee Credit ■ Savings Credit ▨ Private Saving

Figure F.5.e Mid-career self-employed

Medium Saving

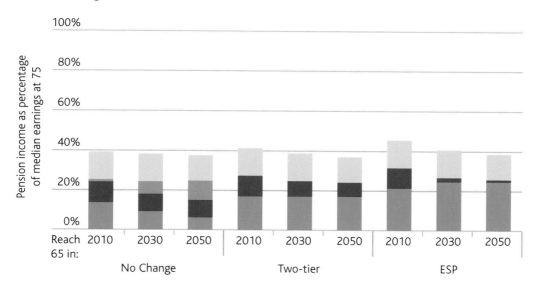

No Saving

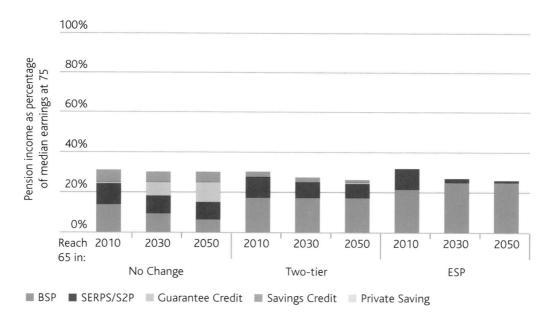

■ BSP   ■ SERPS/S2P   ■ Guarantee Credit   ■ Savings Credit   ■ Private Saving

Figure F.5.f End-career self-employed

Medium Saving

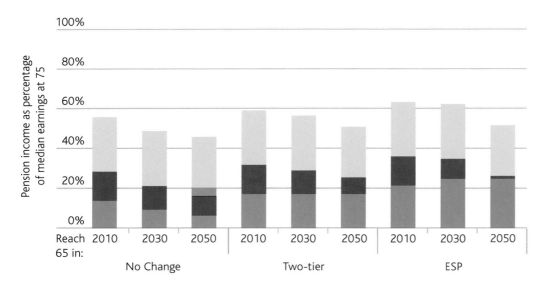

No Saving

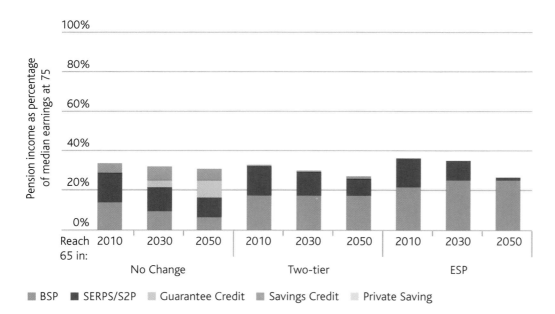

■ BSP ■ SERPS/S2P ■ Guarantee Credit ■ Savings Credit ■ Private Saving

Figure F.5.g Early retiree

Medium Saving

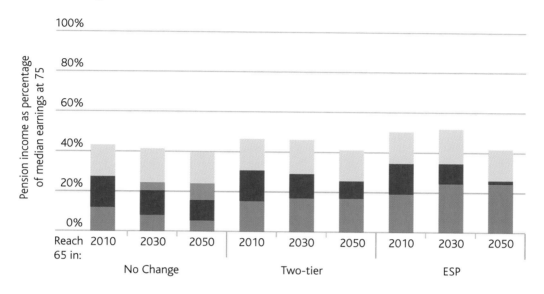

No Saving

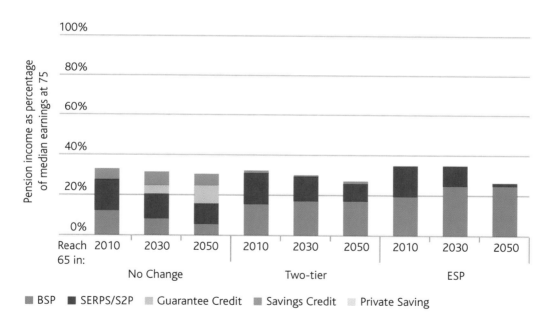

■ BSP   ■ SERPS/S2P   ■ Guarantee Credit   ■ Savings Credit   ■ Private Saving

Figure F.5.h Late entrant

Medium Saving

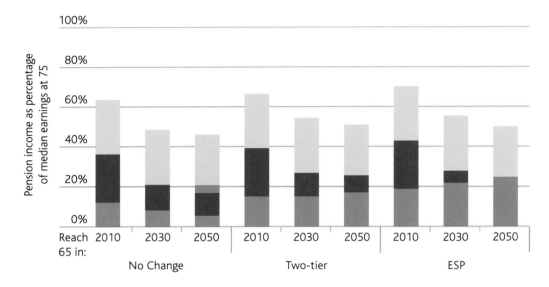

No Saving

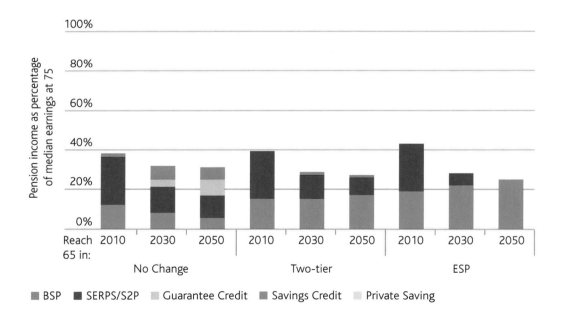

■ BSP　■ SERPS/S2P　■ Guarantee Credit　■ Savings Credit　■ Private Saving

Figure F.5.i Early long-term cover

Medium Saving

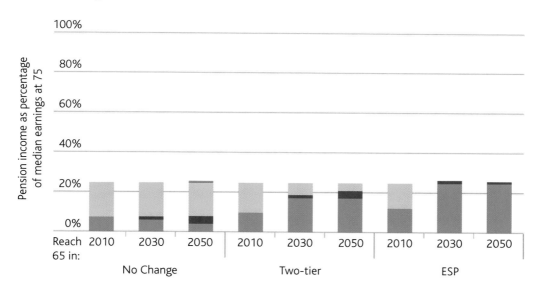

No Saving

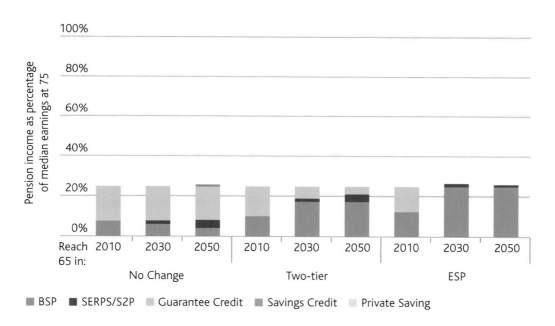

■ BSP ■ SERPS/S2P ■ Guarantee Credit ■ Savings Credit ■ Private Saving

Figure F.5.j Caring responsibilites

Medium Saving

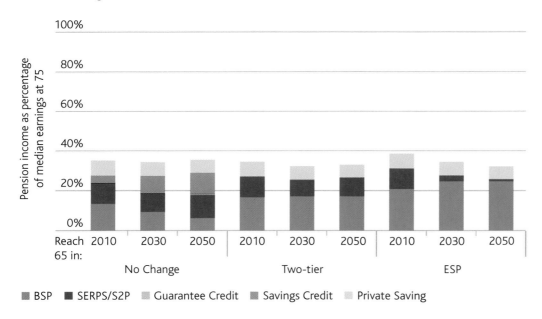

No Saving

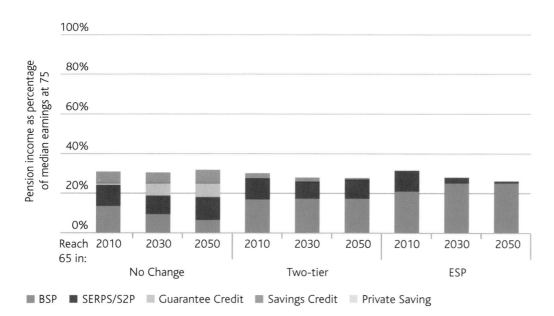

Figure F.5.k Low earner

Medium Saving

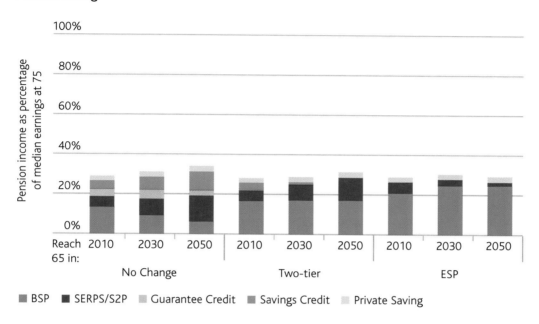

BSP ■ SERPS/S2P ■ Guarantee Credit ■ Savings Credit ■ Private Saving

No Saving

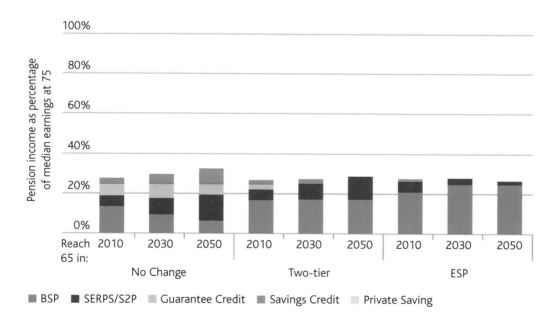

BSP ■ SERPS/S2P ■ Guarantee Credit ■ Savings Credit ■ Private Saving

Figure F.5.l Career break

Medium Saving

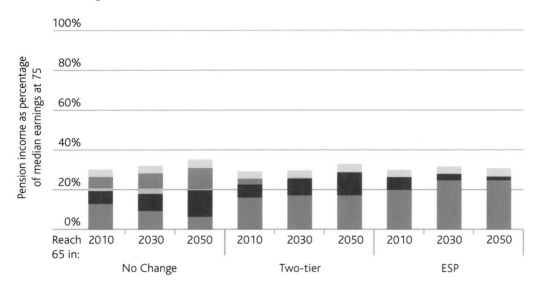

No Saving

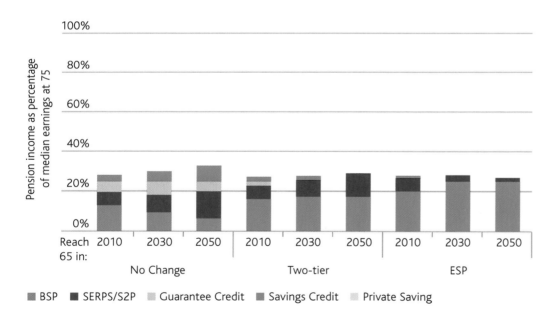

■ BSP   ■ SERPS/S2P   ■ Guarantee Credit   ■ Savings Credit   ■ Private Saving

Figure F.5.m Graduate mother

Medium Saving

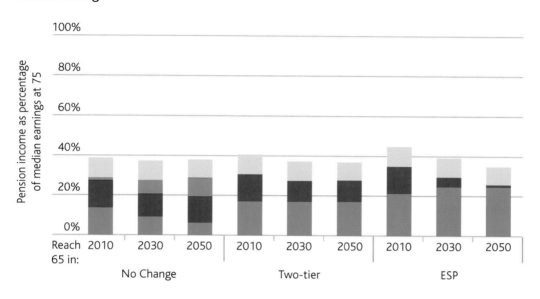

No Saving

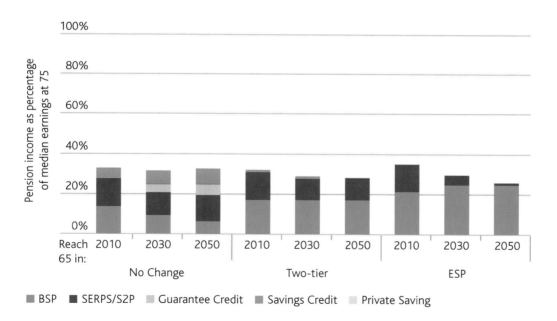

Figure F.5.n Early leaver – carer

Medium Saving

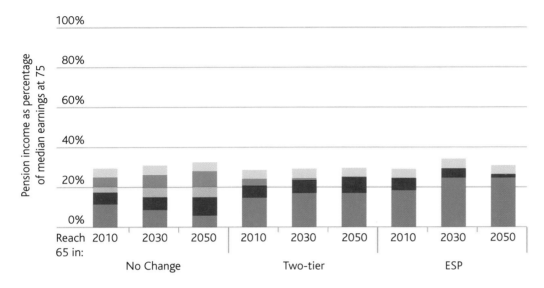

No Saving

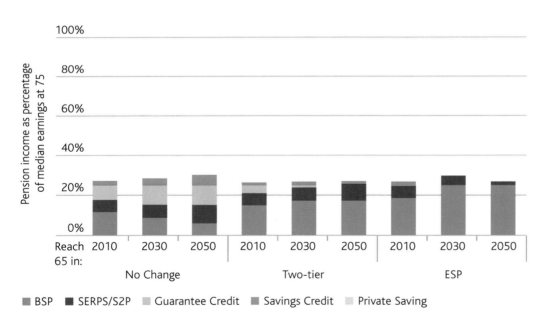

■ BSP   ■ SERPS/S2P   ■ Guarantee Credit   ■ Savings Credit   ■ Private Saving

3. Tax relief modelling

(i) Purpose of modelling

Last year we presented the "effective rates of return modelling" which looked at how the whole pension system interacted to produce an effective rate of return on pension saving over the entire lifetime [see Appendix C of the First Report]. This year we have focussed on the tax relief element of the system to understand how it affects retirement incomes compared to saving via other methods.

(ii) Methodology

This model focuses on individuals with constant earnings to allow us to focus on the specific impact of the tax system, rather than other factors, on outcomes. The model is highly stylised to make it simpler. It assumes that the individual was subject to the 2005/06 tax system throughout their working life, and earnings have remained constant in real terms, to abstract from any movement through tax bands during working life.

The model looks at the accumulation and decumulation of savings in a pension or in an non-pension vehicle, which can either be tax-advantaged (such as in an Individual Savings Account (ISA)) so tax is not paid on any investment growth, or a taxed savings vehicle (such as unit trusts), where it is assumed that all investment income is taxed at the individual's marginal rate of tax.

Pension saving
Individuals save 15% of their income after Income Tax and National Insurance. They receive tax relief at either 22% or 40% depending on their marginal rate. The pension accumulates throughout their working life from the point they start saving.

Employers' contributions are made via "salary sacrifice". In the method we have used, the individual and employer choose to reduce gross pay so that take home pay (gross pay minus Income Tax, National Insurance and pension contributions) remains constant. The employer keeps the total cost of employing the individual (pay, pension contribution and National Insurance) constant, which means a larger pension contribution is made to the pension scheme than would have been possible if the individual had made the contribution, as shown in Figure F.6.

Non-pension saving
The individual pays the same percentage of net pay into their savings account, but does not receive tax relief on that saving. The savings account has the same rate of return and Annual Management Charge (AMC) as the pension fund, therefore the only difference is the tax treatment. If the savings product is taxed, the investment income of the fund is taxed at the individuals' marginal rate of tax. (This probably slightly overstates the tax

Figure F.6 Calculation of level of salary sacrifice

Individual

Gross pay	Income Tax	National Insurance	Pension contributions	Take home pay
£22,000	£3,512	£1,882	£2,491	£14,115
£18,282	£2,694	£1,473	£0	£14,115

Employer

Gross pay		Employers NI	Pension contribution	Total cost
£22,000		£2,190	£0	£24,190
£18,282		£1,714	£4,193	£24,190

Source: Pensions Commission analysis

taken from non-pension saving as capital gains tax has a relatively high tax free allowance.)

Retirement

When an individual reaches state pension age, they receive the BSP and their SERPS/S2P commensurate with their earnings during working life. It is assumed that the individual lives for 20 years in retirement, which is in line with current GAD projections of life expectancy.

Non-pension income in retirement: Non-pension saving is not subject to tax when it is withdrawn from the account. To standardise the treatment of longevity risk we have assumed that the fund is annuitised at the same rate as the pension. However voluntary annuities are subject to a special tax treatment, the element which is assumed to be the return of capital to the individual is not liable for income tax and only the element which is assumed to be investment growth is taxable. To model this treatment we have assumed that 5% of the annuity income is subject to tax. All of the annuity is taken into account in calculating entitlement to means-tested benefits.

Pension income: It is assumed that 75% of the pension fund is used to buy a pension annuity which is fully taxable. As with the non-pension saving the 25% tax free lump sum is used to purchase a voluntary annuity. All income is taken into account for the calculating entitlement to means-tested benefits.

(iii) Results

Figure F.7 sets out the total retirement income (indexed to the income produced from taxable savings) for someone with average earnings during working life.

The increase in income from saving in a pension comes from three different effects [shown in Figure F.8]:

■ Tax free accumulation of income (which is an advantage over non-tax-advantaged saving).

■ The tax free lump sum, which means that not all pension income is required to be annuitised or subject to Income Tax.

■ The "tax rate step-down effect" which benefits pension saving over ISA saving as pension income in retirement faces a lower average rate, than the rate at which tax relief on contributions was given. This is demonstrated in Figure F.9.

Figure F.10 shows how the impact of these elements changes over different income levels.

Figure F.11 shows the impact of salary sacrifice, which increases retirement income, as salary sacrifice leads to significantly higher pension contributions.

Figure F.7 Impact of tax relief on retirement income: basic rate taxpayer

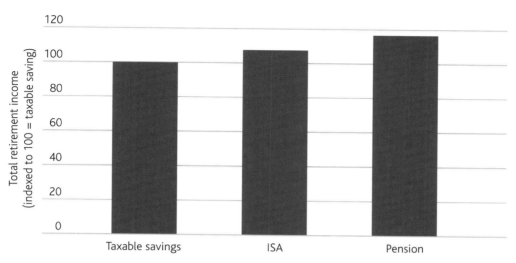

Source: Pensions Commission analysis

Note: Assumes individual saves 15% of salary from age 25. Real rate of return is 3.5% and the Annual Management Charge is 1% during the accumulation phase for all savings products.

Figure F.8 Breakdown of tax relief on retirement income: basic rate taxpayer

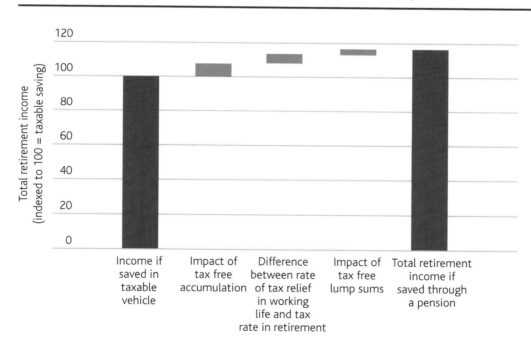

Source: Pensions Commission analysis

Note: Assumes individual saves 15% of salary from age 25. Real rate of return is 3.5% and the Annual Management Charge is 1% during the accumulation phase for all savings products.

Figure F.9 Difference in tax rates during working life and retirement

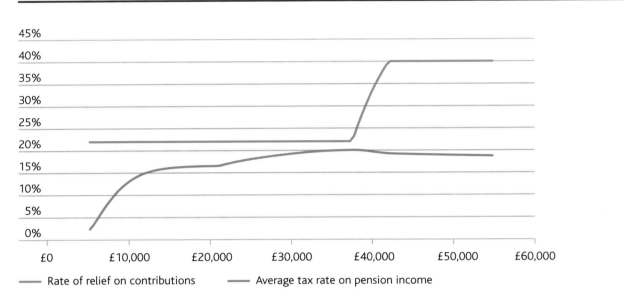

Rate of relief on contributions —— Average tax rate on pension income

Source: Pensions Commission analysis
Note: Assumes individual saves 15% of salary from age 25. Real rate of return is 3.5% and the Annual Management Charge is 1% during the
          accumulation phase for all savings products.

Figure F.10 Impact of tax advantages across earnings bands

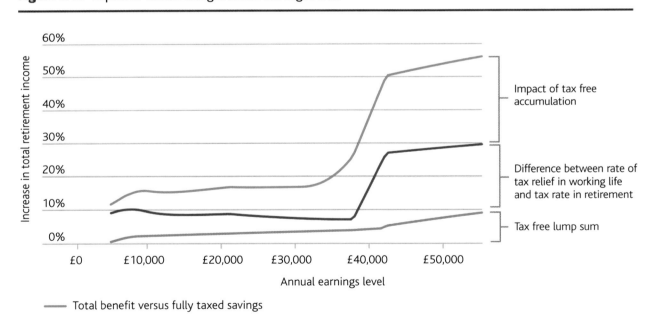

—— Total benefit versus fully taxed savings

Source: Pensions Commission analysis
Note: Assumes individual saves 15% of salary from age 25. Real rate of return is 3.5% and the Annual Management Charge is 1% during the
          accumulation phase for all savings products.

Figure F.11 Impact of salary sacrifice on retirement income: basic rate taxpayer

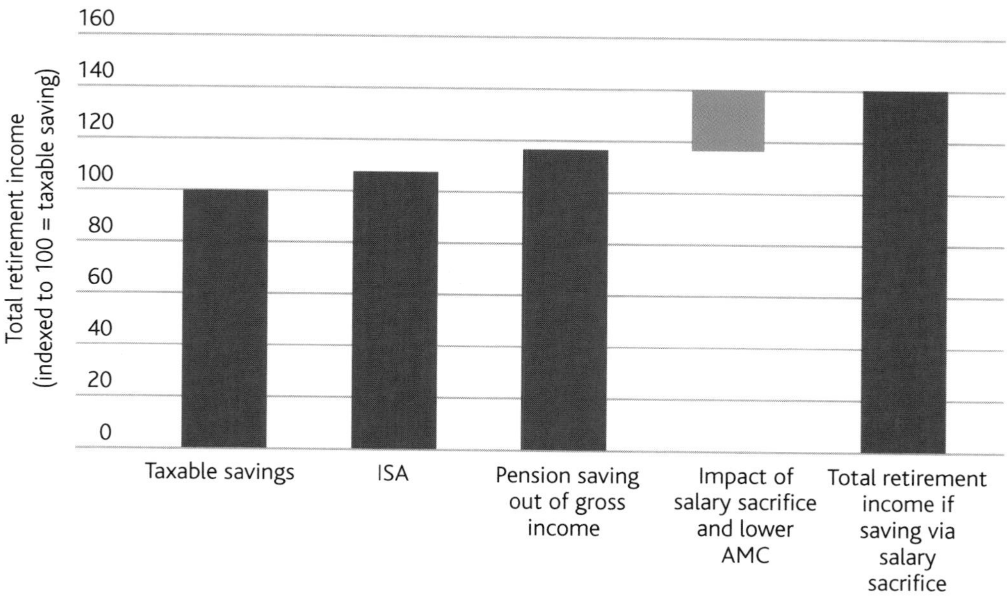

Source: Pensions Commission analysis

Note: Assumes individual saves 15% of salary from age 25. Real rate of return is 3.5% and the AMC is 1% for all savings other than the employer salary sacrifice pension and 0.5% in employer based pension. Salary sacrifice means that the individual takes a cut in gross pay so that take home pay after tax, NI and pension contributions remains constant and the employer puts that pay and the relevant National Insurance contributions into the pension fund as an employer contribution.

4. The Cost of Pension Provision Model

In the UK there are currently 8.5 million individuals aged 21 or over who earn in excess of £5000 per year who do not currently contribute to any form of pension.[1] Yet the insurance industry does not appear to be strongly interested in selling pensions to many of these people, arguing that the costs of providing and administering pensions makes them unprofitable under the present Stakeholder Pension charge cap regime. This is despite the fact that the present price cap is far above the costs achieved in large occupational schemes.

This section of this appendix provides details of our "Cost of Pension Provision Model" which we built in order to understand the drivers of costs within personal pensions and develop proposals for reform, to enable people with low to median earnings to save for a pension cost-efficently. The results of this modelling are discussed in the panel at the end of Chapter 1. This analysis can only be considered as indicative because of the significant assumptions and simplifications we have made in the face of the uncertainties involved.

We set out below the details of our approach in five parts:

i.   Determining potential returns to pension providers from the currently non-pensioned

ii. Estimating the cost of providing pensions to the non-pensioned

iii. Results

iv. Sensitivity analysis

v.   Alternative models of pension provision and their impact on charges and costs

(i) Approach taken in determining potential returns to pension providers

Under the present Stakeholder price cap regime, pension providers can only charge individuals 1.5% of their accumulated pot for the first 10 years and 1% thereafter. Thus in order to assess the returns available from the present under-pensioned market it is necessary to first assess the size of the market and then model the accumulation of funds by individuals.

---

[1]   Source Family Resource Survey 2003/04.

We use the Family Resources Survey 2003/04 to investigate by income band and age the number of people not presently contributing to a pension. We then assess the potential contribution to a pension as a percentage of earnings above £5,000 per year. In our base model we assume that all individuals aged 21 and over make contributions of 8% of gross salary in excess of £5,000 per year. Contributions could come as a combination of employee contributions, employer contributions and tax relief, but for the purposes of this model the origin of contributions is not important.

To work out the size of a pension pot in any one year requires us to make assumptions about the employment and contribution pattern of individuals and the rate of return on invested funds. We have assumed the following:

■ Individuals make contributions on an annual basis.

■ Individuals' earnings, and hence contributions, grow in line with average earnings growth.

■ Some individuals will contribute every year to this pension until they reach State Pension Age, however some individuals will stop contributing due to periods of unemployment, job change, early retirement or because they find a better pension to join. We model this "non-persistence" in contributing using data from the Financial Services Authority (FSA) persistency survey. Once a pension ceases to be contributed to, it becomes "paid-up".

■ In every year 20% of paid-up policies are transferred to other pension providers or are converted to annuities. This process is termed "lapsing".

■ Once an individual reaches State Pension Age their policy is assumed to convert into an annuity.

■ Pensions in receipt of contributions (in-force policies), or those paid-up, achieve a rate of return of 3.5% real per annum.

(ii) Estimating the cost of providing pensions.

To complete our assessment of the profitability of the non-pensioned to a pension provider, we need to model the costs of setting-up and running these pensions.

Due to the complexity of the UK pensions system, provision of pensions is not a cheap business, costs are incurred at many stages in the process and arise due to marketing, selling, advising, administering, investing and complying with the regulatory authorities.

These costs are usually considered under three headings:

- Initial costs which occur in the selling and setting-up of policies; some of these arise per scheme, and some per individual.

- On-going administration costs (e.g. crediting payment to the account, member communication etc.); these are inevitably per account in nature, and

- Fund management costs.

Figure F.12 shows the unit costs we have used in our modelling; these assume that the pension is provided in a Group Personal Pension form and we focus as in previous research in this area on a company of 23 employees, of whom 60% participate in the scheme. In addition we assume that a pension provider must make a market return on shareholder capital invested; thus we discount future profits at a rate of 11%. Our assumptions draw on data provided by different industry participants and are based on those considered by the government as part of the Stakeholder review.

Figure F.12 Unit costs per year assumed in modelling present personal pensions market

	Scheme level		Individual level
	Cost per scheme	Cost per individual	
Number of employees	23		
Participation rate	60%		
Costs embedded in IFA commission			
Prospecting/marketing	£3,220	£233	–
Establishing scheme	£2,990	£217	–
Advising individual whether it is worth saving	–	–	£80
Persuading individual to save in particular scheme	–	–	£80
Initial set up costs for provider			
Sales consultant and staff incentives	–	–	£160
Initial provision of literature	–	–	£10
Marketing	–	–	£15
Compliance with regulations	–	–	£5
Policy set up costs	–	–	£5
Total cost per individual		**£450** +	**£355**

On going costs per policy per year	**In-force policies**	**Paid-up policies**
IFA costs	£0	£0
Compliance costs	£4.5	£4.5
Policy administration	£12	£7
General communication and provider marketing	£3	£2
IT infrastructure	£2	£2
Policy payments	£5.5	£3.5
Premises	£3	£2
Other ongoing costs	£1	£1
Total	**£31**	**£22**

Fund management costs		
Fund management	0.10%	

Source: Pension Commission estimates on discussion with industry experts

(iii) Results

Once we have calculated the potential returns and costs to pension providers of supplying pensions to those without pensions, we can assess what proportion of them would be profitable to the industry.

Figure F.13 sets out our estimates of the combinations of income levels and ages required for individuals to be profitable to the industry under the present charge cap arrangements. We find that only 17% of those currently not contributing to a pension would be profitable to the insurance industry despite the fairly high levels of contributions we have assumed: with lower contributions, as described in the sensitivity analysis below, a far smaller proportion of the market would be profitable. These results also show that at income levels below £20,000 it is difficult profitably to sell pensions at the present charge cap.

This is despite the fact that we have concentrated on a GPP scheme, and assumed a reasonable participation rate (60%) which would only be likely to occur if an employer contribution was made. If we look instead at an individually purchased pension, or at a GPP scheme with no employer contribution rate and thus a lower participation rate, even less of the target market would look profitable.

To understand the source of the high costs preventing profitability we examined a typical individual aged 40 earning median earnings and working for the small company described above. Firstly we investigated what Annual Management Charge (AMC) would make this individual profitable to the industry and then identified how the four main drivers of costs, up-front costs, costs arising due to non-persistency, on going administration costs and costs of fund management individually contributed to this total revenue AMC.

Figure F.14 shows that two of these costs dominate:

■ Up-front costs involved in setting-up and selling pensions.

■ The costs created by non-persistency of individuals, which shortens the time providers have to recoup the up-front costs. This is driven by the common practice of people setting up new pensions when they start a new job, as employers find it administratively burdensome to send contributions from different employees to different pension providers.

Figure F.13 Profitable individuals under present Stakeholder charge cap regime

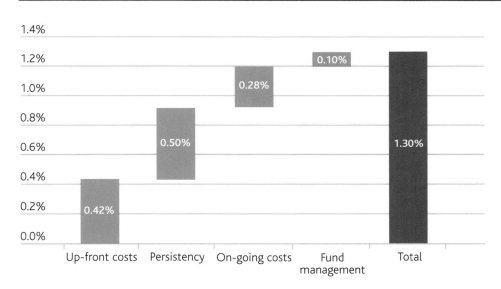

■ Profitable policies under the Stakeholder charge regime

■ Unprofitable policies under the Stakeholder charge regime

A median earner aged 40, marginally unprofitable under the present Stakeholder regime

Source: Pensions Commission analysis

Note: Assumes contributions of 8% of earnings between the Primary Threshold and the Upper Earnings Limit, 3.5% real rate of return and a GPP administered by a small 23 employee firm.

Figure F.14 Sources of costs for the median earner aged 40 in the present Stakeholder Pension system

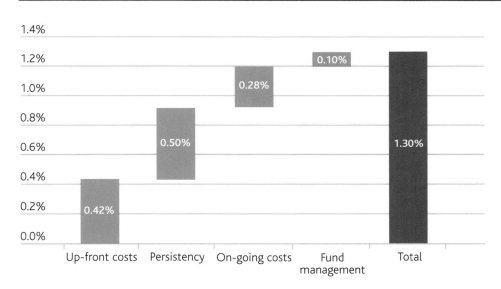

Source: Pensions Commission analysis

(iv) Sensitivity of analysis to assumptions

As the results we obtained in section iii are clearly subject to the assumptions made in the modelling, we have undertaken sensitivity analysis to test the degree to which our results change if we vary our key assumptions. The different scenarios we investigated are explained in Figure F.15.

The proportion of profitable individuals and the AMC required to make our median earner profitable are depicted in Figure F.16. Although these alternative assumptions do affect the number of people profitable under the present regime and the AMC required to make the median earner profitable, even in the optimistic scenario AMCs for the median earner are well above those achieved in large occupational schemes.

(v) Alternative models of pension provision and their impact on charges and costs

Section (iii) demonstrated that there are costs inherent to the UK pension system that prevent the sale of low cost pensions to a large number of low to median income individuals. To reduce costs significantly our results show that two costs, up-front costs and non-persistency, need to be substantially reduced. In this section we consider four models, spanning from minimal to radical change, by which such cost reduction could be achieved.

These models (described in the panel at the end of chapter 1) vary in respect of the location at which individual accounts would be held, the way in which individuals would select funds in which to invest, and the contribution collection mechanism. All the models however involve auto-enrolling individuals into making contributions (which raises participation in the 23 employer company to 80%) and involve a modest compulsory employer matching contribution. All also assume an evolution of the state system, which would avoid the spread of means-testing that would occur if current indexation arrangements were to continue indefinitely.

We investigated the following options:

Option A   A system of auto-enrolment to existing Stakeholder Pensions

Option B   A system of auto-enrolment to existing Stakeholder Pensions with a clearing house to promote and enable persistence in pensions

Option C   A system of auto-enrolment with a clearing house, which coordinates the process of setting-up pension accounts.

Option D   The National Pension Saving Scheme discussed in Chapter 10 of the Report.

Figure F.15 Cost model sensitivity analysis: scenarios studied

	Deviation from base case assumptions
Scenario A	20% increase in all costs
Scenario B	Contributions fixed in nominal terms
Scenario C	25% improvement in persistency
Scenario D	Higher real rate of return (5%)
Optimistic scenario	20% lower costs, 25% improvement in persistency, 5% real rate of return
Pessimistic scenario	20% higher costs, 25% worsening of persistency and contributions fixed in nominal terms

Figure F.16 Impact of scenarios on profitability and AMC required to make median earner profitable

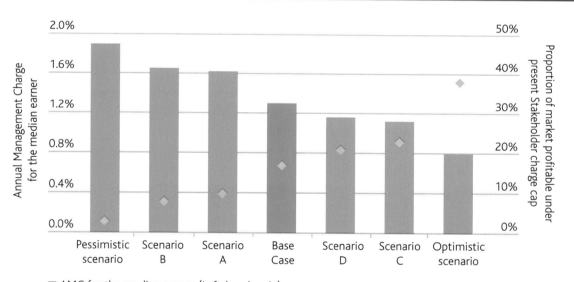

■ AMC for the median earner (Left-hand scale)

◆ Proportion of the market profitable under present Stakeholder charge cap (Right-hand scale)

Source: Pensions Commission analysis

Option A – Auto-enrolment into existing stakeholder accounts

Under this option, individuals earning over £5,000 would be auto-enrolled into an existing Stakeholder Pension designated by their employer. This approach would produce higher participation rates and would thus spread scheme set-up costs across a larger number of participants. In combination with the matching contribution and reforms to state pensions outlined above, the model could eliminate the initial costs arising from the need to advise and persuade individuals to contribute to pensions. But initial scheme set-up costs would not be reduced. Nor would non-persistency costs be cut, since people would still need to join a new scheme when they joined a new employer. We therefore estimate that this approach would cut costs from 1.3% to 1% for the median earner in the small company illustrated in Section (iii). Figure F.17 shows our input assumptions for this model and Figure F.18 our results.

As well as lowering the impact of up-front costs, higher participation has a knock on effect to costs by non-persistency.

Figure F.18 Sources of costs for the median earner aged 40 under Option A: auto-enrolment to Stakeholder Pensions

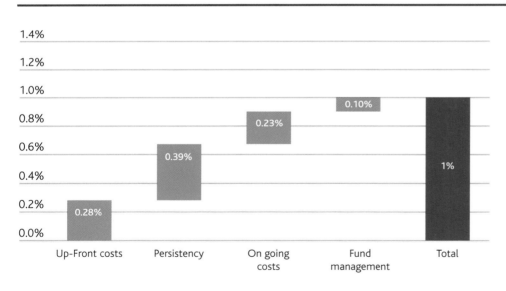

Source: Pensions Commission analysis

Figure F.17 Unit costs assumed in modelling Option A: auto-enrolment to Stakeholder Pensions

	Scheme level		Individual level
	Cost per scheme	Cost per individual	
Number of employees	23		
Participation rate	80%		
Costs embedded in IFA commission			
Prospecting/marketing	£3,220	£175	–
Establishing scheme	£2,990	£163	–
Advising individual whether it is worth saving	–	–	£0
Persuading individual to save in particular scheme	–	–	£0
Initial set up costs for provider			
Sales consultant and staff incentives	–	–	£160
Initial provision of literature	–	–	£10
Marketing	–	–	£15
Compliance with regulations	–	–	£5
Policy set-up costs	–	–	£5
Total cost per individual	£338	+	£195

On going costs per policy per year	In-force policies	Paid-up policies
IFA costs	£0	£0
Compliance costs	£4.5	£4.5
Policy administration	£12	£7
General communication and provider marketing	£3	£2
IT infrastructure	£2	£2
Policy payments	£5.5	£3.5
Premises	£3	£2
Other ongoing costs	£1	£1
Total	**£31**	**£22**

Fund management costs	
Fund management	0.10%

Source: Pensions Commission estimates

Notes: Changes from present system assumptions highlighted in red

Options B and C – Auto-enrolment into personal accounts with a clearing house to reduce non-persistency costs.

In the second and third options employers could be required to auto-enrol individuals into making pension contributions and required to make a matching employer contribution but with the contributions then sent via a clearing house to the different individual insurance companies at which different individuals hold their accounts. We model the assumption that the establishment of a clearing house could reduce non-persistency by approximately 50%. This is because an individual joining a new employer, who also operated a Group Personal Pension (GPP), could continue to make contributions to a pre-existing policy, and could have a right to have employer contributions sent to that policy, without adding to the employer's administration burden requiring them to send money to more than one place. Two variations of this approach are possible.

■ In Option B individuals would still initially join a GPP (or Individual Pension) sold in the current fashion (i.e. via IFAs or insurance company sales forces in direct contact with companies or individuals). But when an individual moved employer, they could continue to make contributions (and to receive employer contributions) into the initial account. The "clearing house" would be essentially an electronic pension payment processing system. This would not radically reduce initial up-front costs, but may lead to some reduction in on-going administration costs as shown in Figure F.19. We also include the costs per policy of an estimated £100 million start-up loan from HM Treasury, repayable over 30 years for the establishment of the clearing house. We estimate that this model might cut costs – for the median earner in the small company to about 0.7% [Figure F.20].

Figure F.20 Sources of costs for the median earner aged 40 under Option B: auto-enrolment to Stakeholder Pensions with an electronic payment processing system

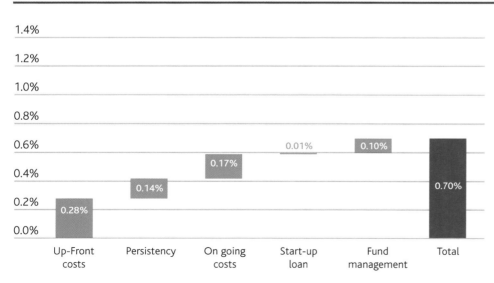

Source: Pensions Commission analysis

Figure F.19 Unit costs assumed in modelling Option B: auto-enrolment to Stakeholder Pensions with an electronic payment processing system

	Scheme level		Individual level
	Cost per scheme	Cost per individual	
Number of employees	23		
Participation rate	80%		
Costs embedded in IFA commission			
Prospecting/marketing	£3,220	£175	–
Establishing scheme	£2,990	£163	–
Advising individual whether it is worth saving	–	–	£0
Persuading individual to save in particular scheme	–	–	£0
Initial set-up costs for provider			
Sales consultant and staff incentives	–	–	£160
Initial provision of literature	–	–	£10
Marketing	–	–	£15
Compliance with regulations	–	–	£5
Policy set-up costs	–	–	£5
Total cost per individual		**£338** +	**£195**

On going costs per policy per year	In-force policies	Paid-up policies
IFA costs	£0	£0
Compliance costs	£4.5	£4.5
Policy administration	£9	£6
General communication and provider marketing	£3	£2
IT infrastructure	£2	£2
Policy payments	£2.5	£2.0
Premises	£3	£2
Other ongoing costs	£1	£1
Total	**£25**	**£20**
Start-up loan of £100 million	£1	£1

Fund management costs		
Fund management	0.10%	

Source: Pensions Commission estimates

Notes: Changes from Option A assumptions highlighted in red

■ In Option C, the "clearing house" would play a more important organising role, and the process of initial account set up would be radically changed. Individuals would be auto-enrolled into making contributions which (together with the employer's contribution) would be sent to the clearing house, which would then contact individuals and ask them to specify the insurance company they wished to open an account. Marketing information from each of the providers might be provided through the clearing house, and insurance companies would attempt to influence the choice via general advertising. But there would be no sales force or IFA direct contact with the employer or the individual. This model is similar to that which we believe New Zealand is now considering. Figure F.21 shows our cost assumptions for this model including a £250 million start-up loan reflecting the increased role of the clearing house. In theory it should be able to achieve significant costs reductions as shown in Figure F.22, perhaps to around 0.5% for the median earner.

Figure F.22 Sources of costs for the median earner aged 40 under Option C: auto-enrolment to pensions invested by insurance companies but arranged by a clearing house

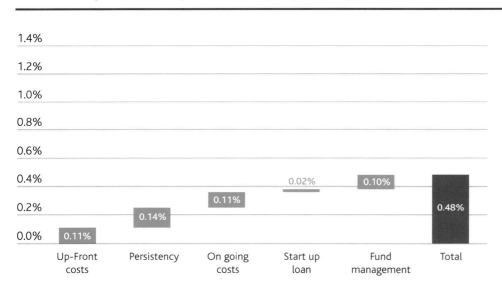

Source: Pensions Commission analysis

Figure F.21 Unit costs assumed in modelling Option C: auto-enrolment to pensions invested by insurance companies but arranged by a clearing house

	Scheme level		Individual level
	Cost per scheme	Cost per individual	
Number of employees	23		
Participation rate	80%		
Costs embedded in IFA Commission			
Prospecting/marketing	£0	£0	–
Establishing scheme	£0	£0	–
Advising individual whether it is worth saving	–	–	£0
Persuading individual to save in particular scheme	–	–	£0
Initial Set up costs for provider			
Sales consultant and Staff incentives	–	–	£160
Initial provision of literature	–	–	£30
Marketing	–	–	£50
Compliance with regulations	–	–	£5
Policy set-up costs	–	–	£5
Total cost per individual	£0	+	£250

On going costs per policy per year	In-force policies	Paid-up policies
IFA costs	£0	£0
Compliance costs	£4.5	£4.5
Policy administration	£9	£6
General communication and provider marketing	£3	£2
IT infrastructure	£2	£2
Policy payments	£2.5	£2.0
Premises	£3	£2
Other ongoing costs	£1	£1
Total	**£25**	**£20**
Start-up loan of £250 million	£2.5	£2.5

Fund management costs		
Fund management	0.10%	

Source: Pensions Commission estimates

Notes: Changes from Option B assumptions highlighted in red

Option D Auto-enrolment into individual accounts nationally administered.

In the fourth model, individuals would be auto-enrolled into making contributions into individual accounts held within a national administered system. The national system would then invest the individual's money, at the individual's instructions, in funds which had been bulk-bought at low fund management fees from the wholesale fund management industry. We feel this model has the capability to further cut non-persistency and reduce lapsing to 25% and 50% of current levels respectively, as individuals would not face marketing pressures to move their account between providers. The associated costs of this marketing would also be removed [Figure F.23]. We estimate, allowing for the financing costs of a £500 million start-up loan, a nationally administered system may be able to operate with an AMC of around 0.3% [Figure F.24].

As stated above, this analysis should only be taken as indicative. If the government is minded to accept a system of auto-enrolment to a nationally administered scheme such as the NPSS outlined in Chapters 5 and 10 of the Report, a full investigation of the possible charges and their sources should be undertaken. We do however feel that our estimates are of the right magnitude as the Swedish Premium Pension Scheme (PPM), an example of this type of system, (though with compulsory contributions), is aiming for costs of 0.33% or lower once mature. And in the US, the President's Commission on Social Security (2001) recommended that a cost target of 0.3% was appropriate for a similar approach for the accounts of people who choose to have some of their Social Security contributions invested in funded accounts (so called "carve-out" accounts) basing these estimates on the already established operation of the Thrift Savings Plan for Federal employees, which achieves still lower costs (around 0.1%) [See Chapter 1 of the Main Report for details.]

Figure F.24 Sources of costs for the median earner aged 40 under Option D: a nationally administered scheme

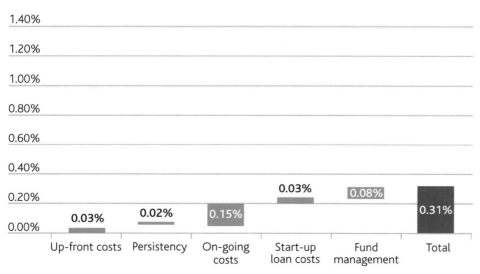

Source: Pensions Commission analysis

Figure F.23 Unit costs assumed in modelling Option D: a nationally administered scheme

	Scheme level		Individual level
	Cost per scheme	Cost per individual	
Number of employees	23		
Participation rate	80%		
Costs embedded in IFA Commission			
Prospecting/marketing	£0	£0	–
Establishing scheme	£0	£0	–
Advising individual whether it is worth saving	–	–	£0
Persuading individual to save in particular scheme	–	–	£0
Initial Set up costs for provider			
Sales consultant and staff incentives	–	–	£0
Initial provision of literature	–	–	£30
Marketing	–	–	£50
Compliance with regulations	–	–	£5
Policy set-up costs	–	–	£5
Total cost per individual		£0 +	£90

On going costs per policy per year	In-force policies	Paid-up policies
IFA costs	£0	£0
Compliance costs	£4.5	£4.5
Policy administration	£9	£6
General communication and provider marketing	£3	£2
IT infrastructure	£2	£2
Policy payments	£2.5	£2
Premises	£3	£2
Other ongoing costs	£1	£1
Total	**£25**	**£20**
Start-up loan of £500 million	£5	£5

Fund management costs	
Fund management	0.08%

Source: Pensions Commission estimates

Notes: Changes from Option C assumptions highlighted in red

5. NPSS employer cost modelling

The purpose of this analysis is to provide an initial snapshot of the potential cost to employers of introducing a modest matching employer pension contribution within the National Pension Savings Scheme (NPSS) for employees with no current employer-sponsored pension. For details of the proposed NPSS see Chapter 10 in the Main Report.

The analysis can only be considered as indicative because of the data limitations and the large number of assumptions that need to be made. In addition the final costs will depend on the final details of the design and scope of the NPSS.

We set out below:

i.   Dividing the employees into groups

ii. Identifying the data source

iii. Assumptions

iv. Using the data

v.   Weaknesses

vi. Results

vii. Sensitivity analysis

(i) Dividing employees into groups

We begin by splitting employees into groups based on the following characteristics by which we want to be able to present the results:

■ Current pension participation

■ Earnings band

■ Age band

■ Number of employees in the company

■ Industry

■ Sector (i.e. public, private, non-profit)

(ii) Identifying the data source

The next step is to identify the people who will be eligible for auto-enrolment into the NPSS. The most comprehensive data source to use for this analysis is the Annual Survey of Hours and Earnings (ASHE) – a dataset that contains information on the distribution of earnings of individual employees, and employer-sponsored pension participation, all provided by the employer. The ASHE samples data from the Pay As You Earn system, and then weights responses. The new methodology used in 2004 produces weighted estimates of earnings where the weights are calculated by calibrating the survey responses to totals from the Labour Force Survey (LFS) by occupation, gender, region and age. (See *Methodology for the 2004 Annual Survey of Hours and Earnings*, Labour Market Trends, November 2004 for more details.)

For our analysis it is important to draw on a large dataset which also contains reliable information on the firm size, industry and sector for estimating the potential employer cost of a matching contribution. Previous analysis has shown that smaller firms are less likely to provide pensions and so they are more likely to be affected by the introduction of the NPSS. (Firms with fewer than five employees do not have to provide access to a Stakeholder Pension for their employees.) The same analysis has also highlighted that there is variation within industries and sectors, with the private sector reporting lower participation rates.

Although ASHE is the most comprehensive dataset available, a number of assumptions have to be made so the analysis is focused on our needs.

(iii) Assumptions

A number of key assumptions are made based on the data available for who is included in the analysis and their associated characteristics:

■ Include all employees whose pay is not affected by absence for the pay period and their average gross weekly earnings for the reference period are greater than zero.

■ Of those whose pay is affected by absence, include employees if they have worked in the same job for more than one year and their annual gross earnings are greater than zero.

■ There are currently two pension participation questions in the ASHE questionnaire: one asks about participation in a salary-related, money-purchase or Group Personal Pension (GPP), and the other about participation in an employer-sponsored Stakeholder Pension. We define an employee as participating in an employer-sponsored pension scheme if they were a member of any of these schemes, including Stakeholder. If a response was either missing or "no" for both questions then we assume the employee was not participating and therefore potentially eligible for participation in the NPSS. This implicitly assumes that members of existing employer-sponsored pensions as described above receive contributions from their employers of at least 3%.

■ As mentioned above, the ASHE weighting is calibrated to the LFS totals. Our analysis is specifically based around pension participation and not earnings so it is important that the results are representative of smaller firms. Figure F.25 illustrates the comparison in 2004 of the usable ASHE estimates for eligible private sector employees to the Small and Medium Sized Enterprises (SME) statistics (published by the Small Business Service) estimates for private sector employees. Based on this comparison, the total numbers of employees are underestimated, particularly for the firms with fewer than five employees. We therefore applied an adjusted weighting to the usable population figures within the ASHE data to make the total number of employees more representative for the smaller firms. Figure F.26 illustrates the adjusted totals of usable private sector employees. (A similar approach was taken for the non-profit and public sectors.) We then look at other characteristics to determine whether an employee is eligible to join the NPSS based on the following assumptions.

■ The earnings thresholds used are for 2004/05 to relate to the ASHE data:

  – Primary Threshold £91.00 per week,

  – Lower Earnings Threshold (LET) £223.08 per week,

  – Upper Earnings Limit (UEL) £610.00 per week.

■ To be eligible to join the NPSS employees should be:

  – aged 21 and over, and

  – have earnings above the Primary Threshold, and

  – not currently participating in an employer-sponsored pension scheme.

■ The employer contribution rate is set at 3% of gross earnings between the Primary Threshold and the UEL.

■ An estimated participation rate is set according to the employees' current earnings:

  – 65% for employees with earnings between the Primary Threshold and the LET, and

  – 80% for employees with earnings at the LET and above.

Figure F.25 Comparison of valid ASHE cases and SME Statistics estimates for private sector employees, millions

	Missing values	1-4 employees	5-49 employees	50-249 employees	250+ employees	All
ASHE estimates						
Pension	0.2	0.1	1.1	1.1	4.6	7.1
No pension	0.2	0.7	2.7	1.5	4.1	9.1
All	0.4	0.8	3.7	2.5	8.7	16.1
SME estimates						
All		1.7	4.4	2.6	9.1	17.8

Source: Pensions Commission analysis on ASHE 2004
Small Business Service Analytical Unit

Figure F.26 Private sector employees with adjusted Pensions Commission weighting, millions

	Missing	1-4 employees	5-49 employees	50-249 employees	250+ employees	All
Pension	0	0.2	1.3	1.1	4.9	7.4
No pension	0	1.5	3.2	1.5	4.3	10.4
All	0	1.7	4.4	2.6	9.1	17.8

Source: Pensions Commission analysis on ASHE 2004

- Total employer labour costs include:

  – total gross salaries, and

  – employer National Insurance (NI) of 12.8% of employees gross earnings above the Primary Threshold.

These are the base case assumptions. Later we undertake sensitivity analysis around our assumptions on the contribution rate and the participation rates.

(iv) Using the data

The next step is to use the ASHE dataset to identify those who are eligible to join the NPSS and estimate the cost to the employer for those employees joining. We will look at how this varies by firm size and industry as we know that variation exists in current pension participation by these factors. We will then look at how the employer cost compares to their total labour costs.

(v) Weaknesses

To identify correctly the number of people who are eligible to join the NPSS, a number of assumptions have to be made. Ideally we need to know who is not currently contributing to an employer-sponsored pension, and of those who are what their total contributions are including the employer contribution if any. At present these data are not available. However the 2005 ASHE data will contain information on both employee and employer contributions potentially allowing more sophisticated analysis (see Appendix A for more details of this change).

We have had to make a number of simplifying assumptions as outlined:

- This analysis is only a snapshot based on the 2004 data. It does not take into account any changing circumstances e.g. in pension participation or the distribution of earnings between now and the introduction of the NPSS.

- We assume that those defined as participating in an employer-sponsored pension scheme have a level of contributions at least as favourable as the NPSS (see Chapter 10, Section 2 for more details). However, in reality this may not be the case for all members. Some of those currently participating in existing provision may not be receiving an employer contribution of at least 3%. If these people were included in the employer costing of the NPSS it could be higher. The extent of any underestimate would be small. When ASHE contributions data are available this would be a useful area for further analysis.

■ Total employer labour costs only include aggregate gross salaries and the employer NI cost of 12.8% on earnings above the Primary Threshold. We have not made any allowances for other benefits such as current pension contributions or health care which the employer may include as part of the remuneration package. Including this would make our estimated total labour costs higher – and therefore make the NPSS cost a smaller percentage of total labour costs.

■ The cost to any individual firm will depend on pension participation of employees, earnings distribution, the number of employees eligible to join the NPSS, and the number who do actually join the scheme.

■ We assume a participation rate of 65% for employees with earnings between the Primary Threshold and the LET and 80% for employees with earnings above the LET. There is very little evidence in the UK in the area of auto-enrolment into a pension scheme to provide an evidence base for this assumption. These participation rates have been assumed to reflect that those on lower incomes could be more likely to opt-out of the NPSS.

(vi) Results

These results are presented in three parts and focus on the private sector only,

■ The total number of employees participating in the NPSS

■ Total employer cost of the NPSS

■ Sensitivity analysis

The total number of employees participating under these assumptions

Overall there are 10.4 million private sector employees not participating in an employer-sponsored scheme [Figure F.26]. When considering the age and earnings characteristics as defined in the section above, the estimated total number of employees who would be auto-enrolled into the NPSS is 8.0 million. Figure F.27 illustrates the distribution of the number of employees who do not opt-out and are contributing to the NPSS under our assumptions and total employees, by firm size and industry under the assumed participation rates.

- Overall 34% (6.0 million) of private sector employees would not opt-out and be participating in the NPSS.

- The greatest impact is on the smallest firm size where half of all employees would be participating. This reflects the current low membership rates in an employer-sponsored scheme relative to the larger firm sizes.

- There is great variation in the percentage of employees that would remain in the NPSS by industry. In particular, the manufacturing, wholesale and retail and business activities industries with the highest number of employees have 29%, 35% and 40% of their employees participating respectively.

Figure F.27 Distribution of employees participating in the NPSS

By firm size:

Number of employees:	Employees participating (millions)	All employees (millions)	Employees participating as a percentage of all employees
1-4	0.8	1.7	50%
5-49	2.0	4.4	45%
50-249	0.9	2.6	37%
250+	2.2	9.1	25%
All	6.0	17.8	34%

By industry:

	Employees participating (millions)	All employees (millions)	Employees participating as a percentage of all employees
Agriculture, hunting, forestry and fishing	0.1	0.2	50%
Mining and quarrying	0.0	0.0	22%
Manufacturing	1.1	3.6	29%
Electricity, gas and water supply	0.0	0.1	10%
Construction	0.5	1.1	42%
Wholesale and retail	1.4	4.1	35%
Hotels and restaurants	0.4	1.1	34%
Transport, storage and communications	0.4	1.2	30%
Financial intermediation	0.2	1.2	14%
Business activities	1.3	3.3	40%
Public administration	0.0	0.0	26%
Education	0.1	0.2	35%
Health and social work	0.3	0.8	41%
Other	0.3	0.8	40%
All	6.0	17.8	34%

Source: Pensions Commission analysis on ASHE 2004

Note: We do not focus on the public administration, education and health and social work industries as most of their activity would be in the public sector.
Analysis assumes that all people who are already members of employers-sponsored pensions receive at least a 3% employer contribution, so they would not be auto-enrolled into the NPSS.

Total costs to employers of the NPSS

This section looks at the distribution of a 3% employer contribution by firm size and industry for the private sector and how this compares to total labour costs [Figure F.28]. (All components of the total labour cost are on an annual basis for all employees, and the 3% contribution is only based on eligible employees under the assumed participation rates outlined above.)

Key results are:

■ The total gross cost of a 3% contribution is £2.3 billion which is 0.56% of the total labour cost (wages and employer NI).

■ As the firm size increases the cost of a 3% contribution decreases as a percentage of the total labour cost.

■ There is variation by industry with agriculture, hunting, forestry and fishing and construction reporting the highest cost as a percentage of their total labour costs, but still this is less than 1%. In cash, the cost of a 3% contribution is highest in the business activities industry but is a relatively lower percentage in terms of total labour costs.

Figure F.28 Distribution of employer contribution of 3%

By firm size:

Number of employees	Total wage cost (£bn)	Total employer NI cost (£bn)	Total labour cost (£bn)	3% contribution cost (£bn)	Percentage of total employer labour cost
1-4	28.2	2.6	30.9	0.3	0.96%
5-49	88.2	8.7	96.9	0.8	0.83%
50-249	58.8	6.0	64.9	0.4	0.60%
250+	201.6	20.5	222.2	0.8	0.37%
All	376.9	37.9	414.7	2.3	0.56%

By industry:

	Total wage cost (£bn)	Total employer NI cost (£bn)	Total labour cost (£bn)	3% contribution cost (£bn)	Percentage of total employer labour cost
Agriculture, hunting, forestry and fishing	2.9	0.3	3.2	0.0	0.98%
Mining and quarrying	1.5	0.2	1.7	0.0	0.35%
Manufacturing	85.3	8.7	94.1	0.4	0.47%
Electricity, gas and water supply	2.9	0.3	3.3	0.0	0.14%
Construction	25.8	2.6	28.5	0.2	0.81%
Wholesale and retail	66.1	6.1	72.2	0.5	0.65%
Hotels and restaurants	11.2	0.9	12.0	0.1	0.79%
Transport, storage and communications	29.7	3.1	32.8	0.2	0.46%
Financial intermediation	38.5	4.2	42.7	0.1	0.18%
Business activities	84.3	8.9	93.2	0.6	0.63%
Public administration	0.1	0.0	0.1	0.0	0.75%
Education	3.8	0.4	4.1	0.0	0.61%
Health and social work	10.4	0.9	11.3	0.1	0.74%
Other	14.2	1.4	15.6	0.1	0.67%
All	376.9	37.9	414.7	2.3	0.56%

Source: Pensions Commission analysis on ASHE 2004

Note   Total employer labour cost include total salaries paid and 12.8% NI on earnings above the Primary Threshold.
Analysis assumes that all people who are already members of employer-sponsored pensions receive at least a 3% employer contribution, so introduction of the NPSS requires no additional employer contributions. It also assumes that there is no 'levelling down' of existing provision. As a result, figures could be under or over-estimates of costs.

■ The "headline" figure of a 3% employer contribution actually represents only around 0.6% of total labour costs [Figure F.29]. There are a number of logical steps which explain this.

■ The 3% contribution rate is only payable on earnings between the Primary Threshold and the UEL, which means it is only about 2% of earnings of the average NPSS member.

■ Around half of employees are already participating in employer-sponsored pension provision so are unaffected.

■ Between 20% and 35% of remaining employees are assumed to opt-out.

■ And finally employers pay NI of 12.8% on earnings above the Primary Threshold which means labour costs exceed wages – so NPSS costs are a slightly smaller percentage of total labour costs.

Thus the 3% contribution on gross wages represents only 0.6% of total labour cost.

(vii) Sensitivity analysis

In addition to modelling the costs under our "base case" assumptions we have undertaken some sensitivity analysis to look at the extent to which our results change if we vary key assumptions. Figure F.30 illustrates the different scenarios where we vary the contribution rate and participation rate.

The results of the analysis under the different assumptions are set out below and only focus on the results by firm size. The results do change under the different scenarios but the overall conclusions are unchanged.

■ Changing the participation rates changes the total numbers of employees participating overall and by firm size. The percentage of employees participating in firms with fewer than four employees under the lower participation scenario is 44% which increases to 67% under the higher participation scenario. In contrast the shift in the percentage of employees participating in firms with 250 or more employees is from 22% to 33% [Figures F.31 and F.32].

■ Figures F.33 and F.34 illustrate how the total cost of the employer contribution and the total cost as a percentage of total labour costs varies by firm size. These figures illustrate that the total annual cost could range under reasonable assumptions from £1.5 bn to £3.1 bn.

Figure F.29 A 3% employer matching contribution costs 0.6% of labour costs

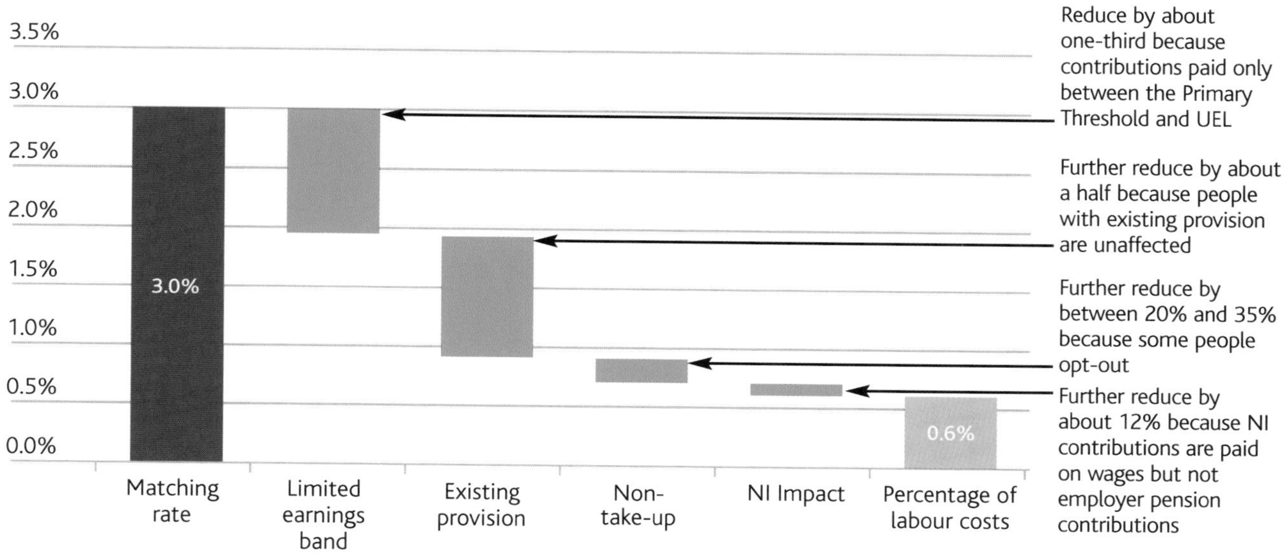

Source: Pensions Commission analysis

Note: Analysis assumes that all people who are already members of employer-sponsored pensions receive at least a 3% employer contribution, so introduction of the NPSS requires no additional employer contributions. It also assumes that there is no 'levelling down' of existing provision. As a result, figures could be under or over-estimates of costs.

Figure F.30 Description of scenarios for sensitivity analysis

Scenario	Key assumptions:	Employee participation rates	
	Employer contribution rate	Earnings between Primary Threshold and LET	Earnings at LET and above
Base case	3%	65%	80%
Lower contribution	2%	65%	80%
Higher contribution	4%	65%	80%
Lower participation	3%	50%	75%
Higher participation	3%	100%	100%

Figure F.31 Numbers of employees participating by firm size: base case and alternative scenarios

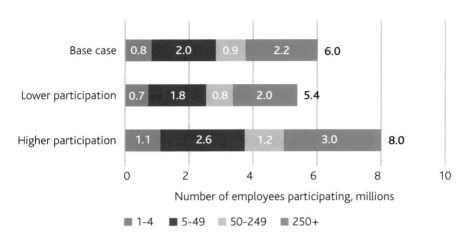

Source: Pensions Commission analysis on ASHE 2004

Note: The "lower contribution" and "higher contribution" scenarios have not been included as they assume the same participation rate as the "base case".
Analysis assumes that all people who are already members of employer-sponsored pensions receive at least a 3% employer contribution, so they would not be auto-enrolled into a NPSS.

Figure F.32 Distribution of employees participating by firm size: base case and alternative scenarios

	Number of employees				
Scenario	1-4	5-49	50-249	250+	All
Base case	50%	45%	37%	25%	34%
Lower participation	44%	41%	33%	22%	30%
Higher participation	67%	59%	48%	33%	45%

Source: Pensions Commission analysis on ASHE 2004

Note: The "lower contribution" and "higher contribution" scenarios have not been included as they assume the same participation rate as the "base case".
Analysis assumes that all people who are already members of employer-sponsored pensions receive at least a 3% employer contribution, so they would not be auto-enrolled into a NPSS.

Figure F.33 Distribution of total annual cost of employer contribution by firm size: base case and alternative scenarios

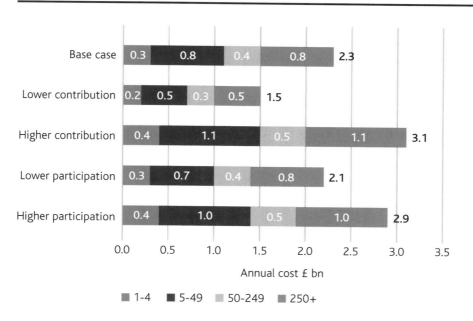

Source: Pensions Commission analysis on ASHE 2004

Note: Analysis assumes that all people who are already members of employer-sponsored pensions receive at least a 3% employer contribution, so introduction of the NPSS requires no additional employer contributions. It also assumes that there is no 'levelling down' of existing provision. As a result, figures could be under or over-estimates of costs

Figure F.34 Distribution of employer contribution as a percentage of total labour cost by firm size: base case and alternative scenarios

Scenario	Percentage of total labour cost				
	1-4	5-49	50-249	250+	Total
Base case	0.96%	0.83%	0.60%	0.37%	0.56%
Lower contribution	0.64%	0.56%	0.40%	0.24%	0.37%
Higher contribution	1.28%	1.11%	0.79%	0.49%	0.74%
Lower participation	0.89%	0.77%	0.55%	0.34%	0.51%
Higher participation	1.23%	1.06%	0.75%	0.47%	0.71%

Source: Pensions Commission analysis on ASHE 2004

Note: Analysis assumes that all people who are already members of employer-sponsored pensions receive at least a 3% employer contribution, so introduction of the NPSS requires no additional employer contributions. It also assumes that there is no 'levelling down' of existing provision. As a result, figures could be under or over-estimates of costs.

6. NPSS macroeconomic modelling

This section of the Appendix provides details of our "NPSS Macroeconomic Modelling," the main results of which were presented in Chapter 6 of this Report. The purpose of this modelling is to provide broad estimates of the potential scale of additional pension saving and income as a result of the NPSS in terms of contributions, fund size, pension income and annuity streams: and to estimate the resulting implications for the total stock of funds. The modelling and results are highly dependent on the assumptions used and should only be taken as a general guide to the scale that could be seen.

We set out below:

(i)   The approach taken;

(ii)   Results;

(iii)   Sensitivity analysis; and

(iv)   Weaknesses of the model.

(i) The approach taken

The approach involves the following key steps:

■ Determining how many people in which income bands are eligible to be members of the NPSS in the first year.

To calculate eligibility in the first year of the NPSS (potentially 2010) we used the ASHE data (as described in the previous section of this Appendix) from 2004 to approximate to the 2010 population. We estimate 8.8 million employees in all sectors in 2004 were eligible to join the NPSS. As in Section 5 the number of people eligible here could be an underestimate as we have assumed that all participants of employer-sponsored pension schemes have provision at least equivalent to the NPSS.

We then split the group of eligible employees into single year age bands and into those earning below the primary threshold (£4,745 in 2004) and those earning above. Using the Family Resources Survey we also found that an additional 1.4 million self-employed people aged over 21 were not contributing to a personal pension and hence might be eligible to join the NPSS.

As in the previous section of this Appendix we have assumed that those people who are earning under the Lower Earnings Threshold (LET) will have a slightly lower participation rate than those earning above. Our central estimate assumes 65% of those eligible between the Primary Threshold and the LET and 80% of those above the LET will contribute to the NPSS.

The participation rate for the self-employed is assumed to be 25% of those eligible (making 375,000 in the NPSS). This is a lower assumed participation rate than for employees as auto-enrolment will not apply to the self-employed and they will not benefit from an employer contribution. [See Chapter 10 of the Main Report for a discussion of the possible implementation of the NPSS.]

■ Establishing how cohorts and pension contributions flow into the model.

Using the GAD 2004-based population projection we took the ASHE and FRS data and pro-rated by the single year age bands to create an estimated 2010-2050 eligible population. The population in the NPSS therefore changes through time as new 21 year olds become eligible and 65 year olds move out of the NPSS and enter the pensioner population.

We then used the ASHE 2004 data to estimate median earnings as a proportion of overall population average earnings by age and used this to assign estimated average earnings to each group in our model. Contributions are assumed to be made from each member's earnings above the Primary Threshold. For simplicity we have combined the employer contribution, employee contribution and tax relief into one single default contribution rate of 8%. Individuals are assumed to contribute until State Pension Age (SPA), or else if they stop contributing they are replaced by a person with equal age and earnings who contributes instead.

We have also assumed an individual or their employer makes Additional Voluntary Contributions (AVCs) in excess of the default auto-enrolled level, of an additional 25% of the default: this increases the average contribution to 10% of gross earnings as our central assumption.

■ Establishing how pensions flow out of the model.

Pension pots are calculated by taking the contribution in each year, adding a year of fund growth and rolling this onto the next year and so on until each cohort retires. The real rate of return used for the central estimates is 3.5%, which represents a reasonable expected return in a balanced lifestyle fund.

From these final pension pots we apply an annuity rate to get the streams of annuity payments (i.e. assuming a price-indexed annuity). To simplify the model we assume annuities are paid for 20 years, with life expectancy kept constant at 20 years after reaching age 65. More sophisticated modelling could adjust for rising retirement ages and changing annuity rates over time, but this would make little difference on aggregate. Pension incomes are calculated from the annuity income generated in each year, based on equal payments over the fixed 20 year period. Where individuals die during working age; we assume that their contributions pass to an equal aged person (who could be their spouse) who inherits the pot on retirement that has accumulated and annuitises then.

(ii) Results

With the central assumptions, that is a 10% total contribution rate (including AVCs), 80% participation of those earning above the LET, 65% participation rate of those below the LET and 3.5% real rate of return, we get the following results:

- Total contributions to the NPSS would be around 0.6% of GDP each year.

- Pension pots leaving the fund would gradually build up to become 1% of GDP by 2050 and around 1.1% of GDP in steady state which is reached in 2070 [Figure F.35].

- The fund size would be of the order of 19% of GDP by 2050 [Figure F.36].

- The stock of annuities in payment would rise to be around 12% of GDP in the long term [Figure F.37].

- Additional income flowing to pensioners from the NPSS would reach 0.7% of GDP by 2050 and over 1% of GDP by 2060 [Figure F.38].

(iii) Sensitivity analysis

The results presented above and in Chapter 6 are all based on the central assumptions discussed above. We have also modelled various deviations from these central assumptions on contribution rates, participation rates and rates of return to test the sensitivity of the results. When changing one set of assumptions we have left the remaining assumptions as in the central case to enable easy interpretation of results.

The rate of return: as the risk and return panel in Chapter 5 of the Main Report showed the range for the rate of return on investments in the fund could vary substantially e.g. to 2% real, if bonds were the main investment vehicle, or to say 4.5% if equities dominate (though of course with the consequence of higher risk). Given that we do not know the risk and return preferences of those assumed to be participating we have run sensitivity analysis around the central rate of return. The fund size could then be as high as 22.5% or as low as 15% of GDP in 2050, although of course in the high equity case there would be more variance around this figure [Figure F.39].

The participation rate: we have modelled higher (100% of all eligible) and lower (50% between Primary Threshold and LET, 75% above LET) participation rates and Figure F.40 shows the results. Obviously the 100% participation rate of all eligible is very much the maximum size of the NPSS and the lower scenario has been included for completeness.

Figure F.35 Inflows and outflows from NPSS as a percentage of GDP

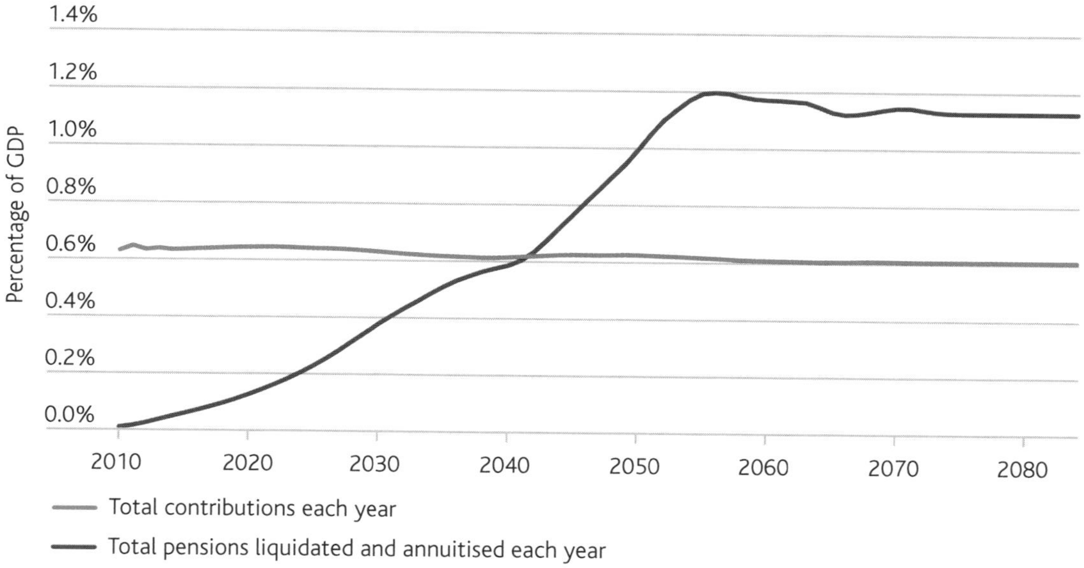

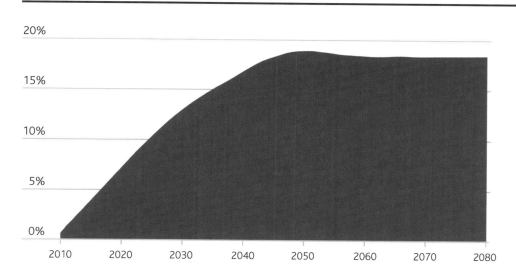

Source: Pensions Commission analysis

Figure F.36 NPSS funds under management as a percentage of GDP

Source: Pensions Commission analysis

Figure F.37 Stock of annuities arising from the NPSS as a percentage of GDP

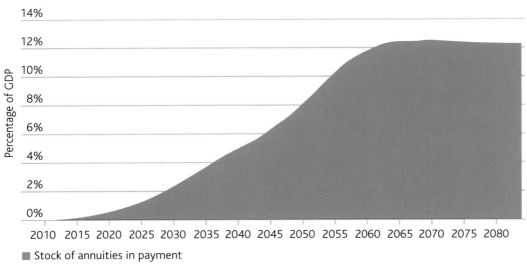

■ Stock of annuities in payment

Source: Pensions Commission analysis

Note: Assumes 3.5% real rate of return.
See Figure 6.35 in the main Report for other assumptions.

Figure F.38 Annual additional income flowing to pensioners as a result of the NPSS as a percentage of GDP

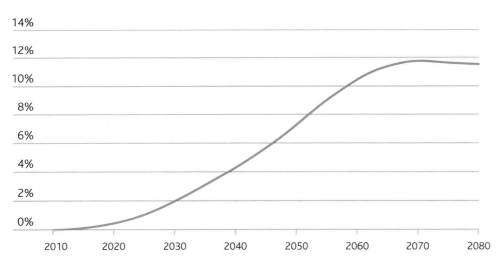

Source: Pensions Commission analysis

Figure F.39 NPSS funds under management with different rates of return: as a percentage of GDP

— 2% real rate of return — 3.5% real rate of return — 4.5% real rate of return

Source: Pensions Commission analysis

Figure F.40 Fund size, contribution rate and pension pots in 2050 with various participation rates, as a percentage of GDP

Participation rate	Fund Size	Annuity streams	Annual contributions	Annual pension pots
High 100% all	37%	11%	0.83%	1.3%
Medium 65% below LET 80% above LET	22%	8%	0.63%	1.0%
Low 50% below LET 75% above LET	20%	7%	0.57%	0.9%

Source: Pensions Commission analysis

Note: Uses central assumptions of 3.5% real rate of return and 10% total contribution rate.

The contribution rate: the actual rate of the default contributions and the amount of AVCs paid would not necessarily be the same as chosen above so we have modelled the size of the fund and pension income with both 8% and 12% average contributions. The results involved move in proportion. [Figures F.41 and F.42].

(iv) Weaknesses of the model

Some could be corrected in a more complex version of the model, but some are inherent.

■ There are very few UK data sources showing participation in auto-enrolment schemes split by age and income and those which are available are not representative of a national auto-enrolment scheme. We have therefore had to make some illustrative assumptions about participation rates. We do not have any large scale data to show the effect of a national scheme on pension participation of other forms so we have assumed this to be negligible and the same percentage of people paying private pension contributions in 2004 is used through out the period. There may be two dynamic behavioural responses to the new scheme which we cannot model. First, people currently contributing to occupational pensions could move into the NPSS, increasing its size. However; this would represent switching of investment between that already in progress and the NPSS, hence the overall impact on national savings will be unchanged. Second, there is also a risk that the NPSS adversely affects existing provision. This is clearly undesirable and we believe the effect can be minimised so we have not modelled it. As it is unclear which of these effects would dominate we have assumed that the overall impact balances out to zero.

We could also make elements of the modelling more sophisticated, e.g. AVCs and opt-out rates could be modelled by age as well as the earnings and contribution patterns of the self-employed.

Figure F.41 Stock of NPSS funds under managment with different contribution rates: as a percentage of GDP

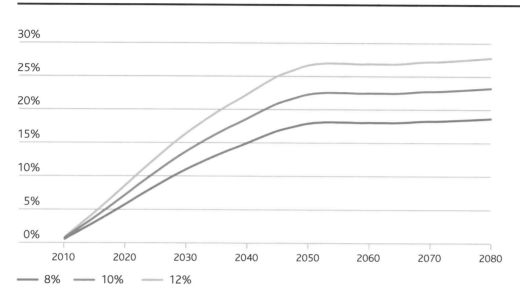

Source: Pensions Commission analysis

Figure F.42 Annual additional income flowing to pensioners as a result of the NPSS at different contribution rates: as a percentage of GDP

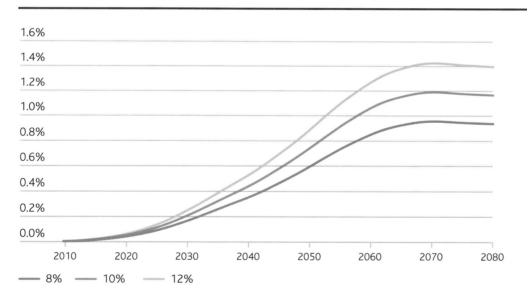

Source: Pensions Commission analysis

List of figures

Glossary

Active members
Active members are current employees who are contributing (or having contributions made on their behalf) to an organisation's **occupational pension** scheme. The scheme may be open or closed but cannot be frozen.

Additional Pension (AP)
A generic term used for the state pension paid in addition to the **Basic State Pension**. From 1978-2002 it was **State Earnings Related Pension Scheme** and from 2002 it is **State Second Pension**.

Additional Voluntary Contribution (AVC)
These are **personal pension** contributions made by someone who is also a member of an **occupational scheme** as a top-up to their occupational entitlement. Additional Voluntary Contributions can be made into the occupational scheme or to a stand-alone product called a **Free-Standing Additional Voluntary Contribution plan**.

Alternative asset classes
Alternative asset classes include **hedge funds**, commodity and managed futures, private equity, and credit derivatives.

Annual Management Charge (AMC)
This is the charge generally applied to **personal pension** plans where the fee is levied as an annual charge on the value of the fund. This charge covers the sales, administration and fund management costs of the fund.

Annuity
Purchased with an individual pension pot, which has been built up in a **Defined Contribution Pension Scheme**, to provide a pension that is usually payable for life. A single-life annuity pays benefits to an individual. A joint-life/survivors annuity pays benefits to the spouse/dependent partner after death of the first. A level annuity pays constant payments whereas an index-linked annuity pays benefits relating to an index (for example the **Retail Prices Index**).

Approved Personal Pension (APP)
This is a **personal pension** which meets certain regulatory requirements, so that it can receive **minimum contributions** (contracted-out rebates from **National Insurance** (NI) payments) enabling an individual to **contract-out** of the **State Second Pension**.

Attendance Allowance
A non-**means-tested benefit** payable to pensioners if they have additional needs because of illness or disability. For more details see Appendix F in the First Report.

Auto-enrolment/ automatic enrolment
A pension scheme where an individual is made a member by default, and has to actively decide to leave the scheme.

Average Earnings Index (AEI)	Average earnings are obtained by dividing the total gross pay by the number of employees paid. The index is a measure of change in average earnings in the UK.
Average earnings terms	Figures have been adjusted to remove the effect of increases in average earnings over time. Thus if something shown in average earnings terms increases then it is rising faster than average earnings, whereas if it is constant, it rises at exactly the same pace as average earnings.
Average salary scheme	A **Defined Benefit** scheme that gives individuals a pension based on a percentage of the salary earned in each year of their working life (rather than the final year).
Baby boom	A temporary marked increase in the birth rate. There were two baby booms in the second half of the twentieth century: immediately following the Second World War and in the early 1960s.
Basic advice sales force regime	Basic advice is a short, simple form of savings and investment advice aimed at people with straightforward financial needs. The adviser should make recommendations about suitable savings products (within his product range) based on the individual's answers to pre-scripted questions. In recommending a **Stakeholder Pension** he must explain the risk and return relationship. The adviser should assess suitability based on other factors such as debt if he is made aware of these circumstances. There is normally no up front fee. Basic advice can be provided face-to-face, over the telephone or over the internet.
Basic State Pension (BSP)	There are four main types of Basic State Pension:

Category A	A contributory based pension requiring 44 years of contributions, credits or **Home Responsibilities Protection**. Payable on claiming at **State Pension Age** at the rate of £82.05 per week (2005/06). Those with less than full contribution records receive a pro rata amount subject to a de minimis of 25%. There is an age addition of 25p per week for individuals aged over 80.
Category B	Pension payable under the same conditions except that the contribution record used is the spouse's contribution record. Widows and widowers receive Category B pension at the same rate as Category A pension. Married women (and married men from 2010) with a Category A pension entitlement worth less than £49.15 per week (2005/06) can top up their pensions to £49.15 per week using their spouses' contribution record, this portion of top-up is called the Category BL pension.
Category C	Now obsolete.
Category D	Non-contributory pension paid to residents of the UK aged over 80 and satisfying a residency test of at least 10 years in any continuous 20 year period before or after the 80th birthday. The pension is £49.15 per week (2005/06)

For more details see *'A guide to State Pensions'*, 2005

Behavioural Economics	A class of economic theories using insights from psychology to understand how individuals make economic decisions (see panel in Chapter 1).
Bond	A debt investment with which the investor loans money to an entity (company or government) that borrows the funds for a defined period of time at a specified interest rate.
Buffer funds (national)	A number of countries have chosen to smooth the age-related expenditure associated with the **baby-boom** generation by establishing national reserve or buffer funds. Most stipulate a certain annual level of contributions or source of income which is then invested. Most countries, with national buffer funds, invest (at least partially) in overseas assets, and in higher return but higher risk assets such as equities [see Figure 5.8].
Bulk-buyout	On winding up an **occupational scheme**, trustees will normally buy out accrued benefits of members and other beneficiaries with immediate or deferred annuities. Where there is a deficit in scheme funding the scheme will be assessed by the **Pension Protection Fund**.
Bulk negotiated funds	The central **clearing house** negotiates specifies a limited number of fund options (by risk or asset class) and then invites tenders from fund managers.
Citizens' Pension	Proposal for a **State Pension Payable** to every individual over State Pension Age who meets defined residency criteria. The level usually suggested is equal to the **Guarantee Credit** component of **Pension Credit** (£109.45 per week in 2005/06).
Clearing house	In relation to pension schemes an agency which collects and distributes information and contributions. The clearing house may also take on some administrative functions.
Cohort life expectancy	See **life expectancy**
Contract proliferation	The acquisition of multiple **personal pension** provision contracts by an individual.
Contracting-out	The system by which individuals can choose to opt-out of **State Second Pension** and use a proportion of their **National Insurance** contributions to build up a **funded** pension. There are four types of schemes, into which an individual may contract-out. The rules and rebate levels are different for each. These are: **Contracted-out Salary Related scheme, Contracted-out Mixed Benefit scheme, Contracted-out Money Purchase scheme** and **Approved Personal Pension**. For more details see Appendix F in the First Report.
Contracted-out Salary Related scheme (COSR)	Schemes **contracted-out** as **Defined Benefit** or salary related schemes.

Contracted-out Mixed Benefit scheme (COMB)	A scheme with distinct sections, one of which operates under the **Contracted-out Salary Related scheme** regime and the other under the **Contracted-out Money Purchase** regime.
Contracted-out Money Purchase scheme (COMP)	Schemes contracted-out as **Defined Contribution** or money purchase schemes.
Council Tax Benefit (CTB)	A **means-tested** benefit through which the UK government helps qualifying individuals meet their Council Tax payments. Qualification criteria include income, savings and personal circumstances.
Decile	The deciles of a distribution divide it into ten parts.
Decumulation	The drawing down of pension assets to fund retirement. In the UK it is permitted to access pension assets partially as a **tax free lump sum** and partially as an income stream (i.e. **annuity** or **income drawdown**).
Default fund	In compulsory or **auto-enrolled Defined Contribution** pension schemes some members do not make a choice of investment fund. These members will have their contributions paid into a default fund, designated for the purpose.
Default rate	In many pension schemes it is possible for the individual to select a level of contributions. In compulsory or **auto-enrolled** pension schemes some members will do not make a choice regarding their preferred level of contribution. These members will therefore pay contributions at a specified default level.
Deferred members	A member of an **occupational pension scheme** who has accrued rights or assets in the scheme but is no longer actively contributing (or having contributions paid on his behalf) into the scheme.
Defined Benefit (DB) Pension Scheme	A pension scheme where the pension is related to the members' salary or some other value fixed in advance.
Defined Contribution (DC) Pension Scheme	A scheme where the individual receives a pension based on the contributions made and the investment return that they have produced. They are sometimes referred to as money purchase schemes.
Direct execution	Where individuals buy a financial product directly from the provider without using a financial adviser.
Disability Living Allowance	A non-**means-tested benefit** which is mainly paid to people under **State Pension Age** if they have additional needs because of illness or disability. For more details see Appendix F in the First Report.

Discount rate	An interest rate used to reduce an amount of money at a date in the future to an equivalent value at the present date.
Earnings-related provision	The pension rights accrued in the scheme are linked to earnings. In a state pension scheme the formula may take account of average earnings over the working life or be based on a certain number of years as well as the number of contribution periods. The alternative to earnings-related provision is **flat-rate provision**.
Economically inactive	People who are neither employed nor **unemployed**, e.g. those who are not doing paid work but caring for children.
Effective pension age	The age at which an individual can achieve the same amount of state pension in earnings terms as he can achieve at the current **State Pension Age**.
Employer-sponsored scheme	A pension scheme which is organised through the employer, enabling pension contributions to be made through the payroll. Often the employer will also make a contribution. An employer-sponsored scheme can either be **occupational** or **group personal** in nature.
European Economic Area	The European Economic Area consists of all 25 countries of the European Union as well as Iceland, Lichtenstein and Norway.
Equity	Share or any other security representing an ownership interest.
Equity release	Equity release schemes give older home owners a way of accessing part or all of the value of the home, either as a lump sum or as an **annuity**, while continuing to have full residence rights during their lifetime.
Executive pension schemes	A **Defined Contribution** pension scheme arranged through an insurance company for the benefit of a senior employee.
Final salary scheme	A **Defined Benefit** scheme that gives individuals a pension based on the number of years of pensionable service, the accrual rate and final earnings as defined by the scheme.
Flat-rate provision	The pension rights accrued in the scheme are on a flat-rate basis. Thus the level of earnings is not taken into account by the formula, which is based on the number of contribution years. The alternative to flat-rate provision is **earnings-related provision**.
Free-Standing Additional Voluntary Contribution (FSAVC)	An **Additional Voluntary Contribution** plan which is separate from the individuals' **occupational pension** fund.

FRS17	FRS17 is the accounting standard for UK pension costs. It is mainly concerned with **Defined Benefit occupational schemes** but applies to all retirement benefits. It requires sponsoring employers to value on a "fair value" basis the assets and liabilities of their occupational schemes. The resulting surplus (or deficit) must then be recognised as an asset (or liability) in the company balance sheet. FRS17 replaced the previous standard SSAP24 on 30th November 2001.
Funded	Pension schemes in which pension contributions are paid into a fund which is invested and pensions are paid out of this pot.
Gilts	An abbreviation for 'gilt-edged securities', also known as government **bonds**. These are **bonds**, loans etc. issued by the UK government. They are often similar in structure to corporate bonds, paying a fixed amount to the owner following a given schedule. Gilts are generally considered to be one of the safer forms of investment so generate a correspondingly lower return than some more risky assets such as corporate bonds or **equities**. Some gilts make payments which are fixed in cash terms, whereas others make payments which go up in line with inflation.
Gross Domestic Product (GDP)	A measure of economic activity in a country. It is calculated by adding the total value of a country's annual output of goods and services.
Group Personal Pension (GPP)	A **personal pension** scheme which is organised through the employer, but still takes the form of individual contracts between the employee and the pension provider.
Guarantee Credit	A **means-tested benefit** which is part of the **Pension Credit** and provides pensioners with a minimum level of income. In 2005/06 the level of the Guarantee Credit for a single person is £109.45 per week. For a couple the level is £167.05 per week.
Guaranteed Minimum Pension (GMP)	The minimum pension that must be provided by a **contracted-out** salary-related scheme for pensions accrued between 1978 and 1997. The GMP is roughly equivalent to the foregone **SERPS** from **contracting-out**.
Hedge funds	An investment fund where the fund manager can use financial derivatives and borrowing. This allows them to take more risk than an **equity** or **bond** fund, in the hope of providing a higher return.
Her Majesty's Revenue and Customs (HMRC)	The new department responsible for the business of the former Inland Revenue and HM Customs and Excise. It is the department responsible for **National Insurance**.
Home Responsibilities Protection (HRP)	This helps protect the **National Insurance** records of people who have caring responsibilities and are eligible for certain benefits. For more details on how this works see Appendix F in the First Report.

Housing Benefit (HB)	A **means-tested benefit** through which the UK government helps qualifying individuals to meet rental payments. Qualification criteria include income, savings and personal circumstances.
Incapacity Benefit	Benefit paid to people incapable of work and who have either paid or been credited with sufficient **National Insurance** contributions, or became incapable of work in youth.
Income drawdown or income withdrawal	Where an individual takes the tax-free lump sum and does not convert the remaining pension fund to an **annuity** but draws income directly from the fund.
Independent Financial Adviser (IFA)	An independent financial adviser is someone who is authorised to provide advice and sell a wide range of financial products. They are distinguished from tied financial advisers, who can only give advice in investment products offered by a specific company.
Indexing regimes	Policy on the uprating of thresholds used in the calculation of tax or benefits. Typically these thresholds increase each year in line with inflation or average earnings. Over the long-term, indexing regimes can dramatically change the impact of taxes and benefits.
Index-linked	**Bonds**, **gilts**, **annuities** and other financial products can be linked to an index and pay an income which increases in line with that index and the capital values of which increase in line with that index.
Individual Savings Account (ISA)	ISAs are accounts which can be used to hold many types of savings and investment products including cash, life insurance and stocks and shares. They are available to most UK residents and there are strict rules regarding the maximum amount allowed for each component and the overall amount you can invest in any one tax year. The returns earned in an ISA (capital growth and income) are tax free.
Inertia	People often accept the situation with which they are presented as a given. As a result **auto-enrolment** increases participation rates, and the **Save More Tomorrow schemes** over time lead to an increase in saving.
Informed Choice programme	The Informed Choice programme is a government programme of initiatives, which aim to foster an increasingly proactive approach by individuals to saving for retirement.
Insurance-managed occupational pension schemes	**Occupational pension** schemes where an insurance company is responsible for the administration of the fund and may also provide some guarantees relating to investment performance.
Investors in People	The Investors in People standard is a business improvement tool designed to advance an organisation's performance through its people.

Jobseeker's Allowance	Jobseeker's Allowance is a benefit paid to people capable of work, who are not in work or are working less than 16 hours a week and are actively seeking work. It is only available to people under **State Pension Age**.
Large firm	For statistical purposes, the Department of Trade and Industry usually defines a large firm as one with 250 or more employees.
Learning and Skills Council	The aim of the Learning and Skills Council is to make England better skilled and more competitive. It is responsible for planning and funding vocational education and training for everyone.
Life expectancy	Life expectancy (or the expectation of life) at a given age, x, is the average number of years that a male or female aged x will live thereafter, and is calculated using age and gender-specific mortality rates at ages x, x+1, x+2 etc. Period life expectancy is calculated using age-specific mortality rates for the period under consideration and makes no allowance for changes in age-specific mortality rates after that period. Cohort life expectancy is calculated allowing for subsequent known or projected changes in age and gender-specific mortality rates after that period as he or she gets older. For example, a period life expectancy calculation for a male aged 50 in calendar year 2000 would use male mortality rates for age 50 in 2000, age 51 in 2000, age 52 in 2000 (and so on). The cohort life expectancy would be calculated using male mortality rates for age 50 in 2000, age 51 in 2001, age 52 in 2002 (and so on). The cohort definition is the better measure of true life expectancy.
Lifestyle fund	An investment fund that has an asset mix determined by the level of risk and return that is appropriate for an individual investor at different stages in the lifecycle. The fund invests in higher return but higher risk assets when the individual is young and gradually moves to less risky assets (i.e. bonds) during the 10 to 15 years before the individual plans to retire.
Limit to life hypothesis	The theory that there is an absolute age beyond which humans cannot live.
Long-dated gilts/bonds	**Gilts** or **bonds** with many years (e.g. 20) left until maturity.
Longevity	Length of life.
Longevity bond	A **bond**, which has an interest rate linked to overall life expectancy rates. It increases in value if **longevity** rises and shrinks if it falls.
Longitudinal	A research study which follows a group of individuals over a period of time.
Lower Earnings Limit (LEL)	The level of earnings at which an individual is treated as if they have made **National Insurance** contributions. In 2005/06 the limit is £82 per week or £4,264 per year.

Lower Earnings Threshold (LET), also referred to as the underpin	For the purposes of calculation of **State Second Pension** anyone earning less than the Lower Earnings Threshold (£12,100 in 2005/06) and above the **Lower Earnings Limit** is treated as if they had earnings at the Lower Earnings Threshold.
Macroeconomics	The study of aggregate economic activity focusing on variables such as **Gross Domestic Product**, economic growth, **unemployment** and inflation.
Major asset classes	The main groups of assets chosen for investment i.e. **bonds** and **equities**.
Marginal tax rate	Highest tax rate paid by an individual.

All individuals receive a tax free personal allowance, which in 2005/06 is £4,895 for those aged under 65, £7,090 for those aged 65-74 and £7,220 for those aged over 75. The higher personal allowances are subject to withdrawal after £19,500 (2005/06). Married couple's allowances are restricted to a narrow age band as they are phased out. Income above the relevant personal allowance is taxed at the marginal rate below:

Taxable income (i.e. income above personal allowance)	Rate of income tax
> £2,090	10%
£2,090-£32,400	22%
£32,400 >	40%

Matching employer contributions	An arrangement common in **employer-sponsored Defined Contribution** pension schemes by which a contribution made by an individual is added to by their employer. A pound of individual contributions might be added to by 50p or £1 up to a limit.
Mean	The average value of a group, calculated as the total of all the values in a group and dividing by the number of values.
Means-tested benefits	State benefits where the amount paid depends on the level of income and capital and other personal circumstances.
Median	The median of a distribution divides it into two halves. Therefore half the group are above the median value and half below.
Medium-size firms	For statistical purposes, the Department of Trade and Industry usually defines a medium firm as one with 50-249 employees.
Micro-employer/ micro-business	In this Report it can either refer to a firm employing fewer than five employees or a firm employing fewer than nine employees.
Minimum contributions	Contributions paid into a **contracted-out personal pension** scheme from the **National Insurance** scheme in place of building up rights to **State Second Pension**.

Minimum Income Guarantee (MIG)	The forerunner of the **Guarantee Credit**.	
National Insurance (NI)	The national system of benefits paid in specific situations, such as retirement, based on compulsory contributions. There are four main classes of contributions.	

	Employment status	Contribution level	Income band
Class 1	Employed	12.8% for the employer and 11% for the employee unless contracted-out.	Pay from **Primary Threshold** to **Upper Earnings Limit** (UEL) but credited from **Lower Earnings Limit** to UEL.
Class 2	Self-employed	Flat-rate payment of £2.10 per week for 2005/06.	If earnings below £4,345, eligible for certificate of small earnings exemption.
Class 3	Voluntary	Flat-rate contribution. of £7.35 (2005/06).	Voluntary for those not contributing through class 1 or 2.
Class 4	Self-employed	8%	Between Lower Profits Limit (£4,895 in 2005/06) and Upper Profits Limit (£32,760 in 2005/06).

There are special rates of class 1 contributions for mariners and of class 2 for share fishermen and volunteer development workers. In relation to pensions, class 1 contributions accrue rights to **Basic State Pension** and **State Second Pension**, while class 2 and 3 contributions accrue rights only to the Basic State Pension. Class 4 contributions do not accrue rights to any benefit.

National Insurance Number	Each UK resident is issued with a unique National Insurance Number. It is used for assigning **National Insurance contributions** and credits to an individual's account and for the administration of **Paye As You Earn**.
National Insurance Recording System (NIRS2)	The **HM Revenue and Customs** (National Insurance Contributions Office) replacement computer system. The majority of the system's functionality is now in place and operational. It collects contributions, holds contribution records, calculates contributory benefits, pays age-related rebates to **occupational** and **personal pension** schemes and can provide data to other government agencies.
National Savings and Investments (NS&I)	A Government Department and Executive Agency of the Chancellor of the Exchequer, its role is to raise funds for the government that are cost effective in relation to funds raised on the wholesale market. It does this by offering savings and investment products to personal savers and investors, and the money placed with it is used to help finance the National Debt.
National savings	The UK's gross national saving represents the extent to which, in any given year, the UK does not consume that year's Gross National Product (**Gross Domestic Product** plus net income from overseas investments), but saves it, either via investment in the UK or via the acquisition of a claim on the rest of the world.
Net Present Value (NPV)	The present value of an investment's future net cash flows minus the initial investment.
New Deal 50 plus	A programme of help provided by DWP for people aged 50 and over who want to work.
Nominal	**Bonds, gilts** or **annuities** which pay an income which is constant in cash terms (i.e. are not **index-linked**)
Normal age pensioners or normal age retirees	Used in this Report to refer to people who are aged at or above the **State Pension Age** and who are retired.
Notionally funded	A form of **unfunded** pension scheme in the public sector, where pension contributions are theoretically paid from the relevant department to HM Treasury to purchase **gilts** but where the future cost still has to be met out of future tax revenue.
Occupational pension	A pension which is provided via the employer, but the pension scheme takes the form of a trust arrangement and is legally separate from the employer.
Old-age dependency ratio	Used in this Report to measure the number of people above age 65 compared with the number of people aged 20-64 in the population.
P14 and P35	Forms sent on an annual basis by employers to **Her Majesty's Revenue and Customs** giving individualised information about **Pay As You Earn** deductions for all employees.

P45 and P46	The P45 is a certificate providing details relating to tax code, pay and tax paid to date and student loan obligations relating to the previous employment. An employee should receive a P45 on leaving an employer and hand it to the new employer. If the employee does not have a P45 he is required to fill out a P46 form. This gives basic information about the **National Insurance** number, whether it is the main job and source of income, and from 2006/07 whether the employee is repaying a student loan.
Pay As You Earn (PAYE)	A collection mechanism used to collect tax, **National Insurance** and some other statutory payments (e.g. student loans) from employees and employers at source. The employer makes the appropriate deductions from weekly or monthly earnings and sends the contributions to **HM Revenue and Customs**. The payments are usually made monthly on an aggregate basis with annual returns of individual information to enable the reconciliation of individuals' contributions and accounts. Pay As You Earn is not normally used as a collection method for the self-employed.
Pay As You Go (PAYG)	A pension system where the pension is paid out of current revenue and no funds are accumulated to pay future pensions. The **National Insurance** system is PAYG.
Pensim2	A model developed by DWP that simulates the future life course of a current population sample to estimate their future pension income. It enables aggregate and distributional analysis of alternative policy, demographic and economic scenarios. For more details see Appendix F.
Pension accrual	The build up of pension rights. In a **Defined Benefit** scheme this may be based on the number of years of contributions.
Pension Credit	The main **means-tested benefit** for pensioners, which combines the **Guarantee Credit** and the **Savings Credit**. For details on how it works see Appendix F in the First Report.
Pension Protection Fund (PPF)	The Pension Protection Fund was established in April 2005 to pay compensation to members of eligible **Defined Benefit** pension schemes, when there is a qualifying insolvency event in relation to the employer and where there are insufficient assets in the pension scheme to cover Pension Protection Fund levels of compensation.
Pensioner Benefit Unit (PBU)	A single (non-cohabiting) person aged over **State Pension Age** (SPA) or a couple (married or cohabiting) where the man, defined as the head, is over SPA.
Period life expectancy	See **life expectancy**.
Persistency	Where someone continues to make contributions to a pension scheme over time.

Personal pension	A pension which is provided through a contract between an individual and the pension provider. The pension produced will be based on the level of contributions, investment growth and **annuity** rates. A personal pension can either be employer provided (a **Group Personal Pension**) or purchased individually.
Pre-funding	Future pension promises are pre-funded by accumulating sufficient funds in advance of retirement. This is the case for all tax approved non-public sector pensions in the UK. It is the opposite to **Pay As You Go**.
Price-indexed	Increasing each year in line with inflation.
Primary Threshold	The point at which employers and employees become liable for **National Insurance** contributions. In 2005/06 the threshold is £94 per week or £4,888 per year.
Protected rights	The element of the **Defined Contribution** pension arising from **Contracted-out** rebates
Protection products	Financial products which provide insurance against specific events, such as unemployment or illness.
Rate of return	The gain or loss of an investment over a specified period, expressed as a percentage increase over the initial investment cost. Gains on investments are considered to be any income received from the asset, plus realised capital gains.
Real terms	Figures have been adjusted to remove the effect of increases in prices over time (i.e. inflation), usually measured by the **Retail Prices Index**. Thus if something shown in real terms increases then it is rising faster than prices, whereas if it is constant, it rises at exactly the same pace as prices.
Reduction In Yield (RIY)	This measures the effect of charges (whether **Annual Management Charges** or implicit costs) on the return an individual achieves on investment. If the rate of return before charges was 6% but the individual receives a rate of return of only 4% after charges, then the Reduction In Yield is 2%.
Regulated advice	Advice from financial advisers certified by the Financial Services Authority and operating within their guidelines.
Replacement rate	This measures income in retirement as a percentage of income before retirement.
Retail Prices Index (RPI)	This is an average measure of the change in the prices of goods and services bought for consumption by the vast majority of households in the UK.
Retirement annuity contract	The forerunner of modern **personal pensions**.

Risk Based Levy	The levy for the new **Pension Protection Fund** (PPF) will from 2006/07 be based risk of the pension fund entering the PPF. Thus it will take into account the scheme's liabilities in relation to its members, the level of funding in the scheme and the risk of the company becoming insolvent.
Risk-free rate	The theoretical rate of return of an investment with no risk. The risk-free rate represents the interest an investor would expect from an absolutely risk-free investment over a specified period of time. In practice the rate of return from a short-term **gilt** is used as a comparator.
Salary sacrifice	An agreement (which **HM Revenue and Customs** requires to be in writing) between the employer and the employee whereby the employee foregoes part of his future earnings in return for a corresponding contribution by the employer into a pension scheme. The advantage for the employee is that employer contributions are free from tax and **National Insurance** whilst employee contributions are only tax advantaged.
Save More Tomorrow Scheme	See "Insights from behavioural economics" panel in Chapter 6 of the First Report
Savings Credit	Part of the **Pension Credit**. It is a **means-tested benefit** for people aged 65 or over, which is withdrawn at the rate of 40p for each £1 of pre-Pension Credit income above the level of the **Basic State Pension**.
Second-tier pension provision	Used in this Report to refer to **Additional Pension** and **contracted-out** equivalents.
Self-Invested Pension Plan (SIPP)	A **personal pension** where the individual chooses where to invest his funds instead of giving his funds to a financial services company to manage.
Self-administered scheme	An **occupational pension** scheme where the administration is carried out directly on behalf of the trustees and not handed over to an insurance company.
Small and Medium Enterprise (SME)	For statistical purposes, the Department of Trade and Industry usually defines a SME as a firm with 249 or fewer employees.
Small firm	For statistical purposes, the Department of Trade and Industry usually defines a small firm as one with 49 or fewer employees.

Socio-economic class	Classification of individuals based on occupation. The Registrar General's Social Class based on Occupation has been used in this Report:	

Class	Description	Examples of occupations
Non-manual		
I	Professional	Doctors, chartered accountants, professionally qualified engineers
II	Managerial & technical/ intermediate	Managers, school teachers, journalists
IIIN	Skilled non-manual	Clerks, cashiers, retail staff
Manual		
IIIM	Skilled manual	Supervisor of manual workers, plumbers, electricians, goods vehicle drivers
IV	Partly skilled	Warehousemen, security guards, machine tool operators, care assistants, waiting staff
V	Unskilled	Labourers, cleaners and messengers

Stakeholder Pension	A **personal pension** product which complies with regulations which limit charges and allow individuals flexibility about contributions.
Stakeholder price cap	The **Stakeholder Pension** price cap is a 1.5% **Annual Management Charge (AMC)** for the first ten years of the policy and thereafter a 1% **AMC**.
State Earnings Related Pension Scheme (SERPS)	The forerunner of the **State Second Pension**, which provides an earnings-related **National Insurance** pension based on contributions. For more details see Appendix F in the First Report.
State Pension Age (SPA)	The age at which an individual can claim their state pension. It is currently 65 for men and 60 for women. The State Pension Age for women will gradually increase to 65 between 2010 and 2020.
State Second Pension (S2P)	The **National Insurance** pension which gives benefits based on an individual's earnings and contributions. For more details see Appendix F in the First Report.

Statutory Money Purchase Illustration (SMPI)	**Defined Contribution** or money purchase schemes are required to send a benefit statement to all members annually. This must include information about current capital value of the fund and an illustration of the pension payable on retirement in today's prices.
Tax credits	There are two main types of tax credit. Working Tax Credit is an income-related credit for working adults and Child Tax Credit is an income-related credit payable to families with responsibility for children, whether they are in or out of work.
Tax relief	Individuals making contributions to tax approved pension schemes receive tax relief at their **marginal tax rate** (e.g. a standard rate taxpayer will receive tax relief at 22%). Individuals contributing to **Stakeholder Pensions** receive tax relief at a minimal rate of 22%. Individuals with very low or no tax liabilities can also receive "tax relief" at 22% on contributions of up to £2,808 per year. Employers' contributions are made from gross profits and thus are both tax and **National Insurance** privileged.
Tax free lump sum	25% of pension saving may be taken as a tax free lump sum. This 25% may include **Protected Rights** but not the **Guaranteed Minimum Pension**.
Tax simplification	Pensions Tax Simplification introduces a new tax regime for pensions which will take effect from 6 April 2006. Simplification will sweep away the eight existing tax regimes and replace them with a single universal regime for tax-privileged pension savings. A key feature is that instead of the annual limits on contributions there will be a lifetime annual limit of £1.8 million (indexed) of tax advantaged pension saving.
Term insurance	Life insurance which covers a specific length of time, for example to cover a mortgage.
Trading down	Buying a home that is less expensive than one's current home.
Unemployment	The number of unemployed people in the UK is measured through the Labour Force Survey following the internationally agreed definition recommended by the International Labour Organisation, an agency of the United Nations. Unemployed people are: without a job, want a job, have actively sought work in the last four weeks and are available to start work in the next two weeks, or: out of work, have found a job and are waiting to start it in the next two weeks. For some of the ELSA analysis unemployment is not so strictly defined.
Universal residency basis	A state pension payable to every individual over **State Pension Age** who meets defined residency criteria.
Unfunded	Pension schemes which are not backed by a pension fund. Instead current contributions are used to pay current pensions along with other funds provided by the employer.

Upper Earnings Limit (UEL)	The upper limit on earnings for the purposes of calculating entitlement to **State Second Pension**. Also the upper limit for most employee **National Insurance** contributions. In 2005/06 it is £32,760 per year or £630 per week. For more details see Appendix F in the First Report.
Upper Earnings Threshold (UET)	An intermediate point prior to the **Upper Earnings Limit**, which affects the accrual of **State Second Pension**. For more details see Appendix F in the First Report.
Withdrawal rate	The rate at which a **means-tested benefit** is reduced for an additional pound of pre-benefit income. For more details see Appendix F in the First Report.
Working age population	Generally defined as those aged 16-59 for women and 16-64 for men. However in some of our analysis we have used a starting age of 20.

Glossary

List of Abbreviations

Abbreviations	Description
ABI	Association of British Insurers
ABI1	Annual Business Inquiry – employment
ABI2	Annual Business Inquiry – financial
ABM	Automatic Balancing Mechanism
ACA	Association of Consulting Actuaries
AEI	Average Earnings Index
AIFA	Association of Independent Financial Advisers
AMC	Annual Management Charge
AP	Additional Pension
APP	Approved Personal Pension
ASHE	Annual Survey of Hours and Earnings
ASI	Alternative Secured Income
AVC	Additional Voluntary Contribution
BBA	British Bankers Association
BBSRC	Biotechnology and Biological Sciences Research Council
BHPS	British Household Panel Survey
BSP	Basic State Pension
CBI	Confederation of British Industry
CMI	Continuous Mortality Investigation
COMB	Contracted-Out Mixed Benefit scheme
COMP	Contracted-Out Money Purchase scheme
COSR	Contracted-Out Salary Related scheme
CPF	Combined Pension Forecast
CPS	Continuous Population Survey
DB	Defined Benefit
DC	Defined Contribution
DH	Department of Health
DWP	Department for Work and Pensions

ECHP – UDB	European Community Household Panel Users' Database
EEF	Engineering Employers' Federation
EFS	Expenditure and Food Survey
ELSA	English Longitudinal Study of Ageing
EMU	Economic and Monetary Union
EOC	Equal Opportunities Commission
EPP	Employers' Pension Provision survey
EPSRC	Engineering and Physical Sciences Research Council
ESP	Enhanced State Pension
ESRC	Economic and Social Research Council
EU	European Union
EU15	European Union 15 Member States
EU-SILC	European Union Survey of Income and Living Conditions
FRS	Family Resources Survey
FSA	Financial Services Authority
FSAVC	Free-Standing Additional Voluntary Contribution
GAD	Government Actuary's Department
GDP	Gross Domestic Product
GHS	General Household Survey
GNP	Gross National Product
GPP	Group Personal Pension
HAS	Household Assets Survey
HB	Housing Benefit
HMRC	Her Majesty's Revenue and Customs
HMT	Her Majesty's Treasury
HRP	Home Responsibilities Protection
IDBR	Inter-Departmental Business Register
IFA	Independent Financial Adviser
IFS	Institute for Fiscal Studies
ISA	Individual Savings Account
IPPR	Institute for Public Policy Research
LEL	Lower Earnings Limit
LET	Lower Earnings Threshold
LFS	Labour Force Survey
LLMDB2	Lifetime Labour Market Database

LS	Longitudinal Study
LSE	London School of Economics
MIG	Minimum Income Guarantee
MRC	Medical Research Council
NAFA	Net Acquisition of Financial Assets
NAFL	Net Acquisition of Financial Liabilities
NAPF	National Association of Pension Funds
NDC	Notional Defined Contribution
NES	New Earnings Survey
NI	National Insurance
NIESR	National Institute of Economic and Social Research
NIRS2	National Insurance Recording System
NPISH	Non-Profit Institutions Serving Households
NPSS	National Pension Savings Scheme
NPV	Net Present Value
NS&I	National Savings and Investments
OECD	Organisation for Economic Co-operation and Development
ONS	Office for National Statistics
OPSS	Occupational Pension Schemes Survey
PAYE	Pay As You Earn
PAYG	Pay As You Go
PEP	Personal Equity Plan
PPF	Pension Protection Fund
PPI	Pensions Policy Institute
PPM	Swedish Premium Pension system
PSTF	Pension Statistics Task Force
RIY	Reduction in Yield
ROW	Rest of the World
RPI	Retail Prices Index
SBC	Small Business Council
SBS	Small Business Service
S2P	State Second Pension
SEK	Swedish Kroner
SERPS	State Earnings Related Pension Scheme

SIC	Standard Industrial Classification
SIPP	Self Invested Pension Plan
SME	Small or Medium-sized Enterprise
SPA	State Pension Age
TAEN	Third Age Employment Network
TSP	Thrift Savings Plan for Federal Employees
TUC	Trades Union Congress
UEL	Upper Earnings Limit
UET	Upper Earnings Threshold
WPLS	Work and Pensions Longitudinal Study

Bibliography

AARP, (July 2005), *International Retirement Security Survey*, USA

ABI, (September 2003), *The Future of the Pension Annuity Market – summary report*

ABI, (October 2003), *The State of the Nation's Savings 2003*

ABI, (August 2004), *Occasional Paper No. 1: Compulsory pensions – an analysis of public attitudes*

ABI, (November 2004), *The State of the Nation's Savings 2004*

ABI, (December 2004), *Occasional Paper No. 2: Making Saving Pay: The Case for Reforming Contracting Out of the State Second Pension*

ABI, (April 2005), *UK Pension Reform – Lessons from Abroad? Pensions in Australia, New Zealand, Sweden and the USA*

ABI, (June 2005), *Bridging the Savings Gap: An evaluation of voluntary and compulsory approaches to pension reform*

ABI, (June 2005), *Serious about Saving: the ABI Agenda for action on state and private pension reform*

ABI, (August 2005), *Contracting-out of the State Second Pension: An ABI Position Paper*

ACA, (April 2005), *UK Pension Trends Survey Report Part 1*

ACA, (May 2005), *UK Pension Trends Survey Report Part 2: Trends in: Scheme provision, contributions and scheme deficits*

Age Concern, (April 2005), *The women and pensions scandal A blueprint for reform*

Allinson, G., Braidford, P., Drummond, I., Houston, M. and Stone, I., (July 2005), *SMEs and Employee Pensions A focus group based study on behalf of the Pensions Commission*, Durham Business School, Durham University

Arnkil, R., Hietikko, M., Mattila, K., Nieminen, J., Rissanen, P. and Spangar, T., (2002), *The National Programme on Ageing Workers Evaluation*, Ministry of Social Affairs and Health Helsinki, Finland

Atkinson, J. and Hurstfield, J., (2004), *Small Business Service Annual Survey of Small Businesses: UK 2003*, IES

Atkinson, J., Evans, C., Willison, R., Lain, D. and van Gent, M., (January 2003), *New Deal 50 Plus: sustainability of employment*, Report prepared for DWP

Banks, J., Emmerson, C. and Oldfield, Z., (October 2005), *Prepared for Retirement? The Pension Arrangements and Retirement Expectations of Those Approaching State Pension Age in England*, IFS Working Paper 05/13

Banks, J., Emmerson, C. and Tetlow, G., (May 2005), *Estimating pension wealth of ELSA respondents*, IFS Working Paper 05/09

Banks, J., Emmerson, C., Oldfield, Z. and Tetlow, G., (October 2005), *Prepared for Retirement? The Adequacy and Distribution of Retirement Resources in England*, IFS

Barclays Capital, (February 2005), *Barclays Equity Gilt Study 2005*

Barrell, R., (2004), *UK Savings and Pensions*, National Institute Economic Review, 190, October, pp55-7

Barrell, R., Kirkby, S. and Riely, R., (2005), *Pensions Saving and the UK Economy*, National Institute of Economic and Social Research

Bateman, H., Kingston, G. and Piggott, J., (2001), *Forced Savings Mandating Private Retirement Incomes*, Cambridge University Press

BCC, (2005), *British Chambers of Commerce Pensions Survey 2005 – Key Findings*

Bellamy, K. and Rake, K., (March 2005), *Money Money Money Is it still a rich man's world?*, Fawcett Society

Benito, A. and Power, J., (Autumn 2004), *Housing equity and consumption: insights from the Survey of English Housing*, Bank of England Quarterly Bulletin

Better Regulation Task Force, (April 2000), *Helping Small Firms Cope with Regulation - Exemptions and Other Approaches*

Better Regulation Task Force, (May 2002), *Employment Regulation: striking a balance*

Better Regulation Task Force, (March 2005), *Regulation – Less is More Reducing Burdens, Improving Outcomes*

Beveridge, W.H., (1942), *Social Insurance and Allied Services: Report*

Bird, D., (November 2004), *Methodology for the 2004 Annual Survey of Hours and Earnings , Labour Market Trends*, ONS

Blake, D. and Mayhew, L., (November 2004), *Immigration or bust? Options for securing the future viability of the UK state pension system*, Discussion Paper P1-0413 Pensions Institute, Cass Business School

Blöndal, S. and Scarpetta, S., (February 1999), *The Retirement Decision in OECD Countries*, OECD Economics Department, Working Papers No. 202

Blundell, R. and Tanner, S., (December 1999), *Labour force participation and retirement in the UK*, IFS

Bodie, Z., (1995), *On the Risk of Stocks in the Long Run*, Financial Analysts Journal 51, No. 3 May-June, pp18-22

Borsch-Supan, A. (ed), (April 2005), *Health, Ageing and Retirement in Europe: First Results from the Survey of Health, Ageing and Retirement in Europe*, Mannheim Research Institute for the Economics of Ageing

Bunn, P. and Trivedi, K., (October 2005), *Corporate expenditures and pension contributions: evidence from UK company accounts*, Bank of England Working Paper No. 276

Cabinet Office, (2000), *Women's income over the lifetime – the mother gap*

Cabinet Office, (2005), *Non-Departmental Public Bodies: A Guide for Departments*

CBI, (July 2003), *Focus on Investment: the impact of pension deficits*, Economic Brief

Cebulla, A. and Reyes De-Bearman, S., (March 2004), *Employers' Pension Provision Survey 2003*, DWP Research Report No. 207

Child Poverty Action Group, (2005), *Welfare benefits and tax credits handbook 2005/06*

Chittenden, F., Kauser, S. and Poutziouris, P., (2002), *Regulatory Burdens of Small Business: A Literature Review*, Manchester Business School, The University of Manchester

Choi, J., Laibson, D. and Madrain, B., (June 2004), *Plan Design and 401(k) Savings Outcomes*, National Tax Journal Forum on Pensions, USA

Choi, J., Laibson, D., Madrian, B. and Metrick, A., (November 2001), *Defined Contribution Pensions: Plan Rules, Participant Decisions, and the Path of Least Resistance*, NBER Working Paper No. W8655

Chung, W., Disney, R., Emmerson, C. and Wakefield, M., (October 2004), *Public policy and saving for retirement: Evidence from the introduction of Stakeholder Pensions in the UK*, IFS

CMI Mortality Committee, (July 2005), *Working Paper 15 Projecting future mortality: Towards a proposal for a stochastic methodology*

CMI Mortality Committee, (September 2005), *Working Paper 16 The Graduation of the CMI 1999-2002 Mortality Experience: Proposed Annuitant and Pensioner Graduations*

Congdon, T., (January 2005), *Tim Congdon on Pensions and Savings*, Lombard Street Research Monthly Economic Review No. 187

Connolly, E. and Kohler, M., (March 2004), *The Impact of Superannuation on Household Saving*, Reserve Bank of Australia, Research Discussion Paper 2004-01

Cooper, D., (August 2005), *Comparing pension outcomes from hybrid schemes*, DWP Research Report No. 269

Datamonitor, (October 2004), *UK IFAs 2004 – Post-Depolarization Strategies*

Datamonitor, (October 2004), *Regulatory Changes – the IFA response*

Datamonitor, (October 2004), *Worksite marketing in UK Financial Services 2004*

DH, (August 2005), *Tackling Health Inequalities: Status Report on the Programme for Action*

Donkin, A., Goldblatt, P. and Lynch, K., (Autumn 2002), *Inequalities in life expectancy by social class 1972-1999*, Health Statistics Quarterly 15, pp5-15, ONS

DSS, (December 1998), *A new contract for welfare: partnership in pensions*, Cm 4179

DTI, (July 2005), *Consultation on the draft Employment Equality (Age) Regulations 2006*

DWP, (2005), *Family Resources Survey 2003-04*

DWP, (2005), *Households Below Average Income 2003/04*

DWP, (February 2004), *Simplicity, security and choice: Informed choices for working and saving*

DWP, (February 2005), *Five Year Strategy Opportunity and security throughout life*

DWP, (February 2005), *Principles for reform The national pensions debate*

DWP, (April 2005), *The Pensioners' Incomes Series 2003/04*

DWP, (July 2005), *Automatic enrolment in workplace pension schemes Guidance on the regulatory framework*

DWP, (August 2005), *Risk sharing and hybrid pension plans*, DWP Research Report No. 270

DWP, (November 2005), *Women and pensions The evidence*

Economic Policy Committee, (2001), *Budgetary challenges posed by ageing populations*, ECFIN/655/01-EN final

Edwards, L., Regan, S. and Brooks, R., (2001), *Age old attitudes? Planning for retirement, means-testing, inheritance and informal care*, Institute for Public Policy Research

EEF/AON Consulting, (2004), *2004 Pensions Survey*

England, J. and Chatterjee, P., (September 2005), *Financial education: A review of existing provision in the UK*, DWP Research Report No. 275

EOC, (September 2005), *Britain's hidden brain drain – Final report*

Equity Release Working Party, (January 2005), *Equity Release Report 2005 Volume 1: Main report*, The Actuarial Profession

Equity Release Working Party, (January 2005), *Equity Release Report 2005 Volume 2: Technical supplement pricing considerations*, The Actuarial Profession

European Commission, (May 2004), *Comparative Tables on Social Protection in the 25 Member States of the European Union, in the European Economic Area and in Switzerland - Situation on 1 May 2004 (MISSOC)*, European Commission, Brussels

European Commission, (2005), *European Economy Public Finance in EMU -2005: A report by the Commission services*, SEC(2005) 723, Brussels

European Commission and European Council, (2003), *Adequate and Sustainable Pensions: Joint Report by the Commission and the Council*, European Commission, Brussels

European Foundation for the Improvement of Living and Working Conditions, (December 2004), *Quality of life in Europe*, Dublin

Federal Republic of Germany, (2005), *National Strategy Report on Old Age Pension Provision*, Federal Ministry for Health and Social Security, Berlin

Fitzgerald, R., Taylor, R. and LaValle, I., (April 2003), *National Adult Learning Survey*, Department for Education and Skills Research Report No. 415

Francesconi, M. and Gosling, A., (2005), *Career paths of part-time workers*, Working paper No. 19, EOC

FSA, (December 2002), *Persistency of life and pensions policies Eighth survey*

FSA, (June 2004), *A basic advice regime for the sale of stakeholder products*, CP04/11

FSA, (July 2004), *Building Financial Capability in the UK*

GAD, (1998), *Government Actuary's Department Survey of Expenses of Occupational Pensions Schemes*

GAD, (October 2003), *Government Actuary's Quinquennial Review of the National Insurance Fund as at April 2000*

GAD, (June 2004), *Occupational pension schemes 2004: Twelfth survey by the Government Actuary and previous editions*

Gale, W. and Sabelhaus, J., (1999), *Perspectives on the household saving rate , Brookings papers on Economic Activity*, Volume 1, pp181-224

Ginn, J., (2003), *Gender, Pensions and the Lifecourse*

Goodman, A., (2004), *Consumer Understanding of Risk*

Gosling, T. and Lewis, M., (2005), *Trust no-one? Public attitudes to raising the age of retirement*, IPPR

Green, E. and White, C., (2005), *Effective means of conveying messages about pensions and saving for retirement*, DWP Research Report No. 239

Gregory, A. and Tonks, I., (March 2004), *Performance of Personal Pension Schemes in the UK*, University of Exeter

Halpern, D., Bates, C., Beales, G. and Heathfield, A., (February 2004), *Personal Responsibility and Changing Behaviour: the state of knowledge and its implications for public policy*, Cabinet Office

Hammarkvist, K., (October 2005), *Difficult Waters? Premium Pension Savings on Course, Extended Summary* (SOU 2005:87), Ministry of Finance, Stockholm, Sweden

Hampton Review, (March 2005), *Final report*

Harrison, D., Byrne, A. and Blake, D., (October 2004), *Delivering DC? Barriers to participation in the company-sponsored pensions market*, Pensions Institute, Cass Business School

Hibbett, A. and Meager, N., (October 2003), *Key Indicators of women's position in Britain*, Labour Market Trends, ONS

Hicks, S. and Lindsay, C., (April 2005), *Public sector employment*, Labour Market Trends, ONS

HM Government, (March 2005), *Opportunity Age – Meeting the challenges of ageing in the 21st century*

HM Government, (October 2005), *Health, work and well-being – Caring for our future*

HM Treasury, (June 2004), *Consultation on "stakeholder" saving and investment products regulations*

HM Treasury, (November 2004), *"Stakeholder" savings & investment products regulations Government Response*

HM Treasury, (December 2004), *Long-term public finance report: an analysis of fiscal sustainability*

HM Treasury and DWP, (July 2003), *Assessing the likely market impacts of charge caps on retail investment products*

Horack, S. and NcNeill, A., (June 2005), *Pensions Commission Attitudinal Research Findings from 10 Focus Group Discussions*, RS Consulting

Horack, S. and Wood, A., (November 2005), *An evaluation of scheme joining techniques in workplace pension schemes with an employer contribution*, DWP Research Report No. 292

Hosty, G., (February 2005), *Pricing risk and potential in the equity release market*, Housing Finance Issue 3/2005, CML

Hotopp, U., (February 2005), *The employment rate of older workers*, Labour Market Trends, ONS

HSBC, (2005), *The future of retirement in a world of rising life expectancies*

Humphrey, A., Costigan, P., Pickering, K., Stratford, N. and Barnes, M., (November 2003), *Factors affecting the labour market participation of older workers*, DWP Research Report No. 200

IDS, (2005), *Pensions in Practice 2005/06*

Inland Revenue, (1998), *The Tax Compliance Costs for Employers of PAYE and National Insurance in 1995-96: A Report by the Centre for Fiscal Studies University of Bath Volume 1*, Inland Revenue Economics Papers No. 3

Irving, P., Steels, J. and Hall, N., (September 2005), *Factors affecting the labour market participation of older workers: qualitative research*, DWP Research Report No. 281

Iyengar, S., Jiang, W. and Huberman, G., (2003), *How Much Choice is Too Much?: Contributions to 401(k) Retirement Plans*, Pension Research Council, Working Paper 2003-10

Kelly, G., Lindsell, W. and Scanlon, D., (November 2005), *Combined Pension Forecasts*, DWP Research Report No. 293

Kempson, E. and S. Collard, (November 2005), *Advice on pensions and saving for retirement: qualitative research with financial intermediaries*, DWP Research Report No. 289

Kempson, E., McKay, S. and Collard, S., (March 2005), *Incentives to save: Encouraging saving among low-income households*, University of Bristol

King, M., (December 2004), *What Fates Impose: Facing Up to Uncertainty*, Paper presented to the British Academy

Leston, J. and Watmough, M., (November 2005), *Providing pensions information and advice in the workplace where there is little or no employer contribution*, DWP Research Report No. 294

Lunnon, M., (July 2002), *Annuitisation and Alternatives*, in 'Actuarial aspects of pension reform', Paper from Seminar for Social Security Actuaries and Statisticians, Moscow

Madrian, B. and Shea, D., (2001), *The power of suggestion: inertia in 401(k) participation and savings behaviour*, Quarterly Journal of Economics, Volume CXVI, Issue 4, pp1149-1187

Manning, A. and Petrongolo, B., (2005), *The Part-time Pay Penalty*, Women and Equality Unit

Marmot, M., Banks, J., Blundell, R., Lessof, C. and Nazroo, J. (ed), (December 2003), *Health, wealth and lifestyles of the older population in England: The 2002 English Longitudinal Study of Ageing*, UCL, IFS and National Centre for Social Research

May, O., Tudela, M. and Young, G., (Winter 2004), *British household indebtedness and financial stress: a household level picture*, Bank of England Quarterly Bulletin

Mayhew, V., (2001), *Pensions 2000: Public Attitudes to Pensions and Planning for Retirement*, DSS Research Report No. 130

Mayhew, V., (2003), *Pensions 2002: Public Attitudes to Pensions and Planning for Retirement*, DWP Research Report No. 193

McCarthy, D., (August 2005), *The optimal allocation of pension risks in employment contracts*, DWP Research Report No. 272

McNair, S., Flynn, M., Owen, L., Humphreys, C. and Woodfield, S., (March 2004), *Changing Work in Later Life: A Study of Job Transitions*, University of Surrey

Mellon, (November 2004), *Key Pension Issues Survey*

Ministry of Health and Social Insurance and National Social Insurance Board, (September 2003), *The Swedish National Pension System*, Ministry of Health and Social Insurance and National Social Insurance Board, Stockholm

Mintel, (2005), *Occupational Pensions, Finance Intelligence*

Mitchell, O. and Utkus, S., (2003), *Lessons from Behavioural Finance for Retirement Plan Design*, Pension Research Council, Working Paper 2003-6, USA

Mitchell, O., Utkus, S. and Yang, T., (April 2005), *Better Plans for the Better-paid: Determinants and Effects of 401(k) Plan Design*, Pension Research Council Working Paper WP 2005-5, USA

Modigliani, F. and Miller, M., (1958), *The cost of capital, corporation finance, and the theory of investment*, American Economic Review, Volume 48, pp261-97

Mody, R., (October 2004), *Middle-ground pension plan benefit design and pension communication to members*, Pensions An International Journal, Volume 10, No. 1, pp25-36

Morris Review of the Actuarial Profession, (March 2005), *Morris Review of the Actuarial Profession Final Report*

Murphy, C., (November 2004), *Public awareness of State Pension age equalisation*, DWP Research Report No. 221

Murthi, M., Orszag, M. and Orszag, P., (1999), *The Value for Money of Annuities in the UK: Theory, Experience and Policy*, Working Paper, Birkbeck College

NAPF, (2004), *Thirtieth Annual Survey of Occupational Pension Schemes*

NAPF, (July 2005), *Pension Scheme Governance – fit for the 21st century*

NAPF, (September 2005), *Towards a Citizen's Pension*

National Research Council, (1997), *Assessing Policies for Retirement Income Needs for Data, Research and Models*, National Academy Press, Washington D.C.

Neale, I., (2000), *Re-Framing 'The Annuity Problem': Can We Afford Retirement?*, Pensions An International Journal, Volume 5, No. 4, pp285-291

Noble, J., (2005), *Micro-employers' attitudes towards pensions for themselves and their employees: A report on small-scale qualitative research with employers*, DWP Research Report No. 266

NTC, (2005), *Pensions Pocket Book*

O'Brien, C., Fenn, P. and Diacon, S., (June 2005), *How long do people expect to live? Results and implications*, Centre for Risk & Insurance Studies, The University of Nottingham

OECD, (October 2003), *Monitoring the Future Social Implication of Today's Pension Policies*

OECD, (October 2003), *Monitoring Pension Policies Annex: Country Chapters*

ONS, (2005), *Trends in Life Expectancy by Social Class 1972-2001*

ONS, (2005), *United Kingdom National Accounts The Blue Book 2005*

ONS, (October 2004), *Annual Survey of Hours and Earnings 2004*

ONS, (December 2004), *General Household Survey 2003*

ONS, (June 2005), *Family Spending 2004*

ONS, (October 2005), *Pension Trends 2005*

Penneck, P. and Tily, G., (September 2005), *Private pension contributions: updated estimates, 1996-2004*, Economic Trends, ONS

Pensions Commission, (October 2004), *Pensions: Challenges and Choices, The First Report of the Pensions Commission*

Pensions Commission, (October 2004), *Pensions: Challenges and Choices, The First Report of the Pensions Commission Appendices*

Pensions Management Institute, (2002), *Pensions Terminology: A Glossary for Pension Schemes (sixth edition)*

Pomerantz, O. and Weale, M., (January 2005), *Are we Saving Enough? The Macro-Economics of the Savings Gap*, National Institute Economic Review, No. 191

Poterba, J., (August 2004), *Population Ageing and Financial Markets*, Federal Reserve Bank of Kansas, Jackson Hole Economic Symposium

PPI, (July 2003), *State Pension Models*

PPI, (May 2004), *Property or Pensions?*

PPI, (October 2004), *Can current pension policy be as good as the alternatives?*, PPI Briefing Note No. 15

PPI, (February 2005), *How big is the life expectancy gap by social class?*, PPI Briefing Note No. 17

PPI, (April 2005), *The gain from deferring state pensions*, PPI Briefing Note No. 19

PPI, (May 2005), *Should the state provide an earnings-related pension?*, PPI Briefing Note No. 20

PPI, (June 2005), *Kiwisaver: Another lesson from New Zealand*, PPI Briefing Note No. 21

PPI, (August 2005), *Can work close the 'savings gap'?*, PPI Briefing Note No. 23

PPI, (September 2005), *A Commentary on the Pension Reform Debate*

President's Commission, (2001), *Strengthening Social Security and creating personal wealth for all Americans: Report of the President's Commission*, USA

Queisser, M. and Vittas, D., (2000), *The Swiss Multi-Pillar Pension Scheme: Triumph of Common Sense*, Policy Research Working Paper WPS2416, World Bank, New York

Rake, K. (ed), (2000), *Women's Incomes over the Lifetime: A Report to the Women's Unit*, Cabinet Office

Redwood, V. and Tudela, M., (2004), *From tiny samples do mighty populations grow? Using the British Household Panel Survey to analyse the household sector balance sheet*, Bank of England

Robson Rhodes, (March 2005), *Pensions in UK Manufacturing*

Rowlingson, K., (May 2004), *Attitudes to Inheritance Focus group report*, University of Bath/JRF

Rowlingson, K., (July 2005), *Attitudes to housing assets and inheritance*, Housing Finance Issue 10/2005, CML

Rowlingson, K. and McKay, S., (July 2005), *Attitudes to inheritance in Britain*, JRF

Sandler, R., (July 2002), *Sandler Review: Medium and Long-term Retail Savings in the UK*, HMT

Savings Product Working Group, (August 2004), *A Future for Work-based savings in New Zealand: Final report of the savings product working group*

Scanlon, K. and Whitehead, C., (March 2005), *The profile and intentions of buy-to-let investors*, CML

Scottish Widows, (June 2005), *UK Pensions Report*

Shiller, R. J., (1981), *Do Stock Prices Move Too Much to be Justified by Subsequent Changes in Dividends*, American Economic Review, Volume 71 No. 3, pp421-436

Siebrits, J., (2004), *Rich or retired? A profile of cash purchasers in the UK*, CML

Small Business Council, (March 2004), *Evaluation of Government Employment Regulations and their Impact on Small Business*

Small Business Service, (August 2005), *Small and Medium-sized Enterprise (SME) Statistics for the UK, 2004*, DTI

Smeaton, D. and McKay, S., (February 2003), *Working after State Pension Age: Quantitative Analysis*, DWP Research Report No. 182

Smith, J., (2004), *Understanding demand for home-ownership: aspirations, risks and rewards*, CML

Social Insurance Agency, (2004), *The Swedish Pension System Annual Report 2004*, Swedish Social Insurance Office, Stockholm

Social Protection Committee, (2004), *Promoting Longer Working Lives Through Better Social Protection Systems: A Report by the Social Protection Committee*, European Commission, Brussels

Social Protection Committee, (2005), *Privately Managed Pension Provision: Report by the Social Protection Committee*, European Commission, Brussels

Sodha, S., (October 2005), *Housing-Rich, Income-Poor, The potential of housing wealth in old age*, IPPR

Stark, J., (2002), *Annuities: the consumer experience*, ABI

Summers, L., (1986), *Does the Stock Market Rationally Reflect Fundamental Values?*, Journal of Finance, Volume 41, Issue 3, pp591-601

Sykes, W., Hedges, A., Finch, H., Ward, K. and Kelly, J., (June 2005), *Financial plans for retirement:women's perspectives*, DWP Research Report No. 247

Talbot, C., Adelman, L. and Lilly, R., (March 2005), *Encouraging take-up: awareness of and attitudes to Pension Credit*, DWP Research Report No. 234

Taylor-Gooby, P., (October 2004), *Public Expectations of Pension Provision*, The Actuarial Profession

Taylor-Gooby, P., (February 2005), *Attitudes to social justice*, IPPR

Thaler, R.H. and Benartzi, S., (2004), *Save More Tomorrow: Using Behavioural Economics to Increase Employee Saving*, Journal of Political Economy, Volume 112, No.1, Pt 2, pp164-187

Thaler, R.H. and Benartzi, S., (March 2001), *Naïve Diversification Strategies in Defined Contribution Savings Plans*, The Economic Review, Volume 91, No.1, pp79-98

The Economist, (January 2005), *Mind Games*

The Employer Task Force on Pensions, (December 2004), *The Employer Task Force on Pensions Good Practice Guide*

The Employer Task Force on Pensions, (December 2004), *The Employer Task Force on Pensions Report to the Secretary of State for Work and Pensions*

The Pension Research Forum, (May 2005), *Effective member engagement – does one size fit all?*

The Pension Service, (October 2005), *A guide to State Pensions*, DWP

The Pensions Advisory Service, (March 2005), *Report on Women and Pensions Helpline*

The Pensions Reform Group, (October 2001), *Universal Protected Pension: Modernising Pensions for the Millennium*

The Retirement Choices Working Party, The Pensions Board and The Faculty and Institute of Actuaries, (2001), *Extending Retirement Choices – Retirement income options for modern needs*

Tily, G., Penneck, P. and Forest, C., (August 2004), *Private Pensions Estimates and the National Accounts*, Economic Trends No. 609, ONS

TUC, (December 2004), *Time for Action*

TUC, (June 2005), *The 80 per cent solution*

Turner, A., (September 2003), *The Macroeconomics of Pensions*, Lecture to the Actuarial Profession

Turner, A., (November 2003), *Demographics, Economics and Social Choice*, Lecture at the London School of Economics

Turner, A., (March 2005), *Pension Policy: Political Choices and Macroeconomic Issues*, Lecture at the London School of Economics

Turner, A., (April 2005), *Pensions, Risks, Uncertainties and Capital Markets*, Lecture at the Cass Business School

Turner, A., (July 2005), *Sectoral and National Savings Discussion Paper*

UBS, (2005), *Pension fund indicators 2005: a long term perspective on pension fund investment*

Utkus, S., (June 2005), *Selecting a Default Fund for a Defined Contribution Plan*, The Vanguard Centre for Retirement Research, USA

Utkus, S. and Mottola, G., (April 2005), *Catch-up Contributions in 2004: Plan sponsor and participants adoption*, The Vanguard Centre for Retirement Research, USA

Utkus, S. and Young, J., (April 2004), *Lessons from Behavioural Finance and the Autopilot 401(k) Plan*, The Vanguard Centre for Retirement Research, USA

Vanguard, (September 2004), *How America Saves*

Wadsworth, M., Findlater, A. and Boardman, T., (2001), *Reinventing Annuities*, The Actuarial Society

Wadsworth, M., (2005), *The Pension Annuity Market*, ABI

Walker, R., Heaver, C. and McKay, S., (2000), *Building up Pension Rights*, DSS Research Report No. 114

Walling, A., (July 2005), *Families and work*, Labour Market Trends, ONS

Watson Wyatt, (January 2003), *Administration Cost Survey 2003*

Watson Wyatt, (2003), *Pension Annuities – Market Dynamics and Implications for Supply*, ABI

Watson Wyatt, (March 2005), *The Uncertain Future of Longevity*, Watson Wyatt/Cass Business School Public Lectures on Longevity

Weaver, R.K., (2004), *Design and Implementation Issues in Swedish Individual Pension Accounts*, Social Security Bulletin, Volume 65, No. 4, Social Security Administration, USA

Wesbroom, K. and Reay, T., (August 2005), *Hybrid pension plans: UK and international experience*, DWP Research Report No. 271

Which?, (2005), *Which Choice? Can the Government's choice agenda deliver for everyone?*

Whitehouse, E., (June 2000), *Administrative Charges for Funded pensions: An International Comparison and Assessment*, Pension Reform Primer Series, Social Protection Discussion Paper 0016

Whiting, E., (July 2005), *The labour market participation of older people*, Labour Market Trends, ONS

Women and Equality Unit, (December 2004), *Interim Update of Key Indicators of Women's Position in Britain*, DTI

Women and Equality Unit, (2005), *Individual incomes of men and women 1996/97 to 2003/04*, DTI

World Economic Forum, (2004), *Living Happily Ever After: the Economic Implications of Ageing Societies*

Yoo, P., (1995), *Age Distributions and Returns to Financial Assets*, Federal Reserve Bank of St.Louis, Working paper 94-002B

Young, G., (2002), *The implications of an ageing population for the UK economy*, Bank of England Working Paper